JACOB:
god's plain man

JACOB: GOD'S PLAIN MAN

Lillian Cantleberry

Publishing House
St. Louis

The Scripture quotations in this publication are from The Holy Bible: NEW INTERNATIONAL VERSION, copyright © 1978 by the New York International Bible Society. Used by permission of Zondervan Bible Publishers.

Copyright © 1984 Concordia Publishing House
3558 South Jefferson Avenue, St. Louis, MO 63118-3968
Manufactured in the United States of America.

All rights reserved. No part of this publication may be reproduced, stored in a retrieval system, or transmitted, in any form or by any means, electronic, mechanical, photocopying, recording, or otherwise, without the prior written permission of Concordia Publishing House.

Library of Congress Cataloging in Publication Data

Cantleberry, Lillian, 1922—
    Jacob, God's plain man.

    1. Jacob (Biblical patriarch)—Fiction. I. Title.
PS3553.A547J3 1984   813'.54   83-23977
ISBN 0-570-03928-2

1 2 3 4 5 6 7 8 9 10 PP 93 92 91 90 89 88 87 86 85 84

contents

preface

It was like just being introduced to someone I thought I had known for years when I read the book *I Have Loved Jacob* by Joseph Hoffman Cohn (New York: American Board of Missions to the Jews, 1948).

Traditionally taught that Jacob was a cheat and a conniver, I had found it enigmatic to think he was chosen by God to stand with giants of the faith like Abraham and Isaac. The best I could decide was that Jacob was chosen so we might be assured God could love anyone!

But the God of Abraham, Isaac and Jacob has given us a carefully written portrait of each of these three men in His Word. Only by reading that account with preconceived notions could one think that Jacob was the least of the three. His circumstances were different, his trials unique, but his faith in God and his devotion to Him were, in the words of Scripture, *perfect.* If this seems surprising, search out the meaning of the word *plain* (or *quiet*) as used in Gen. 25:27. In the original Hebrew it is *tam*--the word is used to describe both Noah and Job, who were perfect, that is, righteous before God.

In the matter of the birthright, Cohn points out that Jacob risked the accusation of being a selfish schemer by negotiating for what was really his already. God had ordained before the boys were born that the younger would rule the older, that is, receive the blessing-birthright accorded to the one chosen to be priest in the family in his generation.

Of special interest is the pottage Jacob cooked and "traded" for the birthright. Cohn quotes Rabbi Herbert S. Goldstein in his *Bible Comments for Home Reading* (New York: Hebrew Publishing Co., 1928) as follows:

> According to the Rabbis, on the day Abraham died, and as is the custom and has ever been, the first meal after the burial is provided for by those who are not mourners themselves. This food is round-shaped to symbolize that the wheel of death is turning and eventually reaches everyone. Hence, Jacob had to boil the food, which could not be done by his parents.

For further information on this, please see "Esau,"*The Jewish Encyclopedia* (New York: Funk & Wagnalls Company, 1925); Louis Ginzberg, *The Legends of the Jews* (Philadelphia: Jewish Publication Society of America, 1961), I, 318; and Targum Pseudo Jon. on Gen. 25:29.

The consensus concerning the red pottage is that it was a ritual meal served at the time of a death. The person preparing it had the place of the firstborn. The one preparing it had to be fasting. Jacob, in fasting, was probably hungrier than the "starving" Esau. He was performing the priestly duties of the firstborn.

In my rethinking of the character of Jacob, his story has so come alive in my mind and heart that I wanted to say, with this book, that "I have loved Jacob"—God's plain/quiet/perfect man.

Part One is written as I believe Rebekah might speak of Jacob—her *Ya'aqob-El.*

Part Three is written as though Rachel were telling about Jacob, her beloved husband.

The other sections are written in narrative form.

As it is written, "Jacob I loved, but Esau I hated" (Rom. 9:13 from Mal. 1:2-3).

íntroóuctíon

Interwoven time lines, important in the story of Jacob-Israel:
- When Abraham was 100 years old, Isaac was born (Gen. 21:5).
- When Abraham was 140 years old, Isaac, age 40, was married (Gen. 25:20).
- When Abraham was 160 years old, and Isaac was 60, Esau and Jacob were born (Gen. 25:26).
- Abraham lived to be 175 years old. At that time Isaac was 75, and his sons were 15 (Gen. 25:7).
- Isaac lived to be 180 years old. He was still living when Jacob returned after 20 years of servitude to Laban; he lived on until after Rachel's death (Gen. 35:28).

From this we can make two interesting observations: (1) Jacob benefited from the teachings and example of both Abraham and Isaac, and (2) Isaac was unduly worried about his death at the time of the blessing bestowal.

The Hebrew word *tam* is used in the following verses:
Gen. 6:9—of Noah—translated "perfect" or "blameless."
Job 1:1—of Job—translated "perfect" or "blameless."
Gen. 25:27—of Jacob—translated "plain" or "quiet."

Part One

Rebekah speaks

The wife of Isaac, mother of Esau and Jacob, speaks of well-remembered things.

Jacob . . . God's plain man!
Jacob . . . my son!

>   Where are you now?
>   Are you well?

Jacob . . . God's quiet man!
Jacob . . . my son!

>   Do you think of Canaan?
>   Do you still love the land?

Jacob . . . God's perfect man!
Jacob . . . my son!

>   We miss you.
>   I miss you most of all!

1

> The Lord, before whom I have walked, will send His angel with you and make your journey a success, so that you can get a wife for my son from my own clan and from my father's family.
>
> *Genesis 24:40*

I dislike this weather! Its unusual chill, mingled with this rain, makes my bones know they are getting older. I don't go out from my tent very often, and I say it's because of the bones.

I have many hours just to think. Some people recall events of long ago more easily than those of yesterday. I *choose* to live in the past, because I dare not dwell on the present state of things.

I think of him whom I love—have loved since before he was born. I think of his brother whom I also loved before he was born—but whose name has become a stabbing desolation in my heart, making the love bittersweet. I think of their father, the man I've loved since before I met him—and I often think of one terrible event that shrouds us all, haunting each in a different way.

But sometimes I try to remember myself as the high-spirited girl who came to Canaan nearly 65 years ago, at the age of 20—was I ever 20?

My father Bethuel, like my grandfather Nahor and our ancestors before them, was a merchant in Haran. My brother, Laban, was continuing the tradition of sharp buying and selling, and I was part of this well-established family.

But with one day's notice I was whisked from my father's house and hurried along to Canaan—to become the wife of Isaac, sole heir of Abraham!

Laban and I grew up hearing stories about our great-uncle Abraham. We were told how, as a young man, he left a high government post at Ur of the Chaldees, lived a while in Haran, then moved on to Canaan—responding to a direct command from the one God. We knew many of the exciting experiences of Abraham's family, and we were impressed by descriptions of the wealth he amassed.

One late summer evening, when Father's conversation had again been about Abraham, he mentioned something we had not known before. In pride tempered with jealousy he said, "Not only does Abraham own multitudes of sheep and goats, hundreds of servants, the finest camels and tents, but beyond all this—the one God has promised the entire land of Canaan to his descendants!"

"The whole land?" Laban was incredulous.

"From the river of Egypt to the great Euphrates."

"Why? Why would Abraham get all that?"

Father tapped five gnarled fingers against five gnarled fingers, remembering more than he would put into words. After a time he said, "God called my uncle—not because he was the wisest or strongest among the descendents of Shem, but because He knew Abraham would obey Him best, trust Him most. The one God knows the heart of each man, and in choosing Abraham He chose rightly."

He was silent for a moment, reminiscing. Then, as if talking to himself, he said, "Father Nahor told me that if God had chosen him to go to Canaan, he would have refused. He had all he wanted in Haran."

"In Haran?" Laban's tone deprecated our city and implied our forefather must have enjoyed dullness.

Father's voice was harsh as he thundered at Laban, "And I know of no one else—not even you, my son—who would give up home, position, friends and comfort to go to that wild land!

"Canaan is only a hub for roads leading to important places. Worse yet—it often serves as a battleground for surrounding countries that prefer to make war on Canaan's plains instead of in their own lands. Would you really like a tent—in barbaric Canaan, Laban?"

My brother was taken aback by Father's anger and shook

his head; he would not want to trade the security of Haran for the uncertainties of Canaan. Even so, he still coveted that vast area and ventured to continue the discussion. "But if Nahor had gone instead of Abraham—then we would own all that land now, instead of Isaac's coming into possession of it." His eyes shone with vicarious joy.

"It's not Isaac's yet. Abraham will leave him only God's promise of it. Isaac may leave his descendants only God's promise. It's uncertain, as I understand it, when actual possession of the land will take place—but it's to be in the future."

His eyes narrowed as he looked disapprovingly at his son. "Be content with what you have, Laban."

"Laban? Content?" I laughed at Father's suggestion. I laughed very loudly and very long to emphasize my derision of Laban. His impatience to be rich was well known. He called it ambition; others called it greed.

During that sleepless night before I left home this long-forgotten conversation about Canaan drifted back to my mind. I laughed again, this time because of how things had worked out. I—Rebekah—was being placed in the line of that Canaan inheritance. I had never cared that it was our great-uncle's family and not ours that was chosen for God's plan. I didn't even understand what that "plan" was all about—but its very mystery intrigued me.

The day before that sleepless night had been amazing. I thought it over during the long dark hours, and I was still reliving it as the first pale light of morning made furniture, walls and ceiling slowly visible—furniture, walls and ceiling I never would see again.

That day had begun with my usual trip to the well. Water had to be carried to the earthenware container that stood in a wooden ring at our front door for washing feet. Waterskins from our kitchen had to be refilled. There must be water for the pitchers beside the wash basins in the bedrooms. Sometimes servant girls went with me, but often I chose to go alone, even if it meant making extra trips. I preferred my own thoughts to their silly chatter.

On this special morning a tall, slightly stooped but distinctively handsome man was standing at the well. A smile lit his weathered face; cascading white hair and beard made him appear radiant. He looked wise and strong, but was as tired and worn as any other traveler. He must have been thirsty, but he made no attempt to draw water or to have his attendants draw it for him.

I felt his eyes on me as I went about my work. Sunlit water shimmered as I let the bucket down into the well, drew it up, and then emptied it into the jug.

After a few minutes he asked if he might have a drink of water. His voice was commanding, but gentle and kind. Without hesitation I dipped the bucket again into the well and carefully poured the water into the cup he held. I managed to smile and said, "Drink, my lord."

He didn't gulp it as most travelers do when tasting cool water after a long, dusty journey. He sipped it with the ecstasy of one sampling the finest wine.

I gave some water to his attendants and then said, "I'll draw water for your camels, too, until they have finished drinking."

I splashed bucketfull after bucketfull into the stone trough for the waiting camels, noticing they wore the grandest leather and brass harness I ever had seen.

Out of the corner of my eye I watched the stranger. It had become an interesting game—waiting on this man with such an unusual capacity for appreciation. If he had been pleased by just a cup of water, he would be in extraordinary good humor about my watering his camels—without even being asked—and doing it so quickly—and with a big smile! The harder I worked, the more honest my smile became. Never before had drawing water been such a delight.

He watched me with a blend of satisfaction and excitement in his eyes. Then to my complete astonishment, he opened a box one of his aides had brought to him and handed me glittering, golden jewelry—carved rings, pendant earrings, slender bracelets. As I marveled at the gift, he asked my name and my family's name. He also asked if my father could find a place at his house that night for himself, his attendants and their camels.

I said I was the daughter of Bethuel, who was the son of Milcah and Nahor. Certain of the wealth and generosity of this man, I told him my father and brother would be honored to have him stay at our house. "We have plenty of straw and fodder, as well as room for you to spend the night."

At that he bowed his head and worshiped his God! He said, "Praise be to the Lord, the God of my master, Abraham, who has not abandoned His kindness and faithfulness to my master."

I was wide-eyed and openmouthed. He had said "Abraham." His master was Abraham! And he prayed to the God of Abraham!

I started to run home, calling over my shoulder that he should wait for my family who would come out to meet him at once.

I found Laban first. He stared at the gleaming bracelets, rings and earrings I wore as I demonstrated with high drama how I dipped the bucket into the well and emptied it into the trough. He was so fascinated by the gold that I wondered if he heard anything I said. But he had listened well, and by the time I finished my story he had planned his strategy.

He summoned our head servants and ordered them to prepare suitable quarters for four men and their camels. Then he ran out to meet Abraham's messenger. I ran with him.

Laban, assuming the role of generous host, bowed low before the messenger from Canaan and said, "Come, you who are blessed by the Lord. Why are you standing out here? I have prepared the house and a place for the camels."

The stranger nodded, smiled, and signaled to his small train that it was time to move on. They followed Laban and me down the streets of Haran, past curious onlookers, and finally to our house.

Laban himself brought water in a basin to wash their feet, then showed the men to rooms where they could rest. Laban himself ungirded the camels and gave them straw and fodder.

Father already had learned of the delegation from Abraham, had instructed the servants to prepare a banquet, and had told mother to oversee each detail.

The grand result was that within a few hours our table was

laden with savory meat, fresh bread, fruit, cheese, onions and cucumbers, and the fine wine kept for choice occasions. Our best plates and goblets added color and elegance.

Laban escorted our visitors to the dining hall, eager to see their response to the lavish fare prepared for them. Abraham's servant was unimpressed. Looking refreshed from his rest he said, "I will not eat until I have told you what I have to say."

My brother paled as he glanced toward the table with all the food ready to be eaten. But with a sweep of his right arm and a slight shrug of his shoulders he said, "Then tell us."

The man began by saying his name was Eliezer. Then he talked at length of Abraham and Isaac. Even though I knew much about these kinsmen, I listened intently, eager to learn more. I became increasingly interested in Isaac. What a singularly brave thing he had done at Mt. Moriah! He had actually given himself to be a sacrifice to the one God! And now how fortunate he was to be so much in this God's favor. I looked over at Laban. He seemed not to be enjoying the story at all.

Eliezer continued, deliberately, as though he had rehearsed his speech. Then he was quiet—but even his silence was filled with an aura of excitement and joy that made the atmosphere of our home glow, at least for me.

I thought his message was over, but the most unbelievable and best came next!

Abraham's urgent desire was that his son not marry a Canaanite woman, but one from his own kindred. Abraham had sent Eliezer to Haran to find a wife for Isaac!

I looked down at my bracelets and rings and felt the earrings brush the side of my face. The jewelry suddenly seemed more significant! Could I be the one he had chosen? Just because I happened to be there to give him a drink and water his camels? My face felt warm, and I knew it was flushed. I was afraid he would think me presumptuous, but he was so caught up in the story he was telling my father and Laban that he seemed not to notice.

"Your beautiful daughter's response to a dusty, thirsty, travel-weary old man speaks of a generous disposition. I am well impressed with her. But the important thing is this: I had asked the God of Abraham to lead me to the woman He wanted for Isaac. The sign I requested was that she offer me and my camels some water. I had scarcely finished asking for this sign before it was given!

"And now I know it is as Abraham told me. He said the Lord would send His angel with me to Haran, to prosper my way and to find the wife for Isaac from his father's house.

"Now if you will show kindness and faithfulness, Bethuel and Laban, give me your answer concerning Rebekah. Will you consent to her becoming Isaac's wife?"

My mind was overwhelmed by torrents of disbelief and joy, hopes and fears! I wanted them to say yes; I wanted them to ask for time to think it over; I wanted them to say no.

The yes became loudest in my mind, as it did in the minds of my father and brother. They said that since the matter came from the Lord, they would not allow personal opinion to enter into their decision. "Here is Rebekah; take her and go, and let her become the wife of your master's son, as the Lord has directed."

Eliezer began to bless the God of Abraham. Anyone hearing him would have known he was accustomed to speaking with the One he called the Most High God—El Elyon.

When he finished his prayer he sent his aides to bring chests of silver, gold and fine clothing. There were more treasures for me and some for my father, my brother, and my mother, who had listened to everything Eliezer said from outside the archway of the room. She stood there, missing none of Eliezer's comments, but also keeping an eye on the servants who were using the extra time to prepare even more food. Eliezer, knowing she was there, called her in to receive her share of the gifts.

Then at last we banqueted. Our family had never set a more festive table, but I was too excited to eat, and later I was too excited to sleep.

Eliezer and I left for Canaan the next morning. Mother begged him to stay a few days before leaving, but we both were eager to be on our way.

My father and brother gave me the customary farewell blessing. They hoped that my marriage would produce many fine children and that my future would be prosperous.

I was given as maidservant my beloved Deborah, the woman who had attended me since the day I was born.

With a poignant profusion of tears, smiles, reassurances and promises I went from my father's house.

I relive those bright hours often; they are priceless keepsakes.

2

> The Lord said to her, "Two nations are in your womb, and two peoples
> from within you will be separated; one people will be stronger than the
> other, and the older will serve the younger." *Genesis 25:23*

Isaac was Eliezer's favorite subject during our
journey to the Negeb country of Canaan. He described Isaac as
handsome, well educated, self-controled and patient. He
seemed to enjoy telling me that Isaac also lived up to the
meaning of his name—"laughter." He said Isaac was a happy
young man, contented with the assurance that God ordered
his days.

We forded the Euphrates and rode over rock-strewn hills,
green valleys and barren tracts. We traveled over sand,
through forests and beside fields of grain. Eliezer avoided
large cities, much to my disappointment; I wanted to see
Tadmor and Damascus.

We enjoyed the songs of the birds and thrilled to the beauty
and fragrance of field flowers. He praised the one God for all
these things, and I began doing the same. Although my family
sometimes talked of the one God and believed in Him, He was
not as real to them as He was to Eliezer—and was becoming to
me! Eliezer was a good teacher.

Finally we came to the southern part of Canaan. Eliezer
said we were home. Home? Could I ever think of this place as
home? A land of adventure—yes! A land of romance—yes!
But . . . home?

He instructed the others in our train to stay behind while
we rode on to a field by a well that he called Lahai Roi. Our
journey was ending, and my happy anticipation was giving
way to panic. I looked to him for reassurance. He was smiling,
and once again I found his joy contagious.

He called my attention to a broad-shouldered, black-haired man kneeling in the field some little distance from the road. It was early evening; the setting sun's golden-rose rays lit his face as he looked heavenward.

As Eliezer helped me dismount, he watched my face register approval. Then he said proudly, "That is my master, Isaac."

"That is Isaac?" I was not doubting Eliezer—just affirming what he said. My fortune was better than I had dared to dream!

Isaac heard us and, letting the distraction end his meditation, he walked toward us. His smile illuminated his face almost as much as the sun had. We looked at each other, and for a wonderful moment we forgot anyone else was around. I had never known there could be such excitement in an exchange of glances. Then we looked away from each other, and I pulled a veil over my face in a belated keeping with custom.

Isaac and Eliezer exchanged warm greetings. I impatiently waited to be introduced to my husband, but Eliezer, in his deliberate manner, decided he would first tell Isaac of his entire trip. He chose to give detailed descriptions and word-for-word reports of conversations. The sunset had given way to evening darkness before he finished.

Isaac and I listened to him, but in the time-honored way we found it possible to speak to each other with our eyes. As Eliezer talked on and on, I thanked the one God for choosing me to be the woman for Isaac.

When Eliezer finally finished his account of the trip, he introduced us to each other, suggesting that all three of us go immediately to see Abraham.

Abraham! I felt as though I was about to meet a legend—an ideal.

I walked beside Isaac as Eliezer led the way. I wanted to turn and run—to go anywhere except to see Abraham. I knew he would never approve of me. I wouldn't know how to behave in his presence, wouldn't know what to say. I glanced at Isaac. Through all our years together he understood—almost always—my thoughts and feelings. He gave me a beautifully reassuring smile, then whispered, "Rebekah, Father is probably uneasy about meeting you for the first time. Put him at ease by being very pleasant."

My dear Isaac knew exactly how to help me out of embarassing self-consciousness. The smile he brought to my face was still there when I first saw Abraham.

Abraham! He was vibrant with the self-assurance of the great, but he evidenced such loving concern that even before arhe spoke I felt accepted; I knew I was home.

By the time Eliezer again told his long story and actually presented me to Abraham, my apprehensions had faded. Never, ever, was my affectionate regard for Abraham diminished!

Isaac and I became husband and wife. We settled into a comfortable pattern of living. Our love grew deeper, and our companionship was sweet. Flock and herds increased. Crops were abundant.

And yet, after 20 years of marriage, my family's wishes for me were only partially fulfilled. Our prosperity was all they could have hoped for, but as for my being the mother of "many children"—that had't happened. I did not have *many* children; I did not have *any* children!

Isaac prayed on my behalf to the Lord God only because of my despair—not because he doubted the promise that "through Isaac" Abraham's line would continue. Isaac, steeped in the teaching and example of Abraham, waited patiently and took God's delay in answering our prayers as a challenge given in love, to be accepted with faith.

In His time the Lord answered. After the long waiting I did become pregnant, and the gladness that had ebbed from our lives because of childlessness returned tenfold! I sang my thanks to Him:

All praise to El Shaddai,
To the God of Abraham and Isaac!
Blessed be His Name.

I will be a joyful mother.
I will instruct the new generation in uprightness.
I called on the Lord, and He heard my supplications.

His merciful kindness is great toward me.
I will praise Him all the days of my life.

Life was good; we were blessed. And the line that would be a blessing to all nations was continuing.

With each succeeding month my physical distress became more severe. I had so wanted a child that now I tried not to complain, but it was almost past enduring at times.

I often thought of Isaac's mother, who died before I came to Canaan. She was much older than I when she had her first and only child. I knew that the God who miraculously restored her youthful health and strength would enable me also to carry my child to full term, but after one particularly exhausting day, I asked Him why my discomfort was so great. He answered that it was because I carried twins who were striving against each other. His actual words burned themselves into my mind:

> Two nations are in your womb,
>> and two peoples from within you will be separated;
> one people will be stronger than the other,
>> and the older will serve the younger.

I related His words to Isaac. We thought about them, talked about them and wondered about them.

"Isaac, why would the older serve the younger? Isn't the eldest son—even eldest by minutes—given the first place in the family?"

"Not . . . always. I . . . wasn't my father's firstborn."

He hesitated for a moment, looking down at the floor; then he continued. "The birthright in our family is a unique trust, having to do with appointing the one through whom God's plan will be carried to the next generation. In the usual course of events the eldest receives this blessing, but God sometimes ordains otherwise, perhaps in order to draw attention to His specific plan."

"Well, my husband, I feel sorry for the son who will be born first, yet must lose his place to the younger. I wish our twins could share the birthright-blessing."

"God will provide for each, as each trusts and obeys Him. Leave their future to Him. He knows each one's heart and potential, and He has chosen the younger one; so be it."

"Yes . . . so be it. Day by day my awe of El Shaddai grows.

He knows, as these twins are being knit together in my womb, how their days shall be and what sort of persons they are. In their most secret place He already knows them! No creature is hidden from Him . . . never, ever hidden."

Our conversations were not always so serious. I remember that Isaac once asked why I seemed to be so deep in thought, and I answered that I was thinking about my new responsibilities. I was nearly in tears as I said, "Isaac, I want to be a good mother. Do you think I will be?"

He didn't want me to think my question was unimportant, but his eyes and his voice were smiling as he answered, "You were a good daughter; you are my good wife—chosen by the Lord God. I have no doubt that you will be a wonderful mother. You probably will humor our children too much, but they will love you for it—just as I love you for all you are to me."

"Isaac, I hope our sons—like you—will love me enough to see only the best in me. Our sons . . . the twins . . . what shall we name them?"

"There will be time enough to name them when they are born. Perhaps the Lord God will name them. He named me."

"He gave you a good name with a wonderful meaning: Isaac—laughter. It suits you well."

Isaac made no further comment. He was given more to silence than to poetic phrases or long conversations; but he spoke eloquently with his eyes—as he had the first day I met him. He drew our conversation to a close with a loving look—a glance with the deepest adoration in it. Then he softly said, "You are the most beautiful, dearest, kindest woman in the world." He said each word slowly, as if choosing the best ones he could find. He kissed me passionately and held me closely— as though he believed I really were all those pleasant things— and as though I were not unbecomingly large with twins!

Day by day my unborn sons occupied my mind almost totally. Twins! The thought was glorious, except for the warning of strife between the brothers. They gave constant evidence of already being at war with each other. Increasingly I longed to be delivered of them—freed from the heaviness and pain. And I was impatient to see them, to hold them in my arms. I loved them both already!

I thanked God for my sons and prayed daily for the strength I needed. I looked forward to our years ahead, rich in the joy of having children—not just a child, but children!

Deborah seldom left my side. She told me again and again about my own birth. She was with the midwife who delivered me, and I was given to her to care for—almost as her own—through the years. Dear Deborah—I depended on her, was comforted by her. She saw to everything my babies would need, discussed every eventuality with the midwife of our camp, and gave me the feeling that all was well.

With mounting anticipation—and impatience—I waited for the birth of my sons.

3

When the time came for her to give birth, there were twin boys in her
womb.   *Genesis 25:24*

After hours of travail and moments of searing
pain—it was done. Two healthy boys were born! Each one was
beautiful, and their first cries sounded musical to me. I knew
there had never been such perfect infants as these before. A
new glowing sensitivity filled me; it flooded my heart and my
mind with new realization of the preciousness of life.

Isaac was with me as soon as they were born. He agreed
with my assessment of the wonders that had been given
us—except that he could hear no lyric quality in their hearty
cries.

Our firstborn child was ruddier than most babies, and his
body was covered with a generous supply of the soft, fuzzy
hair of the newborn. Because of that, we named him Esau,
meaning "hairy." Esau's initial cry was instant and loud. He
announced to the world he had arrived.

Our second baby followed immediately—so closely that
both could have been called firstborn! There was no delay
between them; in fact, the second was clinging to the heel of
the first with his soft fingers. Because of this clinging, we
named our younger son—younger only by seconds—*Ya'aqeb*,
meaning "to grasp the heel," but we always called him *Jacob*--a
short form of the full, beautiful name *Ya'aqob-El*, which means
"may God protect."

Jacob's appearance was very different from Esau's. He was
olive-skinned with just a tinge of the newborn's rosiness. His
hair and eyes were dark. He had to be slapped soundly to get
his first cry, and then, after his responsive burst of exaspera-
tion, he settled down to sleep.

Isaac and I marveled at our sons. We watched them breathe, and were enchanted by the slightest movement of a tiny arm or leg. We saw that each manchild was handsome in his own way. Esau and Jacob—Jacob and Esau—our family was complete, and if we thought of the specter of future strivings between our sons, we did not talk about it. Not talking about it made it seem improbable.

The boys grew rapidly, and we lived in an atmosphere of rollicking laughter, playful antics, times of teasing, skinned knees, and the overall enjoyment of being together. No other pleasure has been greater.

Esau was a boy of inexhaustible energy. He had an insatiable love for the out-of-doors. He was impulsive and had a fiery temper.

In contrast, Jacob possessed quiet stamina. Deep love for his family expressed itself in helpfulness around the camp. He also liked to visit with the shepherds in the pastures and to help care for the animals. He seldom was roused to anger, but when he was, he left no doubt about the robustness of his wrath!

One thing in particular incited Jacob, and Esau made frequent use of it to provoke him—the pronunciation of his name. Jacob guarded his name jealously. He thought it bad enough to be named "heel," but he would not abide having it slurred from *Ya'aqeb* to *Ya'aqab*, changing its meaning to "deceiver." During their quarrels Esau would shout, ' *Ya'aqab*-- Deceiver!" I'm certain many of our servants thought it was one of the right meanings of our younger son's name.

As the boys grew older, they enjoyed going on trips. Along with specially assigned servants, and sometimes even accompanied by Isaac, they made many short journeys.

Esau liked to go where he could learn to hunt game, and Isaac delighted in teaching him how to handle the bow and arrow.

Jacob preferred to visit his grandfather's camp at Mamre. He liked to hear Abraham tell of the splendid houses, shops and libraries of Ur; the dazzling Damascus bazaar; his early days in Canaan; his battle against Kedorlaomer. Most exciting of all to the boy were the accounts of Abraham's meetings with the Lord God. Jacob listened intently while his grandfather spoke of all these things. He was spellbound as he heard the description of El Elyon's voice. Abraham even gave him some insight into the awesome future of our people that God had revealed to him one covenant-making night. Abraham called it a "horror of great darkness."

Sometimes Abraham came back to our camp with Jacob to spend a few weeks with us. In his last years he was with us most of the time. He loved our boys. When they were infants, he had held the one and then the other up toward the one God for His blessing. I had wanted Abraham to live long enough that our sons could know him—and he had.

During his last few years he became periodically preoccupied with thoughts of death and obviously felt it might come to him soon. He didn't look at dying as a fearsome experience, but as a way through which he would be gathered some marvelous day to those who had preceded him—and to his God.

He spoke of the ritual meal to be prepared at the time of his death. As head of our clan he would be honored by having a meal of red stew served in his memory. It must be prepared by someone other than Isaac, for the immediate family was not to be involved in its complicated details. The one designated to prepare it was the eldest grandson.

As Abraham awaited death, he did more than plan the meal to follow his burial. He transferred all his possessions to Isaac. He remained the nominal head of our clan, but Isaac assumed the responsibility for all the property, including the closely guarded olive-wood box.

Isaac knew of the box and the treasure it held, but Abraham couldn't resist making a formal presentation, explaining it to Isaac as if for the first time.

"This box, Isaac, is the most valuable possession you have. In it are records of our family line, of how God has dealt with us, and of how He began the world, destroyed it and then replenished it. These writings have been handed down and carefully preserved. You are to add to them only as the Spirit of the one God directs.

"You will make entries of your experiences and of things concerning your children. Then, when you are old, you will entrust this to the one who, according to God's plan, is the link in his generation to the long line through which God will fulfill His promise of blessing."

Isaac was ready with the words his father wanted to hear. "I know the importance of what you are telling me, Father. You have read those writings to me so many times that I know most of them by heart. I—and my heir after me—will honor and protect this box and its unique contents as you have and will add to them as the Lord God directs.

"He has already given me an entry to make. I must write His words concerning our sons, given while they were yet in Rebekah's womb."

Isaac took the large chest from his father and stood looking at it, awed by his new responsibility. He worked late into the night—praying, thinking about the task of record keeping, then praying some more. At last, when he had peace of mind about what the Lord God wanted written, he began to write—first on clay tablets, then copied onto papyrus. This done, he put the finished writing into the olive-wood box, covered it with a fine linen wrapper, and placed it in its copper chest as he had seen his father do through the years. Finally, he buried it under the floor of his room in our tent, to be protected with his life if necessary.

The next years passed quickly, filled with the liveliness of two vivacious, imaginative, frequently quarrelsome boys.

Our flocks increased; merchandising of wool went well; fields and gardens were abundantly productive. We were grateful to the Lord God.

Esau and Jacob became more obviously opposite as the years went by. Esau was boisterous, given to wild exaggeration. He was full of energy; he was exhausting company. Jacob was steady, predictable and quiet—rather like his father. He was generally easygoing and more comfortable to be around than Esau was. The boys were two different types of people— as the Lord God had said they would be.

———————————————— 4

> The boys grew up, and Esau became a skillful hunter, a man of the open
> country, while Jacob was a quiet man, staying among the tents.
>
> *Genesis 25:27*

Our sons were to have a celebration in their honor, marking the first day of their twelfth year. It was a day to feast with family and friends—a time for them to feel grown up.

They no longer would be considered children. Their study requirements would be substantially increased. In addition to reading and writing, Isaac would introduce algebra, astronomy and medicine—sciences Abraham had learned in the schools of Ur and had taught him. From this time on the boys would also be expected to go with Isaac to the altar when he made sacrifices to the Lord God. They were to learn the traditions of the family, especially those concerning worship and obedience to the Lord God.

As if all this weren't enough, they would be given the responsibility of tending the flocks from time to time. Being 12 was a serious thing.

It was fun, too. Our sons were given servants as companions-three for Esau and three for Jacob. These carefully chosen menservants were young enough to be good company for the boys, but old enough to have basic knowledge in the care of sheep and goats and to be dependable guides through the surrounding countryside.

At the first opportunity Esau planned a trip to his favorite hunting area. Jacob soon was on his way to visit Abraham's camp at Mamre.

As months went by, Esau's hunting trips became almost constant; he traveled farther and stayed longer. Once when he was only 14, he and his companions went on a hunting trip along the Jordan. They were gone more than a week, and we became worried. Isaac sent a scouting party to search for them, but the searchers returned to report no sign of Esau's little group. At the end of the second week he rode hard into camp, dismounted and ran to our tent with shoulders back and head high—walking like a monarch. He had been in the dense forest along the Jordan and had stalked and killed a lion! This whetted his appetite for other daring adventures, and he grew skillful in hunting all kinds of game. He often delighted Isaac by bringing home deer, from which we made his favorite venison supper.

Esau neglected the teaching sessions Isaac planned for him and forgot the times of the sacrifice. He preferred to be off somewhere, riding to the kill. He showed little sensitivity toward the God of Abraham and Isaac, yet his engaging personality could charm his father into excusing him every time.

One day when Isaac and I were discussing Esau, Isaac said, "Esau reminds me of Ishmael. Ishmael was a bold, clever outdoorsman. I wonder . . . if he could have remained with us . . . how things would have been between him and me. I shall never be sure, but because of Esau I can now understand why my father asked whether Ishmael might not stand before the Lord as His person."

"Abraham asked that of God? Isaac, why do you think such a thing?"

"Because he told me so." Isaac began speaking in a matter-of-fact tone, but tears were close to the surface as he continued. "He told me how difficult it was for him to send Ishmael away. . . . He loved him as I love Esau. I was surprised—and disappointed. Of course it was stupid of me to have thought my father could love only me. Now that I have two sons of my own, I see it's impossible to love just one of them.

"I hope there won't be jealousy between my sons, as there was between Ishmael and me."

Isaac had given me an opportunity to bring up something that had been on my mind for a long time. I plunged into it, eager to unload my uneasiness.

"Isaac, my husband, don't you think you might be fostering jealousy? It's plain how much you favor Esau."

Isaac appeared startled at my words. I don't know what he might have said just then, but I decided I wouldn't be interrupted until I had presented a fuller protest.

"I can't understand your attitude toward the boys! Jacob spends more time with you than Esau does. He attends to your teaching and accompanies you to the sacrifices faithfully—yet you show him little of the warmth and joy you have when Esau comes around. You take Jacob's dependability for granted, and I'm certain he senses this."

Isaac thought for a bit and nodded his head slightly as he replied, "I must be more careful of Jacob's feelings, Rebekah."

I sighed with relief. He hadn't become angry; he even seemed to appreciate my counsel—or so I thought! I had only misinterpreted his temporary restraint.

He got up and began to pace back and forth, greatly agitated. He was ready with some counseling of his own.

"Rebekah, you show favoritism, too! You are impatient with Esau's hunting trips, and you dislike his friends. On the other hand, you encourage Jacob's interest in our flocks, you encourage him to supervise our servants, and you deluge him with compliments on his knowledge of the sacred writings!"

I hadn't wanted this to evolve into an argument, but since it had, I kept it going. I raised my voice in defense, "My attitudes toward Jacob are justified because he is making right choices!"

Isaac's eyes narrowed as they always did when he was annoyed. "Even if there is reason to scold Esau and praise Jacob, does that rule out your loving them both?"

I was offended that Isaac could have doubted my love for both my children. Of course I was unhappy about many things Esau was doing and about the companions he was choosing—but I loved him!

"Isaac, things are bad enough without misunderstandings making them worse. Please, hear me—I love Esau, but he shuts me out of his life. Jacob is thoughtful; he talks to me about his interests and dreams. He and I laugh together. Often we work together. We always understand each other.

"But now, enough of this comparing our boys and doubting each other's love for both of them. We are family. We belong together, and we all love each other." Even as I spoke that ideal, I knew it was not fact. The boys seldom got along well. Esau evaded responsibility whenever possible. Jacob assumed responsibility, then resented Esau for not doing his share. There were frequent, sharp confrontations between them.

Isaac spent more time than ever with Esau—when Esau managed to be in camp. I increasingly depended on Jacob for conversation and companionship.

5

See to it that no one misses the grace of God and that no bitter root grows up to cause trouble and defile many. See that no one is sexually immoral, or is godless like Esau, who for a single meal sold his inheritance rights as the oldest son.   *Hebrews 12:15-16*

*t*he boys turned 15. Abraham had been staying with us most of the time but had returned to Mamre to take care of some business, and he did not return for several weeks. We missed him very much. We were to miss him even more.

At the age of 175 Abraham went to sleep one evening in early spring. Eliezer thought he saw an unusual light in his master's tent and went to see what it was—but by then there was only darkness.

Messengers were sent immediately to tell Isaac—and Ishmael. The two half brothers took Abraham's body to the cave of Machpelah in the field of Ephron near Mamre—where Sarah had been buried many years before.

Isaac was not aware of the dramatic event that had taken place between Esau and Jacob just hours before he came back from Mamre. I was aware, and I stood helpless, not knowing what to do. It was to have a powerful effect on our family for all the years to come.

The day Abraham died Esau was on an extended hunting trip. Isaac didn't know where to send a messenger to find him. In his sorrow he turned to Jacob.

"My son, prepare the traditional meal for the mourners— the red stew. I am going now to bury your grandfather, and when I return, we will eat what you have prepared for us."

And so Jacob, heartbroken about Abraham's death but

comfortable in the tradition of his fathers, performed the time-consuming task of preparing this special meal. In accord with custom, he fasted as he cooked it—although the aroma of the simmering food was tantalizing.

I stopped by to see how he was getting along. The stew had a rich, savory aroma—designed to tempt appetites dulled by sadness.

Suddenly we heard that familiar—piercing—yell! We looked out to see Esau riding hard, prodding his unfortunate camel sharply even though it was running fast enough to leave behind a sizeable cloud of dust. The hunter was home.

Esau dismounted, sniffed the fragrant stew and ran toward the tent where Jacob and I were. As he came, I stepped back to a small, curtained-off section of the tent. I needed time to decide how to tell Esau about his grandfather—and how to tell him of his father's frustration at not being able to get in touch with him. I suppose I really didn't want to tell him at all and hoped Jacob would do it.

I couldn't believe their conversation! The symbolic significance of the special food was lost on Esau. He knew only that he was hungry. With great bluster he ordered, "Give me some of that red stuff—now!"

"This is a special meal, Esau . . ."

"And I am especially hungry! I am faint! I am starving! I want food—now! NOW!" His bombastic voice gave no evidence of weakness.

"Our servants will prepare a meal for you, or you can fix something for yourself. There is plenty of other food. You don't need this."

"It will take too long to find the servants and have them fix a meal. I am too faint to cook for myself. I want that food, and I want it now!"

"Over there is fruit and cheese. Eat that until your hunger subsides, then get a proper meal."

"No! You have plenty there. Give me some of it!"

Jacob's countenance changed; he was no longer defensive, but condescending. He folded his arms across his chest and smiled. His next words were measured.

"I will sell it to you."

"I have no money."

"I don't want money."

"What do you want then?"

"The birthright—all claim you might have to it."

Esau's mouth twisted cynically. "The birthright! You want to be Satan-bruiser? You want to be earth-blesser? You want to be family priest!"

"More than anything else."

"I am dying of starvation, and you talk of such things. What profit shall a birthright be to me if I am dead? You can have it. I despise it!"

"Do you swear to give up all right even to contest this in time to come?"

"Yes. I swear it. For me there will be no time to come if I don't get some of that food! Do you hear me?"

I watched through a slit in the curtain amazed. Jacob calmly dished out a large serving of the stew for his ravenous brother, without mentioning Abraham's death or the significance of the food.

Esau gulped it down and ran from the tent. He had not noticed the lentil stew, the round shape of the seeds representing the wheel of death that turns to touch everyone sooner or later. And he certainly did not notice that Jacob was performing a duty required of the firstborn, preparing that ritual meal for the dead.

Jacob stood alone beside the huge kettle that held an ample remainder of the stew. I came back into the room, wondering what to say after the bizarre conversation I had just heard. The only word I could find was a childlike "Why?"

In Jacob's usual direct way he answered, "Because I had been thinking of the birthright as I made this meal—longing to have it, free and clear of any claim Esau might make . . ."

"It is to be given to you anyway."

"So you have told me, but now it will be clear, even in Esau's mind, that he considered it too trivial to care about. He wasn't starving; he was only minutes away from any food in our camp. But, as he said, the birthright was not worth a bowl of stew to him."

Jacob looked pleased with what he had done. He felt he had

proved a point once and for all, and he was satisfied.

"Don't mention this to your father when he returns from Mamre. He will have had grief enough for one day."

"I won't mention it to him; but I won't forget it. Mother, there's no way to explain how excited I feel at this moment! It is as though I actually have received the birthright!"

Young Jacob, a mere 15 years of age, smiled with complacency--believing his life goal had been attained.

We didn't speak of this to Isaac that day or in the days following. Then, as weeks and months passed, it seemed even more awkward to bring it up. The months grew into years. Each year saw our family drifting further apart, perhaps unintentionally—but most irretrievably.

Jacob—I more often called him *Ya'aqob-El*--became overseer of all our flocks. The undershepherds worked well with him; he shared their hardships. Flock tending demanded much strength and stamina, and it called for vigorous health and bravery in the face of danger from thieves, wild beasts and the elements.

Esau became almost totally estranged from both Jacob and me, although he kept in fairly close contact with his father.

"Isaac, I worry about Esau. Speak to him about the way he is living. Remind him that he is a member of a family from whom God expects devotion and purity. He is nearly 30 years old; he should be settling down."

"Rebekah, you fuss too much about him. I enjoy his stories of the hunt and I enjoy the meat he brings back. As for his friends—and the women he sees . . . it is difficult to approach him about these things . . . but I will talk to him the next time he comes home."

Isaac never did succeed in changing the way Esau lived. Against our wishes he married Judith and Basemath, both Hittites. Two wives—and neither from our people! Isaac and I were grieved by these marriages, and our sadness increased as we saw these foreign women draw Esau further and further from the ideals of our home—and from the worship of our God.

We were thankful for Jacob's devotion to Elohim and thankful he had not become involved with pagan women.

Our all-knowing God was aware, before our sons were born, how each would be. And in that perfect knowledge, He also knew our family would reach an unbreachable chasm.

That point was reached one year ago.

6

Then he said, "My son, bring me some of your game to eat, so that I may give you my blessing."   *Genesis 27:25*

Isaac had not been feeling well for several months; his eyes were bothering him. Some days he could see nothing more than vague shapes of things. He believed he soon would die. A part of his physical decline came, I am sure, from witnessing Esau's rebellious attitudes that showed no sign of decreasing as he got older. It was during one of his depressed moods that Isaac made what he must have thought was an attempt to restore Esau to the family—and to God. He called his favorite son to him on the morning of that terrible day.

He was sitting in the doorway of our tent. I was in my own room of the tent, busy weaving wool into cloth for a robe for Jacob. I heard Isaac's voice strained with excitement as he dispatched a servant to bring Esau to him before he left on another hunting trip.

Esau soon came, and I stopped weaving to listen carefully to his father's conversation with him. I did not (and still do not) think that was wrong, because they were discussing a family matter. Even so, I have wished many times that I hadn't heard.

But I did hear, and so I felt responsible to see that their trickery was not successful. Jacob—the God-appointed priest of our family, the owner of a flippantly sold birthright, *Ya'aqob-El*--was in immediate danger of being deposed. Each word cut into my mind as I heard Isaac say, "I am now an old man and don't know the day of my death. Now then, get your weapons—your quiver and bow—and go out to the open country to hunt some wild game for me. Prepare me the kind of tasty food I like and bring it to me to eat, so that I may give you my blessing before I die."

All I could think was, Give Esau the blessing? Never! I had looked forward to seeing Jacob receive the blessing from Isaac. I had planned the great celebration feast to which relatives and friends would be invited. It would be one of the most notable days in Jacob's life.

I drew my mind away from what might have been, wasting no more time thinking of the festivities that should mark so great an event, and concentrated on what must be done to block Isaac's plan that was already being implemented.

I instinctively knew it would be of no use to present Jacob's case to Isaac. I would have to do something more drastic, something more certain to have the right outcome—and every minute counted.

I found Jacob and hurriedly told him what I had overheard. He bowed his head with the desolation of one who had just lost everything of value.

"Jacob, I . . ."

"Please, Mother, sympathy would just make me feel worse right now."

"I have no consoling words, my son. I have a plan. Now listen carefully, and do what I tell you.

"Go out to the flock and bring me two choice young goats, so I can prepare some tasty food for your father, just the way he likes it. Then take it to your father to eat, so that he may give you his blessing before he dies."

Jacob looked at me incredulously. "He will know it's not the wild game."

"No, he won't. I'll simmer it with dried grapes and cover it with almonds and pistachio nuts. It will taste just like the wild game that Esau cooks in the same way."

"Why risk enraging Father by doing this? Why not just tell him that Esau freely gave up his right to contest my claim to the birthright-blessing. He and I were both satisfied that day. I had his promise not to try to assume the office of family priest; Esau had the assurance he wouldn't have to do it."

"My son, there's no time now to talk of that transaction between you and your brother. I am not even taking the time to remind your father of what God Himself told us before you were born. He is, for whatever reason, determined to do this. There is no time to waste."

Jacob was hesitant to undertake this deception, and his face brightened as he thought of a major obstacle. "But my brother Esau is a hairy man, and I'm a man with smooth skin. What if my father touches me? I would appear to be tricking him and would bring down a curse on myself rather than a blessing."

I answered that he should not worry about what he "appeared" to be doing. His interest was to protect what was his and to keep from unduly agitating his ailing father. We were all concerned about exciting or worrying Isaac.

Jacob still did not move. I was never more aware of lost moments. Into the quiet that settled between us I shouted, thinking to convey authority by my raised voice, "My son, let the curse fall on me! Just do what I say! Go and get the young goats for me!"

There were tears in Jacob's eyes and sadness in his voice. "I had not thought it would be like this."

I held my tears back and said firmly, "But this is the way it happens to be. Now go!"

He turned away, and I watched him walk with gradually increasing determination toward the edge of the nearest pasture. When Jacob was convinced that this was the only way, he did not waver again.

While he got the animals, I prepared the rest of the meal. After he brought them back and dressed them, I started them simmering. Next I took the goatskins and covered Jacob's hands and neck with them. We did not speak to each other. Our minds were busy with the immediate task at hand, the risks involved, and the regret that deception instead of celebration would mark so important a moment.

I ran to Esau's tent, found his best clothes, and brought them to where Jacob waited as he watched the simmering meat. He put on the clothes. He was ready; the food was prepared. We had done all we could, and, while we regretted the necessity for deception, at no time did we think it was wrong. Unfortunate? Yes. Exciting? Yes. Dangerous? Yes, perhaps. Wrong? No!

I followed Jacob, and when he went into the tent, I stood outside, guarding against intrusion and listening.

At first there was no sound. I wondered if Jacob had given in to panic and would run out of the tent, ending our plan. Could he think of nothing to say? Then I heard a voice—pitched lower than Jacob usually spoke. He sounded just like Esau!

"My father."

"Yes, my son, who is it?"

"I am Esau your firstborn. I have done as you told me. Please sit up and eat some of my game so that you may give me your blessing."

"How did you find it so quickly, my son?"

"The Lord your God gave me success."

"Come near so I can touch you, my son, to know whether you really are my son Esau or not."

Jacob moved closer, and his father touched him. "The voice is the voice of Jacob, but the hands are the hands of Esau. Are you really my son Esau?"

And I had thought he sounded just like Esau! Isaac's sense of hearing was sharper than his eyesight. For a moment fear caused a sharp pain to pierce my heart. Isaac was suspicious! Would this unsettle Jacob and cause our plan to unravel now?

Jacob waited only a moment, then answered in a voice that betrayed no weakness, "I am Esau."

Then Isaac said, "My son, bring me some of your game to eat, so I may give you my blessing."

Jacob brought it to him and he ate; he brought some wine and he drank. Then his father said to him, "Come here, my son, and kiss me."

So he went and kissed him. When Isaac caught the smell of Esau's clothes, he blessed him and said:

> Ah, the smell of my son
> > is like the smell of a field
> > that the Lord has blessed.
> May God give you of heaven's dew
> > and of earth's richness—
> > an abundance of grain and new wine.
> May nations serve you

and peoples bow down to you.
Be lord over your brothers,
    and may the sons of your mother bow down to you.
May those who curse you be cursed
    and those who bless you be blessed.

There were tears in Isaac's weakened eyes, and there were tears in Jacob's eyes. There was one more warm embrace, then Jacob left his father and walked calmly from the tent.

We walked together back to where the food had been prepared, neither of us speaking. We felt uncomfortable in each other's presence for the first time in our lives—neither knowing what to say.

Once he got into the hastily arranged plan, Jacob found it necessary to say things he never would have imagined possible. My heart ached for him, knowing in what great vexation of spirit he had received the blessing. He picked up his own clothes, went to Esau's tent to return the borrowed things, and dressed again in his own robe. He slowly came back to where I sat staring at the cooking fire. I did not look up.

After a few minutes he spoke, trying to tell me of the desolate feeling the ordeal had brought him.

"I could say I was the firstborn without hesitation, since I purchased from Esau himself the right to stand in his stead. The thing I cannot justify is bringing in the name of the Lord God—saying He gave me success in finding the game so quickly."

"Were the young goats not from God?"

He gave me a faint smile, appreciating that I was groping for words to ease his hurt, his feeling of guilt. "Mother, I feel unclean. The blessing should not have been given under such circumstances. How can I perform the sacred duties of family priest after all this?"

"It was an emergency. How else could God's will in this have been accomplished?"

"We will never know now, my mother."

His eyes flashed with anger, then filled with tears. I tried to speak, but he held up his hand for silence and I was grateful, for I didn't know what to say.

We sat there a long time together, not talking to each

other, trying to sort out our thoughts.

Suddenly our introspection ended. Esau was walking toward Isaac's tent, carrying a large tray of savory meat. We watched in panic as he went in to where Isaac was. Our deception—that is what we had to admit it was—was about to be found out!

Jacob jumped to his feet. "Will Father withdraw the blessing now and curse me instead?"

"He will withdraw the blessing only if he believes it was given to the wrong son."

"He will believe it was the wrong son. Esau won't tell him he sold the birthright."

"But he will remember, I am sure, God's admonition in this matter. Before your brother speaks to him, I believe your father will have been thinking of God's Word, realizing he erred in his plan for Esau.

"And I think that once he realizes he was tricked into doing what was right, he will let it stand. We have all erred, Jacob. You and I ran ahead of God, using a wrong means to a good end, but Isaac must know that he was departing from God's plan in what he was trying to do. No, I don't think he will retract the blessing, Jacob."

"Even so, Mother, our family is hopelessly divided now." Jacob's face became ashen as he tried to express his feelings. "I dread Esau's fury, and I don't want to face my father—ever again. Mine is a hollow victory."

"No! Not hollow! Meaningful! You are God's chosen man; He makes no mistakes. Become the man God knows you can be. He knows your potential as well as your faults, and He has chosen to work through you. That is your victory! And whatever God allows to happen because of today's events will not negate your victory."

"You talk of victory, my mother, but all I see are problems and trouble ahead."

"Jacob, my son, be ready for difficulties from now on! God allows His chosen ones trials and testings to strengthen faith and increase patience. You know that your grandfather and your father both learned this. But remember—you are God's person of most special concern."

_____7

When Rebekah was told what her older son Esau had said, she sent for her younger son Jacob, and said to him, "Your brother Esau is consoling himself with the thought of killing you. Now then, my son, do what I say: Flee at once to my brother Laban in Haran." *Genesis 27:42-43*

Rebekah!" Isaac heard my footstep and shouted my name. It had been several hours since I watched Esau go inside Isaac's tent. Like Jacob, I was afraid, so I hurriedly decided to visit Almon's new baby. Conveniently, Almon lived on the far side of our servants' quarters. My walk over there was refreshing, and I stepped briskly. The baby was a beautiful little girl, and I found reasons to stay to help the young mother for a while, thinking it would have been nice to have had a daughter of my own.

I started home—slowly. I was emotionally and physically spent. Each step dissolved some of the distance protecting me from an unavoidable confrontation with Isaac.

He was standing at the door of our tent, and because I did not answer his first call, he shouted again more loudly, "Rebekah! We must talk! Now!"

I still did not answer but walked past him into the tent. He followed and motioned for me to sit on the floor cushions, then he dramatically paced back and forth across the room for an undue length of time. He seemed as willing as I was to postpone the words that had to be said.

His patience always outlasted mine, so I was the first to break the silence. "Isaac, I'm waiting for you to speak. You have much to say. Tell me what you want; ask me what you want; but talk to me. End this smothering silence!"

In a voice too sad for anger he began. "Why, Rebekah? Why

did you do it? It must have been your idea; Jacob never would have thought of it."

"Yes, it was my plan, and Jacob was not willingly part of it. I pleaded with him and commanded him. Then he complied.

"Now, about the why—it was because I knew the blessing belonged to Jacob and would not see him tricked out of it. It was his by God's decree—and by the barter."

"Barter?"

"Indeed, yes."

"What are you talking about? Barter? Concerning the birthright? What do you mean?" Isaac's voice trembled.

"Jacob so wanted the blessing that, although God decreed it would be his, he secured his right to it by offering to buy it from Esau. Esau accepted Jacob's terms without hesitation.

"You were not told of the barter, my husband, because it happened the day you returned from burying Abraham. I felt it would add too heavy a load on top of the grief you already carried then. And afterwards . . . I don't know . . . there never seemed to be an appropriate time to discuss such an unhappy subject.

"We were wrong in not telling you of it, but even had it not taken place, why did you arrange in secret to bless Esau when you yourself recorded years ago that God had ordained our younger son to be above the elder?"

I waited for his answer as he struggled to find the words. We each had tears in our eyes; each stood in error; each had contributed in a different way to a situation that never should have developed. We had no defense for our actions. In this time of grief we had no solace for each other.

I never have possessed the ability to endure strained silence. "Isaac . . . Isaac . . ."

"Be still, Rebekah! I cannot answer your question, but I can tell you what happened when Esau came to my tent with the savory meat.

"I smelled the blend of the herbs and nuts in which the meat had been cooked before I realized my eldest son was there. I wondered why I was being served meat twice. I called out, asking who it was. He answered 'I am Esau, your firstborn.'

"I was trembling mightily as I asked again, 'Who?'

"At first I thought my trembling was due to this illness, but then I realized I was shaking with rage at having been tricked." Isaac's voice had been under control until this point, but now it became so choked with tears that words ceased for a time. He roughly wiped his tears away with the sleeve of his robe, then continued. "More than that . . . I was shaking . . . overcome by fright at what I had done. I realized I had been going against the one God's command.

"I explained to Esau about the meat I had just eaten and the blessing that had been given. In confessing this to Esau I also confessed it before God. And then I found the courage to say with boldness, 'Yes, and he shall be blessed!'

"Rebekah, Esau knows beyond any doubt—the blessing I gave Jacob stands. I told him, raising my voice over his bitter tirades, that Jacob had been made his lord."

I tried to fathom what it had meant to Isaac to deny his fond affection for Esau, to humble himself before his favorite son—and before his God and now before me.

Having said all this, Isaac sat on the cushions beside me. We reached for each other's hands. We had held hands as young lovers, as happy parents, as companions in good and bad times. As our hands met, we affirmed all our years together and our love for each other, even in the face of our present heartbreak. Whatever became of the relationships between us and our sons—or between our two sons themselves—we loved each other, and this gave us comfort.

"You spoke bravely and well to Esau, my husband, my beloved Isaac."

We said nothing for a while, neither mentioning Esau's response. Those were the last moments without the desperate fear that has possessed me for the rest of my life.

"Rebekah, do you remember what Esau used to call Jacob when he was angry with him, when they were boys?"

"Of course. It was Ya'aqab--deceiver—instead of his given name—Ya'aqeb--heel. I have no doubt which name he used today—it was Ya'aqab, was it not?"

"It was that, among others. Esau shouted that his brother was a thief, a sneak, a cheat and a liar."

"No! Isaac, it was Esau who was cheating! He knew the blessing belonged to Jacob. Of his own free will he had traded it away because he didn't care about it. But if he resorted to name-calling, perhaps that served to free him from the frustration he felt, just standing there holding the savory meat that was as untouched by you as if it weren't there."

I thought of Esau, outwitted and outmaneuvered this time, and I couldn't suppress a faint smile.

From the tight line formed by Isaac's mouth and the wrinkles that covered his forehead I knew there was more to hear, and I asked, "Do you think he will stop at name-calling, or might he become violent? Do you think he might harm Jacob?"

Isaac, recalling the terror of that moment, answered slowly and with great care. "The rage of his words was less frightening than the sudden quiet that followed. He stopped pacing back and forth; he no longer shouted his tirades. He was standing close to me, breathing heavily and mumbling to himself. I reached out, thinking to sooth him. My hand felt his right hand. It held a dagger. He pulled away from me shouting 'Ya'aqab,' and ran from the tent. I have not seen him since.

"Rebekah . . . do you know . . . where Jacob is?"

"He was going into the fields with the flocks."

"Send for him. He must not be in dagger range—or arrow range—of Esau today; tonight he must sleep in our tent. By tomorrow Esau's temper will have cooled, and things will be better between them."

That was the longest night I ever remembered. Jacob was safe in our tent, but I did not sleep. A cold, aching heaviness settled over me, and I have not been free of it since. But at that point I had not yet given up hope.

By morning I had reached a logical solution to our immediate problem. I knew how to protect Jacob without having it look as though he were being protected. He never could abide being watched over. With my plan he would be safe and have a happy adventure as well. It would mean having him away from home, but probably only for a short time—until Esau could be diverted from his passionate hatred.

After breakfast we learned Esau had left camp at daybreak,

going off on a hunting trip. That was good news! The hunting trips he still made frequently were a joy to him. By riding hard and shooting big game he worked off agitations. Because of his rage this time, I hoped he was going after lion—bagging that great a prize might change his mood.

Jacob went back to the flocks before I told him the solution I had for the dangerous situation between him and Esau.

It was quiet that morning, and for some time I thought about my two sons. I pictured them as they pursued their typical vocations—Esau sauntering in with his lifeless trophy draped across his proud shoulders and Jacob sometimes with a wolf-torn sheep or lamb that he carried gently to where he could care for it, restore it to wholeness and return it to the flock.

By midmorning I decided to tell Jacob of my plan, and I walked the long distance out to talk with him, thankful for occasional spots of shade where I could stop to rest. I finally came to where he was—on a grassy slope beside a flock of choice lambs.

It seemed right, having Jacob here with the flocks. I wondered if I should forget my idea. Would that terrible yesterday cloud our lives from now on, or would we be able to get back to some kind of normal living once the rough edges of people's pride and nerves had worn smoother? To have a family that could not live as a family was worse than being without one!

Jacob saw me coming and jumped up from where he was sitting, calling in surprise, "Mother, is something wrong?"

How could I answer a question like that? Everything was wrong! He knew that. Not knowing how to answer, I pretended I hadn't heard him. He ran to meet me.

"Mother, what has happened? Is Father all right?"

"He is as well as when you left him a few hours ago."

"Good. Then what would cause you to walk all the way out here—alone?"

"Nothing more has happened. I want to keep it that way, and that's why I've come. I want to discuss a plan with you, and I want to talk where no one else will hear me."

"Maybe you should not plan any more things for me for a while."

"Jacob! I did what I felt I had to do yesterday. You can't possibly know how sorry I am that it worked out as it did. But yesterday is gone, and I am again doing what I feel I must. Let me tell you what seems best to me. You can judge it for yourself. I have not spoken to your father about it, wanting your reaction first. Will you listen?"

"Of course. I'm curious to know what is so urgent that you would walk all the way to this pastureland. Please begin, but first let's sit on that large rock under the almond tree over there."

The almond tree was in full blossom. I looked up through its pink-white clusters to bright blue sky, catching sight of a flash of red as a bird darted to its nest. It seemed wrong to intrude on such beauty with any words except those of praise to God for His marvelous creation. I drank in the beauty as nourishment for my unhappy heart.

"Mother, will you tell me what is on your mind?"

"Oh, yes, yes, Jacob. I was just taking a minute to remember it's springtime. Now—I have been thinking . . . that you might go on a trip to visit some of your relatives that you have never seen—those who live in Haran. My brother, Laban, should see what a fine man you are. You should meet your cousins, Leah and Rachel.

"It will be good for you to see more of the world than pasturelands, Gerar, Beersheba and Mamre. On the way to Haran you could stop at Damascus. It is a great, exciting city. Do you remember your grandfather telling about visiting there on his way to Canaan from Haran? I always thought of that city as special because it was there that he purchased faithful Eliezer, whom he sent to Haran to find a bride for his son."

"I know the story of Eliezer finding you and bringing you here, Mother. Are you sending me to Haran to look for a wife for myself, since you don't have an Eliezer?" Jacob was smiling as if the idea appealed to him.

"You might find a wife, but that's not my chief intent. Jacob, you have to get away from here before Esau returns from his hunting trip. While he carries this crazed attitude of vengeance towards you, there is no safety for you here. When his temper mellows, I'll send for you right away.

"Go to Haran. Meet your relatives. Have an interesting trip. Find a wife—whatever pleases you. But go! And leave before tomorrow night.

"Parah can oversee your flocks while you are gone. You need have no worry with him looking after them."

Jacob offered no argument, made no comments, asked no questions. He looked toward his sheep and walked over to them. He called them by name and patted each one affectionately.

As I watched him, I marveled that one so gentle could also be so bold. He never mentioned it to us, but other shepherds told us of his killing wolves and running off would-be thieves on several occasions.

After some time he returned to where I was sitting, and without any trace of emotion he said, "All right, it is settled in my mind. Send Parah as soon as you get back to camp. If I must go, I want leave-taking to be as short as possible. I'll be on my way as soon as I can pack."

He helped me get up from the low stone that had been my not-so-comfortable seat.

"Believe me, your leaving home for a while is for the best for all of us. Perhaps it will be possible for you to return before the autumn rains.

"I'll go back now to send Parah—and to ask your father's permission for this venture to Haran."

It might have been my imagination, but I thought I heard Jacob laugh ever so softly—and sadly—when I mentioned asking Isaac's permission. It was a stinging comment. Even Jacob sensed the luxury Isaac allowed himself—his relaxed, unhurried, almost indifferent approach to things. It demanded that someone else take responsibility, out of sheer desperation to get things done! I had made this plan, walked out to discuss it with Jacob, and was hurrying to dispatch Parah. Only then did I consider how to approach Isaac with this possibility of averting a murder!

Isaac had taken the olive-wood box out of its place and was

busy with preliminary writing on clay tablets, bending close to the table to see.

"Isaac! You are not writing what happened yesterday!"

"Yes, I am."

"Why? For future generations to know our family troubles?"

As bad as it already was, this made things worse, almost beyond enduring. For the first time since all these traumatic events began I broke down and really cried. I sobbed. I allowed myself the freedom of a tantrum. It had been years since I had allowed myself such a release of emotion. The wilder I became, the more stone-like Isaac became. He would not give me the satisfaction of knowing I disturbed him. There was not the slightest chance of my changing his mind about the writing. Worn out by hysterics, I had to quiet down. I scarcely had strength left to ask, one more time, why.

"Because God decides what is placed in the sacred record. I am not writing willingly of our distress. If it were my own choice, I would write only the good.

"After breakfast this morning I went to our altar with an animal sacrifice. I wanted to tell the Lord God that I was repentant for everything that each member of my family did yesterday that was contrary to His will. Then I wanted that day to be remembered no more.

"During the hours I waited at the altar, He impressed on me that He wanted a full account to be written down."

Again I asked why. It was a childish question, but it held the bewildered hurt of an old woman.

"I wondered why at first, too. Then the Lord God led me to think of the generations who will read these words. They must see us as people who erred and yet were not discarded by Him. They must learn from our experiences not to allow sins and mistakes to keep them from making what amends are possible and then go on being His people."

Isaac's answer gave both of us much to think about. After a while I said, "Those are more than your own thoughts, Isaac. You couldn't have been that objective, at least not this soon, about our heartbreak. This reasoning is truly from God.

"Even so . . . I still would rather keep it private, my husband!"

"So would I. But the Spirit of God gave me a restlessness until I began to write these things. And since it's distasteful to me to do it, please don't delay me any longer. I want to get it done and pack the box away again."

"Can you wait a few minutes—so I can tell you something very urgent?"

"If it's urgent, how could it have waited while we talked about the writings? If it isn't urgent—it has waited already and it can wait some more."

"It is urgent! It is just that in my shock at what you were writing I left it temporarily unsaid. Please, hear me now."

"All right. My train of thought has been so disrupted that it will take me some time to come back to my writing anyway. What is so pressing?"

"First, think of how, even before our present crisis, we had been troubled by Esau's heathen wives. They have made our lives miserable, and they have influenced Esau further away from our family and from the worship of the Lord God."

"Rebekah, that is a long-standing problem, hardly one that must be dealt with in the next hour."

"I know. That's why I said it was only the first of the things I must say. What if Jacob also decides to take a Moabite wife, or a Hittite? Your father took no chances with your future. He sent to Haran for one of your own people. Should you not be as concerned about Jacob's mate?"

"You want a suitable wife for Jacob. Fine. But that, too, is something that hardly must be handled within the hour. What, I ask you specifically, is the urgency of your interruption?"

"You know what it is, Isaac! It's Jacob's life! He cannot remain here while Esau is in his violent rage! Jacob would not want to appear to be running from Esau as a fugitive. So we can choose this time to send him to visit his uncle Laban in Haran—and perhaps while he's there he can find a wife from our people."

At last I had captured Isaac's full attention. He sat for a while, thinking of the proposed trip to Haran, nodding his head slightly in agreement. I pressed the point.

"If Jacob stays here and is killed, or if he stays here and

takes a foreign wife, my life is worthless to me. I cannot stand any more trouble."

Isaac's forehead wrinkled. He folded his arms across his chest, and his fingers rhythmically tapped his upper arms.

I prayed he would decide the matter in the way that would most easily solve our immediate problems—and I was certain what that way was! My prayer ended; Isaac's silence did not.

I waited, prayed again, and waited again. When it seemed he was not going to say anything more I got up to leave. As I was at the doorway of the tent, he spoke in a very tired voice—a voice that held a hint of tears, "Send Jacob to me."

8

So Isaac called for Jacob and blessed him . . . .   *Genesis 28:1*

It was late in the afternoon when I saw Jacob coming in from the pasturelands. I went out to meet him and told him his father was waiting to see him—that all was well regarding the trip to Haran. I walked with him to where Isaac waited in our tent, and, since Isaac did not ask me to leave, I stayed to listen to what he would tell our son.

"Do not marry a Canaanite woman. Go at once to Paddan Aram, to the house of your mother's father Bethuel. Take a wife for yourself there, from among the daughters of Laban, your mother's brother."

He had not spoken to Jacob the night before when he had slept in our tent, hiding from Esau. These were his first words to his younger son since he unknowingly gave him the blessing. He merely gave Jacob leave to go to Haran. He had not accused him of being a cheat and did not even refer to events of the day before. His words and his tone of voice had a healing, calming effect on Jacob. As he sensed his father's acceptance of him, he relaxed, and the tension lines around his mouth disappeared to allow him even to smile a bit at the prospects of the trip ahead of him.

But Isaac had saved the most important part of his communication with his son until last. Tears he had been holding back now ran across his face, giving eloquent testimony of his love—and of his sorrow over all that had happened. Placing his left hand on Jacob's shoulder, he raised his right arm as if to reach to the very hand of God. By now there were tears in Jacob's eyes, too, and in mine.

In a clear, steady voice Isaac began to speak. His words

made Jacob's eyes shine and caused him to stand taller than before.

> May God Almighty bless you and make you fruitful and increase your numbers until you become a community of peoples. May he give you and your descendants the blessing of Abraham, so that you may take possession of the land where you now live as an alien, the land God gave to Abraham.

The blessing truly had been given now—without deception and without duress. It was given from a heart brimming with faith; it was received with gladness and hope!

Jacob decided to travel with as few possessions as possible—only what he could carry. He did not take a camel or donkey. He wanted no attendant. He took barely enough money for the food and lodging he would need along the way. But he did take with him the priceless appointment to be God's person in the line of promise.

I helped him sort through his things, storing some away and putting essentials into his backpack. His only comment while we worked was, "I will be going opposite from the way my grandfather traveled. He came from Haran into Canaan; I will go from Canaan into Haran. It does seem that I'm going in the wrong direction.

"I don't want to stay long in Haran; I won't feel at ease there."

"You will feel perfectly at home—you will be with family," I assured him, adding that I, too, hoped his stay would not be long.

He left early the next morning, before we awakened. At first I was disappointed at not being able to say good-bye, but then I felt relieved that we were spared one last emotionally exhausting experience.

I spent the rest of that day and the days following in partial numbness to my surroundings. I have never felt fully alive since—part of me has died.

Esau came home from his hunting trip. The lion he had stalked escaped. He had torn his right arm badly on a thorn bush and was in sharp pain. He was angrier than ever. And when he discovered Jacob had gone to Haran to visit his uncle and to find a wife, he was livid!

He ordered his servants to get ready immediately for another journey—a very long one. He did not stop to see Judith or Basemath but hurriedly ate some food, repacked his saddle bags and remounted his camel. He rode past our tent, stopping long enough to shout his feelings.

"Jacob has gone to Uncle Laban. I will go to Uncle Ishmael! Jacob will secure a wife from Laban's house? Let him! I will secure a wife from Ishmael's! I have heard my uncle has a daughter named Mahalath. If she is as beautiful as I have heard, I will marry her. If she is not, I will find another woman!"

Isaac and I were alone. We were grateful we had each other, but we realized that each of us was diminished with our sons gone. Each had taken part of our very life with him.

"Rebekah."

"Yes, my husband?"

"The Lord God has always known . . . which of the two would be worthy of His calling."

"Yes."

"Rebekah."

"Yes, Isaac?"

"I will go now to the altar. I want to pray for God's protection for both of our sons."

When Esau came back, he brought his new wife, Mahalath. His other wives were jealous, and strife was added to strife.

He seldom comes to our tent to talk with us, and when he does, we are careful not to mention Jacob's name. He always wears his dagger now, and he has the disconcerting habit of tapping its handle with his large, hairy right hand. And as he taps it, a smile devoid of joy comes to his lips.

It will be a long, long time before it will be safe to send for Jacob. Surely we can't plan on it before the autumn rains— probably not before the spring rains next year!

O, my son, Jacob. How I have loved you, since before you were born!

I shall always love you.

May God protect—*Ya'aqob-El*!

Part Two

JOURNEY TO HARAN

Jacob sometimes remembered his mother's voice. It had sung, scolded, soothed and taught throughout his life. And now it was strange, not hearing her any more!

Jacob . . . God's plain man.
Jacob . . . chosen by God.

> Exiled from Canaan,
> Lonely, exhausted, hurting.

Jacob . . . God's quiet man.
Jacob . . . kept by God.

> Given a glimpse of glory,
> Granted the voice of God.

Jacob . . . God's chosen man.
Jacob . . . loved by God.

> Stranger in a foreign land,
> Led—to Rachel.

9

Jacob left Beersheba and set out for Haran.   *Genesis 28:10*

Jacob poured out the last of the water he had carried in a special jar all the way from the well at Lahai Roi. It splashed softly into his cup. He looked at it with excitement and despair—emotion that had battled each other in his mind since he left home.

The thrill of being independent of family and servants was waning. He had chosen to go alone to Haran in spite of his mother's urging him to take at least the three servants who customarily went with him into the Negeb, Beersheba and—in former days—to Hebron and Mamre. In some ways it would have been easier to have the servants along, but his brain reeled from the recent, bizzare events, and he did not want companions who might wonder about what had happened and try to pry explanations out of him. Explanations? There were none! There was only confusion.

Jacob needed the healing goodness of quiet. Human company would have robbed him of hours for meditation and prayer. More than ever before, he longed for a personal fellowship with his God.

Sometimes he thought of his mother's repeated warnings about traveling alone. "It's too dangerous! There are robbers! Wild animals—even lions!"

He smiled with a little pride as he recalled his answer. "Alone with flocks by day and night, I already have fought off robbers and wild animals. You see, I'm trained for this journey. Anyway . . . in the pasture or on the road—even in the presence of Esau—I claim God's protection. Do you yourself not call me *Ya'aqob-El?*"

Her answer came from her fear of imminent trouble. "Go! Alone or not—go! I fear Esau more than wild animals or robbers. Go, my son, go with God."

Rebekah's voice had echoed and reechoed in his mind as he plodded over miles of pathways and trade routes. How many days had it been? Four? Five? It didn't matter. His sandals were as dusty one day as another, and his feet as tired.

Once he slept under a giant oak, another night under an ancient olive tree. One night, when he found himself in a desolate area with no trees—not even a sizeable bush—he had shouted to the barrenness, "When I come into possession of this land, I will have trees planted in every idle field, on each vacant hillside—pomegranate trees, olive and almond trees. Perhaps I will even plant some cedars!"

"When I possess the land . . ." His words haunted him. He was leaving it—for who knew how long. Would he ever see it again? The vow to plant trees and the fear of never returning to Canaan—these were evidences of the opposing emotions still warring inside him.

Jacob shook his head to banish the thoughts of despair. He still held the cup of water, allowing the sun to reflect on it and make it sparkle. Then, thinking of Abraham, he drank the water as if performing a ritual.

He looked down at a mass of boulders piled waist high. They were the essence of calmness and permanence—suitable symbols of his grandfather, Abraham. Here, on this hill overlooking the town of Luz, he felt nearer to the old patriarch than he did to his family just 60 miles away.

Abraham had never tired of telling young Jacob about the stone altar he built on this hill. He had built an altar at every place he camped, but this one was especially meaningful to him. It was one of the first he built in Canaan; it was the one to which he returned after he brought his family back from their misadventure in Egypt.

Jacob touched the stones reverently and sat down beside them, wondering if this mound were really part of that altar built so many years before.

He began to realize how tired he was. It felt good to rest; and this huge, flat hilltop provided a wide view of the sur-

rounding countryside and made an interesting vantage point—
a pleasant place to stop.

The hill was surrounded by large almond plantations,
which at this time of year were in abundant blossom. The
acres of white flower-covered trees seemed to provide a festive atmosphere for his arrival there. He thanked Elohim for
their beauty. He reflected on his decision to walk through the
land; it had been a good one. It had given him the feeling of
being one with it, branding it his own with each press of his
foot. For some moments he was at peace, thinking of the
beauty of Canaan, thinking of Abraham and of the God of
Abraham.

Then taunting, unsettling thoughts overtook him again.
God spoke to Abraham long before he came to Luz. He had
never spoken to Jacob. Was it also significant that Jacob was
reversing the route his grandfather had taken? Suppose he
never got back from Haran. Would the Lord God ever speak to
him?

Jacob softly voiced a prayer: "Elohim—God of Abraham
and of Isaac, You talked with my grandfather and with my
father. You gave and affirmed covenants—everlasting covenants! But . . . am I truly the next covenant person? Will You
speak to me?"

He continued, now to himself, "No, surely not to me . . . not
to me. My life is chaos. I received the blessing—after a
fashion—but if I'm God's chosen person, why am I running?
Should I turn and go back home? Or would that make my
mother ill with worry about my being murdered? Would my
going back without a wife disappoint my father?

"And Esau . . . would he think I was afraid to finish the
journey to Haran? And what would Esau do? Would he actually try to kill me?

"Oh, I can't go back to all that! If having the blessing is a
good thing, why is my mind in this turmoil? Where are you,
Lord God? Only in Beersheba? Where should I be? My grandfather went on a wrong path once into Egypt. Am I going in
the wrong direction? How can I know? How can I know?"

His scarcely audible words ceased. He looked at the imper-
sonal sky, the mute trees, the silent stones. When he spoke

again, his voice was not a whisper but an agonized shout, "How can I know?"

After a while he thought of his sack of provisions. He knew he must eat, but nothing in that sack tempted his appetite. He poured out another cup of water from a recently refilled goatskin bag and sipped it slowly.

He tried not to think of anything. He tried to concentrate only on the setting sun. Canaan's sunsets are brief and spectacular.

How could the same sunset be seen also by his family from the fields around Beersheba? Even though he had not been on the road many days, his home camp seemed part of another lifetime. It was incredible that his family shared this sunset.

And the same sunrays fell around that old cave of Machpelah at Mamre where Abraham and his beloved Sarah were buried. Jacob stopped at that cave on his way to Luz. It had seemed the thing to do, but the experience left him unmoved, unable to shed a tear. That cave-tomb, standing in a field like any other field, had not spoken to him of Abraham. His pilgrimage merely fulfilled a duty.

The lowering golden sun would illumine something else— a craggy hill outside Salem, Mt. Moriah. He knew the fearful story of Mt. Moriah well. That hill would always be associated with Isaac and with Abraham—and with the awesome sacrifice they enacted there. Jacob had gone aside from his path to see that hill. He had stood at the foot of it, transfixed. As he had been told, it had a rock outcropping on the east side, and it looked like a skull. He did not go to the top of the hill, for he felt he would be trespassing on holy ground. But seeing that stark place drove him to his knees, and he wept at such devotion to God and at so great a deliverance.

And now Jacob had come to this other hill near Luz intentionally and eagerly. It was a further acknowledgement of Abraham and the large part he had played in Jacob's early training.

Here in this delightfully high and wide place the vivid red and gold and purple sunset seemed appropriate. From this spot Abraham must have watched the sun go down—and rise. Here he had sweat as he pulled and lifted large grey stones into a sizeable altar—and had felt his legs and arms ache afterwards from the strain of it. Here was the vibrancy of Abraham that Jacob had not sensed at his tomb. How he longed to feel the joy that filled Abraham in his first days in Canaan when God talked to him. God . . . talked . . . to him!

Jacob thought perhaps he should build an altar here, too. He walked to the opposite side of the hilltop expanse and began to look for suitable stones. Then he stopped short. Build an altar? Who? *Ya'aqeb*, the hanger-on to his brother's heel? Or was he, in the sight of the Most Holy God, just *Ya'aqab*, the deceiver? No! No! Only Esau had ever called him that detestable name, and Esau knew better! He was *Ya'aqeb*. He was— even as his mother called him—*Ya'aqob-El*.

Questions swirled in his mind, and apprehensions mounted as darkness fell. Jacob called out to the One to whom he belonged:

Lord, God, who am I? Who are you? Where are you?

Hear me, I pray! I have done things I should not have done; and there are things I should be doing now, instead of running away. I should be caring for the flocks, trying to make peace with my brother.

Do you hear me, God of Abraham and Isaac? I am alone, afraid to admit that I am afraid. I need to hear your voice.

There was no voice, no response. Jacob kicked one of the scattered boulders aside, and it hurt his toes. He took long strides back to the mound that Abraham had placed there. He looked intently at its stones, noticing that they had been placed with devoted care and had symmetry of design. He knelt and prayed his yearning prayer again. As he prayed this time, he felt more confident of his closeness with the one God.

He prayed for a long time, and when he finished, he believed he would hear that divine Voice. He stayed on his knees, quite still, until he was exhausted. The only sound was the faraway cry of a night bird.

The birdsong pierced Jacob's heart. As it continued, it seemed as though a shroud of gloom had fallen over him, separating him from any real hope for the life he had planned.

That bird had a nest, knew where it belonged, glorified its

Creator in soaring song. Jacob seemed worse off than the bird. He had no home, did not know where he belonged, and most certainly did not feel he was bringing glory to his Creator.

Jacob was getting used to the sound of his voice and began to speak aloud again. "If Abraham were sitting here with me, he would have looked up quickly, listened hard, and told me what kind of bird that was, what kind of nest it built, and what it liked to eat. He knew every bird, animal and plant in Canaan.

"More important, if Abraham were here, he would advise me what to do. But he is not here . . . and God does not answer me. I need—desperately need—some direction.

"I feel I'm no longer a person, only part of this vastness." He paused and assessed that idea; it intrigued him. To be part of the earth would demand no response, no words, no actions. Could one become like these unfeeling, uncaring stones?

The shroud of despair smothered him, tied with the cords of self-pity and fatigue.

It was almost dark. Only the slightest color remained on the western horizon. The sun had long since passed from sight, leaving behind a pale lavender afterglow, as though it tried not to desert this lonely traveler.

But as inevitably as the sun had set—as surely as its rays were disappearing—Jacob's indomitable nature made him stir himself from melancholy brooding. He had fought these moods before, but never one so all-encompassing. He knew that the longer he indulged in it, the more difficult it was to overcome it.

He remembered that his father often called despair—not doubting—the chief enemy of faith. That never had meant much to Jacob before, but now he understood.

Sitting and watching the sun go down had not helped; he must move around. Slowly, like a man twice his age, Jacob arose from his place beside the old altar, walked across the level ground of the hilltop to a place just above its steeply sloping edge, then made a complete, deliberate circle around the whole expanse.

It was dark except for scant light of a first-quarter moon showing now and then between billowing cloud banks. He could not see the landscape below, but he recalled assorted images in the eye of his mind.

Looking south, he remembered Beersheba, Gerar and Mamre. Westward was the Great Sea that he had never seen. Abraham had seen it and had told him of its endless bright blue waves. Between that sea and where he stood was a wealth of land he wanted to walk across—when he returned. To the north lay more of the Jordan River than he had yet seen. Following its meandering course, he would pass through a wide valley of rich farms, orchards, pasturelands and caravan trails—and he would come to a lovely inland sea called Kinnereth. He knew that parts of the Jordan's banks were heavily overgrown and densely forested—Esau had hunted lion there. To the east stood a chain of mountains still visible in the late evening.

A feeling of confidence rose within him that was stronger than his present situation seemed to warrant. All that land was to belong to him and to his descendants. Beyond human reasoning stood the covenant of God! Without any doubt he believed that the revelation given to his forefathers was from God. He claimed the covenant. The land! The glorious land! God said it was for Abraham's descendants—forever!

He sat on one especially large boulder and thought of one of the last conversations with his mother. Rebekah had said he should be ready for difficulties because God's men were tested in order to grow in faith and patience. He had thought it trite at the time, but now the idea encouraged him. Of course! The present disquieting situations were tests. But the despair inside him argued that if this were so, he was not meeting the tests well at all—he was failing!

"Think of the land!" he told himself aloud. "Think of the land and of the unimaginable possibility that one day I may hear the voice of God." Jacob was almost happy.

He also was at the point of exhaustion from days of walking, days of doubting, and days of turmoil. He was tired of wondering, of hoping—even of praying. All he wanted was to sleep for hours.

He looked around for a low, flat rock—as he had done many other nights in pastures near home. When he found the right size stone, he moved it to a grassy spot and covered it with a folded scarf. He wound his robe tightly around himself and lay down with the stone for a pillow. The warmth of his robe felt good, for hilltop breezes were cool after dark. The softness of the scarf over the stone was comforting.

He purposely placed himself so he would face in the direction of Haran as he slept. Whatever his personal inclinations, whatever doubts remained by morning, whatever second thoughts battled for first place, there would be no turning back. At daybreak he would set a straight course to Haran.

Meanwhile he would sleep.

10

He had a dream in which he saw a stairway resting on the earth, with its top reaching to heaven, and the angels of God were ascending and descending on it. There above it stood the Lord, and he said: "I am the Lord, the God of your father Abraham and the God of Isaac. I will give you and your descendants the land on which you are lying." *Genesis 28:12-13*

*W*ith a shepherd's practiced awareness of sound and light, Jacob usually awoke in the first pale gray of early morning. It shocked him to sudden alertness when he saw intense light all around him—light so bright it had facets of rainbow colors in it. The light was gently warm—invigorating. It dazzled his eyes, not with painful brightness but with a soft luminous glow.

At first he had an impulse to jump up from his hilltop bed and run for the sheer joy with which he was bathed by the light. But to his amazement he could not move a muscle. It was not that he was constrained by force, but rather he was totally relaxed and so comfortably supported that he just could not move, lest he disturb the perfection.

Jacob was content and quiet, yet his mind was pervaded with keen anticipation, for he knew beyond any doubt that this was only a prelude to something far more wondrous. Then he saw it!

He could not believe what his eyes told him was there. A magnificently wide ladder reached from the earth on which he lay to the heavens! Radiant beings were ascending and descending on it. Even at a considerable distance, they transmitted an aura of strength, serenity and wisdom. He realized that they must be the very angels of God!

Jacob was gripped momentarily by a holy fear as to what all

this meant. Then a spirit of peace entered him, and he understood that the ladder and the angels represented vital, constant contact between earth and heaven. These were divine messengers going back and forth—purposefully, consistently. For this brief moment he was being allowed to see the "invisible."

Even then his old enemy, despair, sent a fleeting alarm through his mind. Elohim had spoken directly to Abraham and to Isaac. Was he God's man in the sense that they were? Surely his faith did not match theirs. Perhaps God would speak to him only through angelic messengers. Jacob's heart beat faster as he thought of the ecstasy even such an indirect message as this would be! He ached to hear the voice of Elohim, but he would be satisfied with words delivered by His angels.

His heart raced and pounded with the energy he would need if he tried to climb that ladder himself. He had no sensation of time; he never knew how long he watched the ladder and the angels in the crystal clearness of that light—in absolute, golden silence.

Then there came an indescribable sound, as of cascading, rushing water. He felt drenched by it. The sound was a Voice from beyond the vastness between earth and heaven; it came from the firmament! It was the voice of—dare he think it?—yes, there was no doubt—it was the voice of Almighty God, El Shaddai!

The Voice brought no craven fear to Jacob, but a deep, always-remembered awe. The words were understandable, yet different from ordinary language. It was a mystical speech—beyond his power to describe or to copy.

Jacob was struck breathless! He saw El Shaddai standing above the ladder! The thunderous Voice spoke:

I am the Lord, the God of your father Abraham and the God of Isaac. I will give you and your descendants the land on which you are lying. Your descendants will be like the dust of the earth, and you will spread out to the west and to the east, to the north and to the south. All peoples on earth will be blessed through you and your offspring. I am with you and will watch over you wherever you go, and I will bring you back to this land. I will not leave you until I have done what I have promised you.

Jacob awakened out of his sleep. He heard a sound like the roar of rushing waters. He sat bolt upright. The sun was high in the sky, and its beams made the dust on the path nearby look like grains of gold.

"Surely the Lord is in the place, and I was not aware of it."

He looked into the heavens. There was no sign of the Lord God's glistening form at the top of the ladder—not even a ladder!

He was afraid and said, "How awesome is this place! This is none other than the house of God; this is the gate of heaven!"

He lay back down again, trying to sort it out in his mind. Had he actually seen Elohim? Or had he only dreamed it? He slowly got up, looked toward the heavens, and then ran to the old altar. His face shone with joy that was anchored in assurance. He . . . had . . . seen . . . his God! In a dream, yes, but he had seen Him!

Jacob's tiredness was gone. Morning air had never been this exhilarating before! He saw new shades of colors in the trees, in the flowers, even in the limestone rocks.

He was freed from the nagging concern about leaving his family and about the journey before him. Despair over his mistakes and his inadequacies had been lifted from his mind, for the Lord God had not uttered one word of accusation against him—only encouragement and affirmation. God had heard his prayers, seen his tears, and would be his faithful Keeper.

As tears streamed down his face, he raised his arms to heaven in elation. With sharp eyes he scanned as much of the universe as he could. His adoration of the Lord God, his thankfulness to Him for His unfailing love—these were beyond words. He tarried there in joy-filled silence, knowing that the angels would tell the Lord God all he could not say.

Jacob thought of each precious Word he had been given. Every time he recalled them, they grew richer in meaning. Each time he repeated them, he treasured them more.

The sun's angle was slightly west, so Jacob knew it was past midday. He had stayed a long time at the altar, reluctant to end so perfect an experience. But at last he walked away, thinking of what he must do before leaving this hilltop.

He went to the place from which he had seen the ladder, heard the Voice, and seen the vision of the Lord God. He picked up the stone that had served as his pillow and set it up as a monument. He went over to his sack of provisions and took out his bottle of oil. He brought it back, took out the stopper, and lavishly poured its contents over the top of the pillar, symbolizing consecration.

He named the place Bethel. To Jacob it would always—in a most personal way—be the "House of God."

Finally, he called out to the Lord God in a strong voice, ringing with gladness and trustfulness:

> If God will be with me and will watch over me on this journey I am taking and will give me food to eat and clothes to wear so that I return safely to my father's house, then the Lord will be my God. This stone that I have set up as a pillar will be God's house, and of all that You give me I will give You a tenth.

Jacob felt that he could have stayed on that hilltop, contented for the rest of his life. That one glimpse of his God would have sustained him.

It would have been even more difficult for him to leave if the Lord God had not promised that he would be allowed to return.

It would also have been more difficult to leave if he had known the hardships he would face in Haran. Even so, the Lord God promised He would watch over Jacob wherever he went, and so it would be.

—————————————————————————————**11**

Then Jacob continued on his journey and came to the lands of the eastern peoples.
Genesis 29:1

Jacob fastened his pack of belongings to his back, picked up his staff, and walked down the hill with a spring in his step. The aching weariness of his trek from Beersheba had vanished. He was refreshed and eager to reach Haran—to stay only as long as God directed, then return home. He already was homesick for Canaan, and he had not even left it!

Just now he was going to see what could be found in Luz in the way of provisions for the next phase of his journey. He also hoped to purchase a meal. He imagined the fragrance of roasting lamb, the pungent taste of cheese, the delight of a cake made with dried grapes.

As it turned out, Luz consisted of only a few mud brick houses. Their flat roofs obviously were used as storage areas for all sorts of things; some were used as sleeping quarters when the little houses were too crowded or too warm for comfort. The many-purpose roofs were reached by outside staircases. The houses had small windows, either latticed or shuttered for privacy and security. Most had just one room.

The first house where Jacob saw someone outside belonged to a potter. He was sitting in the doorway of a small shed, intently shaping a clay lamp. His wheel, turned by foot power, was an indented stone that revolved on a stone pivot set into the ground. He deftly shaped the clay as it turned around and around. He worked with the unhurried air of a true artist, and he seemed exceedingly pleased with what he was making.

When he was finished, he looked away from his work and

nodded a friendly greeting to Jacob, acknowledging his audience of one.

Jacob responded with a spontaneous smile and an eager question. "Where can I get bread and water for my journey, sir?"

"Where are you going?"

"To Damascus, then to Haran."

"Are you walking? Alone?"

"Yes, walking—alone. Will you tell me about the bread and the water now?"

"Do you know how far it is to Damascus and how far it is from there to Haran? Have you been to those places before?"

"I have a good idea of how far it is and how long it will take me to walk there. No, I have never been to those places before—and I may never get to them if I can't find some bread and water to take with me."

"My wife made some barley bread today. You may have a little of it. We have goat's milk cheese and some olives—more than we need."

"Fine. I will take two loaves of bread, some cheese and olives."

"You have money to pay for them?"

"Yes. Here." Jacob held up his money pouch with a flourish, glad the old man could not see the small amount that was in it—an amount that had to last all the way to Haran.

While the potter had been asking questions, he had also been watching Jacob with discerning eyes. Now he relaxed his shoulders, leaned back and smiled genially. "I have decided I like you.

"You are welcome to my home. Yes, you may have the bread and other provisions, and you will have supper with us tonight. Since by then it will be too late to start out for Damascus, you are welcome to sleep on our roof.

"My name is Rekem. Will you stay with us this night?"

"My name is . . . Jacob. I will stay, very gratefully."

Jacob was certain that this unexpected kindness was a sign that the Lord God was keeping him, protecting him, blessing him. He took Rekem's hospitality as from God.

The plain supper that evening was like a celebration to

him—a poignant reminder of the sumptuous banqueting that should have marked his receiving the blessing from Isaac. No matter—Jacob was in excellent humor. His host proved to be an interesting conversationalist, telling exaggerated stories of his town and the people who lived in it.

Later, Jacob slept well on the rooftop. That night there were no dreams, just deep, restful sleep.

In the morning he breakfasted with his host, packed food and water, and began the walk toward Damascus.

"Peace to you, Jacob, and a safe journey."

"Peace to you, Rekem, and good health."

He had gone only a short way when he heard sandaled feet coming up fast behind him. He turned to see a face wrinkled with concern. His new friend, breathing hard from his brief run, said, "You should not go alone. It is too far to walk all the way. Do you know there are robbers? They especially attack travelers who are alone—and walking!"

Jacob shrugged and lifted his hands in mock helplessness. "I have no one to go with me. I have no camel and no money to buy one."

Then he smiled, wanting to ease the old man's mind of worry. "Don't be afraid; my God is with me—to keep me well and bring me safely back home."

"Your God?"

"Yes, Elohim is one of His names. He is with me."

"You carry your God in your pack?"

"No, Rekem. He is not a god of clay or stone, made with hands. He is the one God—all-powerful and all-knowing. He, in a very special way, carries me; that is, He is aware of where I am and He helps me, guides me."

"Stay another night. We will talk about your God, Jacob."

"I can't stay now, but when I come back I will stop at your house, and we can talk then. I will tell you of my God and of how He helped me safely to Haran and back. And I will introduce you to my wife."

"You are married?"

"No, not yet, but I'm going to Haran to get a wife."

"Oh!" Rekem laughed. "Is that why you are in such a hurry? I am glad. I thought . . . well . . . when you came to my house and said you were traveling alone—so eager to be going and with little money—I thought you must be running away from someone."

Jacob was caught off guard by his words. They hurt and his face registered the pain, but he only said, "Do not worry about me. As I told you, my God will protect me."

Rekem began to speak again, but Jacob held up his hand for silence and gave his new friend a most engaging smile. "I must go, Rekem. Peace to you."

"And to you. Come back soon. We will talk."

The two men parted with the customary embrace, then Jacob resumed his walk with the invigorating feeling of someone about to accomplish what others said he could never do. It was really quite simple—just put one foot in front of the other, then do it again—millions of times.

He passed the twin mountains of Ebal and Gerizim. He noted with some surprise how they contrasted with each other—Gerizim with its green mantle of trees and grass and terraced vineyards, and Ebal stark and barren. He then went along the Jordan valley and followed it to the Sea of Kinnereth—glorying all the more in the beauty of his land. Each change of scene was a delight, another incentive to return as soon as possible. No other land, anywhere, could be as beautiful with such a variety and abundance of plant and animal life. Yes, it seemed good to him, walking the land, learning of it firsthand. His love of Canaan grew with his knowledge of it.

Jacob lay down whenever he grew tired, filled the goatskin bottles whenever he found water, and stopped along the way to buy bread and other essentials. North of Kinnereth he caught sight of a rushing waterfall. It hurled streams of water that surged with power. He stood for a long time watching its grand extravagance. It was the essence of exultant energy. It reminded him of God's voice, and as he turned to resume his walk, his step was lighter.

It was late afternoon when he came to Lake Huleh, a place of quiet beauty along the northern section of the Jordan, and it proved to be a restful place to spend the night. Just a few strides from the lake was a large, flat area that was ringed by trees and low-growing shrubs. Daisy-like chamomile flowers were blossoming in spring's profusion. Jacob chose the shade of a symmetrical carob tree as the exact place he would camp. He sat down, sighed deeply, and a wide smile spread across his face. How little it took, really, to be comfortable—sometimes just a grassy field and the opportunity to rest one's feet! He leaned against the tree and listened to the gentle lapping of tiny waves against stony banks. It was a soothing sound, both physical and spiritual balm to the tired traveler.

Jacob was so satisfied with this camping place that he thought he might stay all the next day and the following night. He would get some much-needed rest and give himself time to think about the days ahead. Here in the placid region of the lake, Haran and even Damascus seemed impossibly far away. In his relaxed state it was easier to remember the past than to plan for the future, but Damascus was his next goal. He must think of Damascus.

He remembered his grandfather's description of that city and of the terrain on both sides of it. After crossing the fertile Euphrates valley Abraham had led his people through stony desert land where vegetation was sparse and the sun's heat intense. Not until he neared Damascus had the pasture been better, the climate more bearable. Abraham had enjoyed telling about Damascus and its impressive setting—high on a green plateau, nourished by the mighty Pharpar and the lovely Abana rivers.

Jacob's journey had been difficult enough, but he knew the last part would be more strenuous. He would encounter that same desolate area through which Abraham had traveled. He was aware of the added danger of traveling alone with not even a pack animal to carry extra water and food. He forced himself to face his problem more fully; he wondered if there might be an easier way for him.

He walked down to the lake, absentmindedly threw small stones into its smooth blueness, and watched—childlike—as wavering, widening circles appeared around the spot where the stones splashed in.

For a brief moment he thought of just staying in that haven by the lake, of not going on to Haran at all. But his parents had wanted him to go. Surely it was God's will also since his vision had not given any sign of deterence, but rather encouragement. He would go on—but how?

Jacob began thinking of Damascus as an important stopping place on the caravan route between Egypt and the Mesopotamian cities of Babylon and Ur. Many caravans even originated in Damascus itself—loaded with produce from its surrounding farms and lavish silks and tapestries made by its renowned artisans. Caravaneers would be commonplace at Damascus, and a person would have a fair chance to find work helping with the tents or with the inevitable flocks of sheep and goats that were part of every caravan.

Being with a caravan would mean no more uncertainty about a night's lodging or provisions. It would also mean companionship. Jacob felt ready now for the company of other people—especially as he thought of the barren stretches between Damascus and the Euphrates. It seemed the most logical thing in the world to him; he would see about work on a caravan that would take him as far as Haran.

For a moment his mind was at peace. The next moment he was puzzled. Was this the thinking of a prudent planner, or of one who wanted to reject the discipline of hardship? Was it brave to continue walking alone—or foolhardy? Why did every problem have so many choices, each of which seemed right—and wrong?

He remembered Rekem's warning about the long distance and the danger of robbers. If Rekem's hospitality was from the Lord God, why not his advice?

Common sense battled with pride, and in a short while Jacob determined common sense to be the winner. He would swallow his words about accomplishing the long, lonely walk by himself. He would take the advice of his parents—and of the friend God had given him at Luz.

He threw one more stone into the lake—this time not thoughtlessly but to punctuate a new resolve. He would go to Damascus as planned. Once there, he would find a caravaneer who needed a willing and able worker.

He was almost too excited to sleep that night and wished it were morning so he could begin sooner. He covered a stone with his scarf and pillowed his head on it as he lay down to rest on his grassy bed. He began to sense the gentle rhythm of the surface swells of Lake Huleh slapping the shoreline. It was soothing and refreshing. It eased him to sleep.

In the morning, after a scant breakfast of dates and bread, he made his way to the main road and directed his feet and his attention toward Damascus. The deep physical rest of the previous night had been good, and things had been brought into his mind that were of immense help in planning the next part of his journey. He walked with head high and praise to the Lord God on his lips.

Days of walking ate up the distance. Jacob stopped briefly at the village of Laish and again in the city of Mazaca—but only long enough to secure necessary food and water. He saw the towering grandeur of snowcapped Mt. Hermon. He wanted to go to the top of that mountain when he returned to Canaan—to see the view from its summit and to touch and taste the snow.

He generally followed the main trade route and made good progress for a time, but as he neared Damascus, he was covering fewer miles in a day. Water had become more difficult to find, and his money for food was nearly gone. A few shrewd merchants, noting the inexperienced traveller's desperate need for food, had charged excessive prices. They sensed he would pay rather than argue, and they considered it a small probability he would ever pass by again. Such a person was fair game for sharp tradesmen.

In the distance he saw a towering ziggurat and a gigantic city wall. There was heavier travel now on the road. Although he had been straining toward it for many days, he felt surprise that he was at last actually approaching Damascus!

The vegetation on either side of the road had become more plentiful, and the wide fields of wildflowers that had so delighted Sarah's eyes were a joy to him also. He noted the productive farms that had caught the patriarch's eye. The area around Damascus was beautiful, and this added to the excitement of his first visit to a large city. Now the possibility of going the rest of the way to Haran in a caravan—not having to worry about finding food, water or shelter—delighted him.

He spent four days and nights in Damascus. He found parts of it beautiful, parts bewildering. He stared open-mouthed at the temples of the moon god and goddess. Such grandeur for nongods! He remembered, in contrast to this, the simple stones that he, his father and his grandfather used to build altars for the God of all things! It did not seem right. Surely his God should have the finest temple of all. He resented the lavish display that the moon god's worshipers had built. He wanted to tear them down but settled for clenched fists and deliberately turned his back on them.

Jacob walked through the bazaar with its colorful, aromatic confusion of merchandise. Some of the items for sale were tempting, but the small amount of money in his pouch let him enjoy the wares only by sight, smell and touch. Some day, he hoped, he would come back with money enough to buy many things. He saw an embroidered silk shawl that would be a perfect gift for his new wife, whoever she was. That, too, would have to wait until later.

One sight in Damascus appalled him. In addition to the food, clothing, furniture, jewelry and trinkets that were bought and sold, he saw the buying and selling of people. Although Abraham had told him of this, he had never thought much about it. Families were divided. Strong men were sold to work like animals, and beautiful young women were sold into harems to provide children for wealthy men who would count both the women and the children born to them as their property. Hiring out to a taskmaster on a caravan to Haran seemed bad enough! What if such servitude were for a lifetime?

Jacob's mind was soon satiated with the things of Damascus. He eagerly approached each caravaneer he saw, asking if he were going to Haran and if he had a place for another worker. Late in the morning of his fourth day in Damascus he found a caravan that was bound for Haran. The leader was a robust man who shouted orders in a voice one would not dare to disobey. He had been pointed out to Jacob as the man to see if he wanted a job; his name was Ishan.

"Sir, you are going to Haran?"

"Haran, Babylon and Ur. Why?"

"I would like to be part of your caravan. I am an excellent shepherd. I take good care of the healthy sheep and can heal sick ones. I don't sleep when I'm guarding flocks . . . and I don't scare easily when wild animals come sniffing around. I am strong. Do you have a place for me—as far as Haran?

Ishan's eyes narrowed. He looked Jacob over from head to toe and apparently was pleased with the amount of work he could expect from this man. "There might be. Do you know about putting up tents and taking them down—and are you good at it?"

"Yes."

"Yes, what?" Ishan roared, more to intimidate than to ask for information.

Jacob drew himself taller and forced a calm answer. "Yes, I know about tents, and yes, I am a good worker."

"You will do, since I need someone before we leave—tomorrow morning at dawn. I can't chance finding someone better. You will do. No wages, though—just your food and transportation to Haran. Understand?

"I understand."

"Be back here by sunup in the morning. What did you say your name is?"

"I am . . . Jacob."

"Jacob—an unusual name. I have never heard it before. Well, Jacob, you will help with tents, and you will help with the flocks. Agreed?"

"Agreed. I will be here—and before sunup in the morning!"

Jacob was not certain he liked or trusted Ishan, but the situation was temporary, and it was the best way he had found to get to Haran. He thought of how his mother called him *Ya'aqob-El*. He certainly hoped Elohim would protect him now.

At daybreak Jacob took his place among Ishan's other shepherds. It was good to be with sheep again. He gently patted a lamb and thought of his flock at home in Parah's care.

He mounted a scraggy donkey Ishan loaned him for the trip. He would ride slowly, at the pace of the sheep, for a while.

"It's strange," he mused later as the city of Damascus became a small spot on the horizon. "Esau never wanted to stay home, and I did. Now he is home—at least when he wants to be—and I travel to new places almost every day! I wonder if he stays home more, now that I'm gone. Does he think of me often? In anger?"

He straightened his shoulders and raised his chin higher as he thought of his brother. Esau should be happy! He had all his father's servants at his command and Isaac's wealth to insure him a fine living. He didn't have to attend to the duties of family priest. He had all he wanted, and had escaped the responsibility he didn't want. Why should he be angry?

As he thought of Esau's anger toward him, he was aware of that same emotion in his heart for Esau. Deep inside himself Jacob cried, "He tried to cheat me out of what was mine by God's gift and by his own agreement—then accused me of cheating him!"

With his mind full of tumultuous thoughts about Esau, the peace that had been his during the past weeks faded away. He became so agitated that he prodded his donkey too hard. It snorted and balked. Jacob dismounted, talked to the animal, patted its neck and head, and led it for a long while before trying to ride it again.

He decided that anger spent on Esau was wasted emotion. It was worse than wasted, for it turned in on himself and made his mind restless. This time it even caused him to walk when a much-desired ride had been available! He vowed to control his anger.

The caravan trip was routine, but it meant a new pattern of living for Jacob. He did his work well, thrived on the meals provided, and had good conversations with the herdsmen and other caravan people. The terrain they crossed was arid and monotonous. Pasture was good near the occasional streams, but the grass was short and brown in most places.

The caravan made an overnight stop at Tadmor, a junction point for wayfarers from many directions. Then travel resumed, bringing them at last to the Euphrates River. Jacob found fording this river with the flocks was challenging work. It demanded quick action and strength of arms, legs and back. He respected his grandfather all the more as he thought of how he, too, had waded waist-deep in water, keeping track of animals as they swam across, reaching with his crook to pull in those in danger of drifting downstream. Makeshift rafts supported by inflated animal bladders carried persons who could not swim and things that could not float.

Once across the Euphrates and beyond its luxuriant, water-blessed valley, they moved into semiarid places—green only along the banks of the Balikh, a tributary of the Euphrates, and along the Kara, a tributary of the Balikh.

The closer they came to Haran, the more brown replaced green as the landscape color. There were almost no trees. Jacob never imagined a land without abundant trees; he would be desolate without them.

Ishan ordered the caravan to halt late one afternoon. Haran was just ahead. Its high ziggurat could be seen on the horizon. They would encamp along the road, then in the morning before daylight they would move again, going into the city gate where Ishan would fill out identification papers, pay taxes, and arrange to unload the cargo. He would also have to get permission to pasture the caravan's flocks temporarily near the city wall by the commonly used well.

Jacob took his place with the herdsmen, guarding the flocks through the night. He was glad for the starlit quietness. He had several hours now to think about Haran—and to pray.

12

While he was still talking with them, Rachel came with her father's sheep, for she was a shepherdess.   *Genesis 29:9*

*t*he darkness of the morning sky was diluted to a dusky gray before the sun turned it gold and blue. At the first hint of light Jacob awakened herdsmen who still drowsed; they must get the flocks moving.

Ishan and his assistants alerted the others, and by full sunup the caravan was on its plodding way to the main gate of Haran.

The morning was hot. Its hours dragged by, and Jacob lost all sense of time while Ishan took care of the necessary paper work with city officials. He felt as though he had been awake for at least a week. Nothing seemed real. Where was the eagerness, the sense of elation he had expected to feel when he reached his destination?

He helped with unloading as local merchants sent servants for their part of the cargo. This was not his required work—once at Haran he was free to leave the caravan—but Jacob was glad to find something to take up more time and divert his thoughts. He was reluctant to leave Ishan's group, not because of any particular attachment to them, but because leaving them meant facing Haran—finding Uncle Laban and his family. No matter how often Jacob tried to picture his meeting with them, he always imagined that it would be awkward and difficult. He would postpone it for at least a few hours.

The caravan was unloaded at a large, rambling building. Its numerous rooms were not connected, but each had an opening onto the city square. Stalls were filled with merchandise, and the shopkeepers were responsible for selling it by day and guarding it by night. Their motto was "A good price is a price that is good for the wolf and good for the sheep," but the odds that a "wolf" and a "sheep" would mutually benefit from a sale were small.

By midafternoon the unloading was finished. Jacob looked for Ishan. He found him still talking with the merchant who had purchased most of the tapestries from the Damascus artisans. Not wanting to interrupt and still not caring about hurrying away, Jacob stood at a discreet distance from the men and waited. When the conversation ended and the merchant left, Ishan sat quietly for a few moments with his eyes closed. Jacob wondered if he were praying—and to what god? He knew little about the man. Probably Ishan was just napping, tired from the tensions of a long journey and the details of business he had handled that day. Jacob had decided to find a shady spot somewhere and take a quick nap when he noticed Ishan had risen and was coming toward him. He called out in a strong voice, "Jacob, you have been a good worker. We will miss you."

"I am glad you were pleased."

"You are free to go now. Go in peace, my friend."

"And peace to you, Ishan. May you have good fortune in Babylon and Ur. I wish you well."

They parted as friends, yet they scarcely knew anything about each other except their names. On the trip they had talked only about the work at hand. Jacob laughed to himself as he thought of all the things people say—from tradition or habit—that protect them from sharing anything meaningful from their deepest personal thoughts.

While he wondered what Ishan might be thinking as he said his casually polite good-bye, Jacob knew what he was thinking himself—something so heavy he thought Ishan could have heard it if he tried! He was thinking that he would rather go on to Babylon and Ur—or turn and go back to Canaan without ever seeing his relatives. He still had not decided on a suitable way to introduce himself, let alone to ask Laban that one of his daughters might become his wife! Suppose the daughters were already married, or suppose he didn't like them. They might be shrewish, stupid or ugly—or all three.

Suppose they didn't like him. They might consider him presumptuous, dull or unattractive—or all three!

He wasn't sure he even liked their names. He remembered his mother repeating them with pride: "My nieces, Leah and Rachel." She had reminded Jacob that Leah was the older of the two, and if she were not already married, she would be the one his Uncle Laban would want him to marry. Jacob's response had been a suppressed bristling resentment that the matter of older and younger would cast a shadow on his marriage. Why did it matter who was older or younger? Years—or minutes—of difference in age surely were of less importance than the sharing of interests, mutual respect and attraction.

Soon a decision would be made, and either Leah or Rachel would be his wife. Wife! The more he thought about it the less he wanted to pursue the matter.

Such were his thoughts as he left the caravan. He walked through the city streets for a time and, like all newcomers to Haran, went to where the ziggurat towered above everything around. He stared at the beautiful architecture, feeling the usual awe of those who saw it for the first time. Then he turned from it, as he had from the larger one in Damascus, unable to understand how people could worship a god that they had made with their hands. It would certainly take a great temple to honor his God. The world itself could not contain it!

He had seen the bazaar, the ziggurat, and some of the beehive-shaped houses of Haran. He had no desire to see more, so he walked toward the city gate and out past the fortress that guarded it.

By now it was late afternoon, and there were three flocks of sheep in a nearby field. They were gathered around a large well, but their shepherds had not removed the heavy stone from its mouth so the sheep could be watered. That puzzled him, and in curiosity he walked toward them. He might not feel comfortable around caravaneers or people in cities like Damascus or Haran, but he understood shepherds and could talk easily with them.

"My brothers, where are you from?"

"We're from Haran." Apparently the tallest one spoke for all three.

"Do you know Laban, Nahor's grandson and the son of Bethuel?"

"Yes, we know him."

"Is he well?"

"Yes, he is, and here comes his daughter Rachel with the sheep."

The panic that had been building in Jacob reached higher intensity. Rachel, the younger of Laban's daughters, would be beside him in a matter of minutes!

What would he say? Most especially, what would he say to her with these herdsmen watching and listening? He glanced over his shoulder in the direction his informant indicated and saw a shepherdess with a small flock coming toward the well.

He must get these men on their way. He blurted out what to them must have seemed a surprising assumption of authority over their work. They could not have known he spoke out of desperation.

"Why don't you water the flocks so they can get back to grazing? They will be hungry if you stop their feeding so early in the day."

The tall spokesman calmly answered, "We don't roll away the stone and begin watering until all the flocks and shepherds are here. Then the stone only has to be removed and put back once—and all who use it can help lift it." He spoke condescendingly, as if explaining to a young child. Then he grinned rather knowingly, as if to say he would not miss the meeting between this stranger and Laban's beautiful daughter—not for anything!

As they talked, Rachel arrived with her flock. She did not speak to the shepherds, and she took no apparent notice of Jacob. By long practice she knew how to seem totally preoccupied with her sheep; it was a way to prevent unwelcome conversation.

No one spoke. The herdsmen watched Jacob and Rachel with increasing interest. Jacob stood still, absolutely certain that he was looking at the most beautiful girl in all of Mesopotamia! Rachel was finding it difficult to pretend that she did not notice the man who regarded her with such an adoring look. Still, no one spoke.

One of the herdsmen cleared his throat. Rachel risked a full glance at Jacob and definitely liked what she saw. Jacob, not knowing whether to introduce himself to his cousin or wait until she spoke first, found the tension too much to bear, so he resorted to action. He moved the stone to get the sheep watered and the other shepherds on their way—and to demonstrate for this lovely lady how strong he was. It usually took two or more men to move the cover off the well, but Jacob rolled it away himself.

The herdsmen watched in wonder. Not one of them—or anyone else they knew—could have done that. A jubilant Jacob ignored them now and began to shepherd Rachel's flock to the well. He gave the impression that he was preoccupied with the sheep, as Rachel had done at first. He carefully tended them, making sure each one got sufficient water. And still no one had spoken.

Rachel's curiosity finally overcame her customary shyness; she walked toward this unusual visitor. She was about to ask who he was and where he was from when he suddenly turned and faced her. He moved closer, and she didn't turn from him. He forgot all about a proper introduction. He kissed her.

Jacob's heart was overwhelmed with so much emotion that he burst into tears—tears of joy at having reached his destination; tears over the lonely, arduous weeks he had spent on the way; tears of homesickness; and tears that he could not explain, but that were inspired by the special beauty of this girl.

Tears! What would Rachel think of him? And what would she think of a man so bold as to kiss her like that? It had gone all wrong. Jacob felt embarrassed and defeated. He tried not to imagine what she must be thinking.

When he regained some of his composure, he began as simply as possible to explain things to her. "I am a nephew of your father, Laban. I am the son of your father's sister, Rebekah. I am your cousin. I have just arrived from Canaan, from my home in Beersheba. I am . . . Jacob."

Without one word in answer to his belated introduction, Rachel turned and ran.

The herdsmen proceeded to water their flocks and lead them back to pasture. Since Jacob was so strong, they left the stone cover off the well for him to replace. He heard them laughing as they walked away and felt their derision.

Jacob was alone again. He sat by the well, his head in his hands. He went over in his mind each step of this unbelievable meeting with his cousin. He wondered whether she would ever speak to him if he went on to his uncle's house now. He knew that, for the time being, he would have to watch the flock she had abandoned because of him. And he had better struggle with that stone cover and get it back in place before the next shepherds came. He didn't want to anger any more people, and he knew the shepherds wanted their water supply protected both from the sun that evaporated it and from debris that could contaminate it.

Rachel had run home as fast as she could to tell her father of Jacob's arrival. Her home was not like the beehive-shaped, one-room huts that made up most of Haran. Laban had inherited his father's fine house, two stories high, with cane-latticed windows and wide balconies. The house proclaimed wealth.

Laban's principal income was from his large flocks of sheep. He never had been a shepherd, but he hired the most capable ones he could find. He allowed his younger daughter to care for a small flock of choice sheep that were pastured on rented land close to the city wall, a short distance from the fortress. He also owned a meat shop in Haran that his sons tended. He looked forward to seeing his daughters make desirable marriages. He wanted them to select men who could enhance his fortune and help manage his enterprises.

He was taking a late afternoon nap and was abruptly awakened as Rachel ran through the house calling him. Her face was flushed, and he had never seen her as excited as this before.

"Here I am, Rachel. What has happened? Why are you home this early?"

"Father, listen! You will not believe this, but it's true! I went to the well with the sheep, and a man I never saw before was there. He lifted the stone off the well all by himself! He watered the sheep for me. Then he told me he is the son of Rebekah, your sister. He has come from Canaan. He is Jacob."

"Jacob, my nephew?"

"So he said."

Now Laban was almost as excited as Rachel. "Why did you leave him at the well? Why didn't you bring him on home? My own flesh and blood, my own sister's son, here in Haran and you left him waiting at the well!"

"I'm sorry, Father. I didn't think to ask him to come with me. I was overwhelmed with the surprise of . . . of seeing him."

"And where, Rachel, are the sheep?"

"I forgot about them! I suppose Jacob is watching them."

"You foolish daughter, let's go to him as quickly as possible. No, I will go. You stay and tell Leah about this visitor of ours. Tell the servants to prepare a fine meal of roast lamb and . . . and everything that will make this evening's dinner an appropriate celebration. And, Rachel, see that the servants prepare a room for him quickly. Now I will go to meet him properly and bring him back with me."

"And the sheep?"

"The sheep?" Laban shrugged his shoulders as if to say he could not be bothered with such trivial things. "Send a servant for them, girl! What are servants for?" Then, thinking of the value of the prime sheep and the incompetency of some of the servants, he added, "Send three servants! And quickly!"

Laban went to his room and changed into his best robe and sandals. He walked briskly to the well, thinking even faster than he walked. He was eager to meet his nephew—Isaac's heir!

13

As soon as Laban heard the news about Jacob, his sister's son, he hurried to meet him. He embraced him and kissed him and brought him to his home. *Genesis 29:13*

Laban ran the last few yards to impress Jacob with his great joy in greeting him.

"Peace be to you, Jacob, son of Isaac and Rebekah."

"And peace to you, my uncle."

There was an awkward silence for a moment, then Laban embraced his nephew, kissed him, and said, "Your coming has brought me such joy. There is much we have to talk about. I have many questions about my sister and am most interested in what brings you to Haran."

"I look forward to talking with you—answering your questions and telling you of what brings me here."

The servants Rachel sent for the sheep had arrived and were proceeding to move them to their fold.

"I am afraid my daughter did not welcome you properly . . . and even left you to tend the sheep while she went to tell me of your arrival. Rachel is young; you must forgive her."

"Rachel is young—and most beautiful. I watched her leading the sheep to the well. She is a skillful shepherdess."

"Yes, she keeps this small flock of my choice lambs—pasturing them here during the day and leading them home in the early evening. She loves the animals, and they love her."

They had begun the walk back to Laban's house and found it easy to talk with each other, Laban pointing out places of interest along the way or remarking about the weather, Jacob encouraging him to talk by being an attentive listener.

When they arrived at the house, a servant washed Jacob's

feet and showed him to his room. Jacob sank down blissfully on the comfortable mat and closed his eyes—but his time of restful quiet was short. Uncle Laban was at the door.

"Jacob?"

"Yes, Uncle Laban?"

"I want to make certain you are comfortable in your room."

"I am comfortable, thank you."

"Our home is not elegant, and the furnishings are not new, but you are welcome to the best we have."

"Everything is very good." Jacob decided he might as well get up; he sat on one of the floor cushions and indicated that his uncle should sit on the other.

Comfortably seated, Laban spoke with glib politeness and studied humility. His mind was filled with visions of the jewelry Eliezer had brought many years ago when he came to take Rebekah to Canaan as a bride for Isaac. He was sure that Jacob was in Haran now because he knew of Leah and Rachel and was ready to take a wife. Laban thought it was commendable for him to come for the girl himself instead of having a servant do it for him. He wondered if Jacob had gold and jewels in his pack. The dowry Eliezer brought for Rebekah had done much toward extending the family's business interests. It was difficult for Laban to think of one thing and talk about another, but he did it well.

"And how is my beloved sister, Rebekah?"

"She is well. She is a devoted wife and mother; she sees to things around our home camp very efficiently. She wove this tunic I am wearing. She sends her love to you."

Laban reached over, touched the hem of the tunic, and managed to squeeze out a tear. "I have touched the garment she made . . . Jacob, I have missed my dear sister these long years. Canaan is a remote place. It is not easy to have a loved one move there—probably never to be seen again by the family in Haran."

"Yes, it is difficult for families to be separated." Jacob thought first of his own separation from his family; then he remembered the slaves being sold in Damascus. Would he be causing similar sadness by taking a beloved daughter from his uncle? He felt Laban knew the reason for his visit to Haran and was warning him that he didn't want any of his family taken from him, as Rebekah was taken from her father's house.

Laban, noticing the dismay on Jacob's face, hastened to make sure he didn't think his uncle was hopelessly sentimental. He came to the point, "If anyone wants to take one of my daughters as far as Canaan, there would have to be a larger dowry than Eliezer brought for Rebekah!" He forced a laugh that he hoped would say he had not meant to sound greedy.

Dowry! If Jacob had appeared dismayed before, he now looked devastated. Dowry! Jacob had not once thought of a dowry. He had come this long way to claim a wife but had nothing with which to claim her! It was all in Canaan! What good was Isaac's wealth—or his share of it? He had not one gold piece to offer Laban for Rachel. And Laban did not look, even at first glance, like someone who could be paid with promises.

Laban had made a feeble attempt to make Jacob laugh, but instead his nephew seemed at the point of tears. He wondered what was causing this young man such distress and was irritated that he didn't know enough to laugh when his host expected him to laugh. He decided Jacob probably knew no social graces at all. He was used to the coarse life of shepherds who live in tents. But—he could learn. Laban would teach him manners—and much more.

"We have talked long enough for this time, Jacob. Rest a while, and at supper we will talk further."

Jacob was tired enough to rest, even though his peaceful mood of a few minutes earlier had dissolved in his uncle's unsettling presence.

While Jacob rested, Laban checked to see how the welcoming feast was progressing. He ordered his servants to treat his nephew with great respect. As long as he remained with them, there would be celebration in his house—the best food and the finest wine. Then he went to his own room, intending to finish the nap that had been interrupted by Rachel several hours earlier. But he could not sleep.

He was restless and waited impatiently for the late dinner to be prepared. He had important things to discuss with Jacob.

His mind wandered to thoughts of how to invest the dowry. Isaac would be at least as generous with the gift for his son's wife as Abraham had been with the gift for Isaac's wife. Dear Rebekah! How good of her to send her son back home to take a wife. He would make certain she was not disappointed; he would give Jacob a very fine wife. He might even persuade Jacob to take two wives!

Laban's delight was boundless as he thought of how much two doweries would be. If Jacob had not brought enough for two, Isaac could send sufficient gifts for the second wife by messenger. After all, Laban of Haran could be a patient, trusting man. This thought made him wince. He would be hard pressed to find many who would agree with his opinion of himself.

Whatever would be, would be—one wife or two. Meanwhile, he must be a genial host. Perhaps it would be better to talk of lighter things during suppertime. He might ask about Jacob's travels from Beersheba; no doubt he would have many experiences to relate. Some of them could possibly be interesting.

Later, when the two men enjoyed a very late but sumptuous dinner, they did talk of many things. Laban began by apologizing. "So scant a meal to welcome my nephew! If only I had known you were coming, I would have prepared a large banquet for this night. As it is, we will have the banquet another time."

Jacob was amused. It was no scanty meal, and even if later there were a banquet, it could not have finer food. He thought of his farewell to Ishan—trite words to keep meaningful ones safely unsaid. Even families did it. Laban apologized for the food according to custom; Jacob accommodated him by replying according to custom.

"My uncle, this is excellent food. As anyone can tell, it is the choicest meat and the best wine. Surely no one in all of Haran sets so fine a table. I am honored to be your guest."

Laban nodded, accepting the compliments. Jacob knew more about acceptable manners than he had thought.

"When we have your real welcome dinner, my four married sons, who work in the bazaar, will be here—and of course

Leah and Rachel. There are also other relatives you should meet while you are here. Would you like that?"

"Oh, yes, very much. You are most generous."

"Now, Jacob, eat."

Jacob ate heartily. He had been too excited to eat breakfast, too confused and troubled to eat lunch, so he was desperately hungry. It really was excellent food.

After the servants cleared away the supper things, Laban leaned back on a large leather cushion, patting his stomach and smiling contentedly. He, too, had eaten well.

"We have talked about my sister, but I have not inquired about Isaac. Is your father well?"

"No, he is nearly blind. He is weak and unable to supervise the camp or the flocks. We think he may not live much longer."

The thought of Isaac's dying sharpened Laban's craving to get to important matters of business. Gone was his resolve to let that evening be a time of pleasant conversation about family interests. Gone was his good intention to be a ready listener to the story of Jacob's adventures along the way from Beersheba to Haran. Isaac was dying!

He sat up straight, wiped his mouth with the sleeve of his robe, and looked intently at Jacob for a moment. He leaned toward him and asked, as gently as his eagerness would permit, "Your father—he inherited all the land of Canaan from your grandfather Abraham?"

"Not exactly. The land of Canaan, Elohim has said, will belong to our family and to our descendants forever; but we have not yet possessed it. Other tribes and nations are settled on it. We will be led by our God; when it is time to take the land, we will do it."

"How? When?"

"I can say only that it will be according to God's plan and in His own time. Meanwhile, we live on sufficient portions of the land, and we claim His certain promise for the future."

"It sounds rather vague."

"It is assured by Elohim!"

Laban looked disappointed but forged ahead with his questioning, hoping to salvage something more solid than promises, even if they were from Elohim. "You and Esau are Isaac and Rebekah's only children?"

"Yes."

"Which one of you is the older?"

"Esau, by less than a minute."

Laban looked more disappointed. "Then he will receive the birthright share of Isaac's legacy?"

"No. It is mine."

"How can that be?"

"It was God-given, and then . . . I purchased it. It is a long, unusual story. My uncle, I will have to tell it to you some other time. Tonight it is late, and I'm very tired. With your permission I'd like to go to my room to sleep."

"Of course. We have many days to talk. I have assigned a servant to attend you; let him know if you need anything. His name is Abri. I trust you will rest well. Good night, Jacob."

After Jacob left, Laban sat alone for some time. His eyes closed, and he tapped his chin with his right forefinger. Anyone who knew him recognized this meant he was thinking deeply and was not to be disturbed.

He was thinking at that moment of his two daughters. There was no doubt Jacob already was attracted to Rachel. Of course he would be. Rachel! She could have her pick of all the eligible men. In many ways she reminded him of Rebekah—especially her eyes. Rebekah and Rachel both had eloquent eyes. Laban supposed that was the wrong word to describe them, yet they were indeed eloquent; they could speak wordlessly across the room and command a person's attention, or they could speak intimately and say more than any combination of words. Rachel was like her aunt in other ways, too. She had a quick mind, alert to things going on around her. She was ambitious and self-reliant. Rachel—worth much gold and many, many jewels.

Jacob had not yet seen Leah. Leah was an obedient daughter. She kept her thoughts to herself, and although she seemed lonely, she did not try to be companionable, even to her sister. She seemed unable to make conversation interesting or even possible. Leah was a good girl. She assumed, quietly and naturally, the overseeing of the household and servants after her mother died. Laban was pleased with Leah; it was unfortunate she didn't have the beauty of her aunt or her sister. Leah's eyes were narrow, and since her vision was not good, she made them even narrower when she squinted to see anything very far away. The squinting was already making traces of wrinkles in her forehead. Before many years they would be more than traces. Once you knew Leah, you loved her for her gentleness and dependability, but to see her together with her dazzling sister was not to see her at all.

Leah would be a fine wife for Jacob. She would adapt well to the rigors of Canaan's tent living. Rachel was too fragile for that. She needed the comfort of a house and the care of servants who understood her high-strung temperament and her tendency to try to do more than her strength would allow.

He knew from the look on Rachel's face when she came to announce Jacob's arrival that she was impressed with him. She had never before looked so delighted, so grown up. He had not thought seriously of her marriage to anyone yet. She was too young. Leah was of marriageable age—had been for a few years.

Either of the girls would find Jacob to be a good husband. Laban had assessed him carefully in the short time he was with him and found him likeable. There was no doubt he had excellent parents; he had inherited his father's wealth. Yes, Laban would be happy to treat him like a son.

Laban had heard just that day of some fields for sale in the northeast, near the Tigris River. He must make a trip there to look over the land soon—in the event he received some gold to invest.

Jacob had gone to sleep quickly. He slept soundly and awakened early. He got up from his sleeping mat and walked to the latticed window of his room. He could see a small courtyard and a few bright flowers blooming along its edge. Above the yard and the flowers was a bright blue sky—no clouds at all.

Abri had brought in a pitcher of water and placed a basin beside it. Jacob splashed the cool water on his face and arms; it was almost as refreshing as another night's sleep. He stretched his arms high, breathed deeply, and believed he was ready to talk with Laban about the obvious purpose of his visit. He knew his uncle had already guessed it, for he had mentioned the dowry. The dowry! What would he do about that? He felt less ready to face his uncle after that word came back into his mind.

Unsettling questions put his mind in a tumult. Why had Isaac not thought to send a dowry? Why had Rebekah not remembered how important it was to her family? Why had he not thought of it himself? He knew the reason but did not like to remember that all three of them were in a frenzy of fear and could think of only one thing—escape from Esau.

But what should he do now? He could not go back to Beersheba without a wife. He could not go anywhere—without Rachel.

Jacob stopped pacing the floor of his small room. He had been behaving as though his God were not with him. Elohim had said, "I am with you and will watch over you wherever you go."

Elohim already knew his problem and would be his Sustainer. This being without a dowry was a way to grow in faith. Would he ever learn to recognize these hard situations as tests of faith immediately? Once he recognized them as tests, would he ever learn to pass them as competently as his grandfather and father had—especially at Mt. Moriah. The remembrance of that rocky hill came clearly into his mind and made him reevaluate the difficulty he was facing. He would entrust the matter of the dowry to God—as he entrusted his very life to Him.

Meanwhile, he had another urgent problem that he should solve right away. He must find a way to speak to Rachel alone, to apologize for the unconventional way he had greeted her and, if possible, to talk with her at length—to find out what sort of person she was in addition to being an outstandingly beautiful young woman.

He supposed he must meet Leah also and wondered if she were as well favored as her sister. He dismissed that thought, for no one else in all the world could be as lovely as Rachel. He experimented with making a word picture of her eyes. "Large" and "luminous" were fair beginnings. He tried without success to define the classic bone structure of her face, her long black hair, her slender arms and expressive hands. No words he knew were adequate. She was altogether lovely. She was—Rachel.

How long had he been daydreaming? He jumped to his feet and found his way to the kitchen. There were dates, goat cheese and small wheat cakes for his breakfast.

He had stayed in his room so long that the others had eaten and were out of the house already. Servants told him Laban had gone to purchase sheep. Leah had gone to the marketplace to buy provisions for the day's meals. Rachel had taken her flock out to pasture near the well by the city wall.

Jacob ate hurriedly, then he also left the house. He knew where to find that pasture near the well!

Part Three

Rachel Remembers

Patterns of joy and sorrow . . . settings for her constant love for her beloved.

Jacob . . . God's plain man!
Jacob . . . my beloved.

> Deceived by Laban,
> Befriended by God.

Jacob . . . God's quiet man!
Jacob . . . my husband.

> Captive in Haran,
> Canaan in his heart.

Jacob . . . God's chosen man!
Jacob . . . my life!

> Gladdened by Joseph,
> Son of our love.

14

After Jacob had stayed with him for a whole month . . .   *Genesis 29:14*

had been thinking of Jacob all morning—as I ate breakfast and as I led the sheep to pasture. The morning hours passed; I still thought of him. I had seen him only for a few moments, but that was long enough to know he was strong, impulsive, exciting, thoughtful—and very, very handsome. I decided that when I saw him the next time, I would be aloof or haughty because we should have been introduced before he kissed me! I smiled at the thought of teasing him with a few words and looks of disdain. Then, remembering his eyes brimming with tears as he tried to explain his impulsiveness, I was not sure it was a good idea.

From time to time I watched the road leading from the city gate, hoping I would see him coming. One of the lambs wandered too far from the rest of the sheep, and I picked up my crook and went to bring it back. It was frisky and gave me a good chase, demanding full attention for a time. The diversion was welcome, for I was able not to think of Jacob for several minutes. Why should I think of him anyway? He was only an interesting stranger who happened to be a cousin on a journey to somewhere—stopping off at Haran to see his relatives.

And then I saw him crossing the open space between the grazing land and the road with long strides, almost running. I sat perfectly still and turned my head in the opposite direction to practice the expression I wanted my face to wear. The other time we met I hadn't said one word to him—not one word. He must have thought I was dumb! This time I wanted to be witty and charming.

I heard his footsteps but still did not turn to face him. An unusual shyness seemed to stifle me.

"Rachel." He spoke just that one word, but his voice said, "Hello, I'm sorry. I care very much about you." At least I thought it did.

"Jacob." I smiled and spoke the name I never tired of saying. Now this was sparkling conversation—just each other's names! I couldn't think of anything more to say, felt my face grow warm, and knew it was flushed.

"Good morning, Rachel. The servants told me I would find you here."

"You came to water the sheep again?"

"If you want me to, I will—but I came for another reason."

"To meet your new shepherd friends from yesterday?" I couldn't resist teasing, and Jacob enjoyed it, for he smiled broadly at my impertinent questions.

"I did not come to water sheep or to talk with shepherds. I came to find a lovely shepherdess and to apologize to her for the way I behaved yesterday. Rachel, I am sorry. I have no excuses. To think I didn't even tell you who I was before I kissed you . . . I can't believe I could have been that bold and clumsy. Will you forgive me?"

His smile had faded and now he looked so worried that I wanted to tease a little more so he would stop taking the situation so seriously.

"Do you always kiss girls the first time you see them?"

His smile returned to erase the worry lines, and he began to laugh. Then he answered deliberately. "Always—every time I have been on the road for many weeks, feel lonely in a strange land, and have in front of me the most beautiful girl in the entire world, who happens to be my cousin."

"Then it doesn't happen often?"

"Rachel, yesterday was like no other day—ever."

It was a simple statement but I gladly read into it all that Jacob implied. I was special to him from that first moment—as he was to me.

I could not voice the things I wanted to tell him—not yet—so I asked trivial things like, "How did you like your room, Jacob? Did you sleep well?"

He didn't answer, so I tried one more question. "Did you find enough to eat for breakfast?"

"Rachel, we were talking about yesterday."

"I know."

"Why did you change the subject?"

"I thought we had finished with that subject, and I want to know if you are comfortable at my father's house. I'm concerned about you."

"Then be concerned that I don't enjoy dull conversations."

"Sleeping well and eating well are important."

"Yes, but talking about such things is dull. Have you ever noticed how people talk about nothing when they don't want others to know their thoughts? It is a waste of words."

"I should be insulted, Jacob. You think I'm dull and a word waster."

"I never meant to say that . . . ." Jacob looked confused. I had teased long enough.

"I am dull. It comes from being out here talking to sheep too much of the time. I'm not good at conversation, but talk to me. Tell me about your home and your family—especially your mother, my aunt Rebekah."

Jacob talked to me for hours. I felt I really did know him well—knew his family and his land. He even told me of his God. There was nothing dull about Jacob—or his conversation.

We shared the lunch I had brought with me.

"Do you always bring this fine a lunch to share with passersby?" Now Jacob was teasing and we both laughed easily.

"Only when the passerby is a lonely traveler from a strange land, who happens to be Aunt Rebekah's handsome son."

I wanted that delightful day never to end, but sunrays angled down to remind us that time was not standing still, no matter how much we wished it would. I looked toward the well and saw the other shepherds had gathered their flocks for watering.

"Jacob, it's time to go. Look, the other shepherds have gone to the well. They are always ahead of me."

Jacob wanted them on their way before he and Rachel

watered her flock. "They seem to be just standing around. Why don't they get their sheep watered?"

"They are probably waiting for you to remove the stone."

Jacob shook his head and laughed. "Not today, at least not by myself." He reached his right arm around to rub his left shoulder and winced as he remembered his strained muscle.

We led the sheep to the well, and he helped the other men remove the stone to water all the animals. No one spoke of the day before. Aside from customary greetings, no one spoke at all.

When Jacob and I led the sheep back to their fold, we walked silently. We did not bore each other with what Jacob called "dull conversation." Neither did we tell each other our thoughts. I was thinking I was glad he had come to Haran. I was certain his thoughts were the same.

By the time Jacob had been in our home for a month I could scarcely remember what it had been like before he had come. I dared not think how it would be without him.

My father liked the way Jacob found opportunities to be useful. He tended two of my sheep that became deathly sick from eating lupine weed, then he combed the field and rooted out every trace of that noxious plant. Once a shepherd from grazing lands in the north came in carrying one of Father's prized ewes. She had fallen into a ravine and broken a leg. Jacob set the bone, and the leg healed so well there was hardly a limp when the sheep was taken back to rejoin the flock.

He had become acquainted with my brothers at the great banquet Father gave in his honor soon after he came to be with us. They didn't see him often, for they were extremely busy overseeing meat stalls in the marketplace and supervising Father's large herds and flocks that were the source of the meat. My brothers and their families lived in large houses on the other side of Haran; Jacob was never invited to visit them.

Jacob and Leah got along well. He took time to talk with her often. He was friendly, kind and considerate toward her—as he was toward everyone. She smiled more in that first month after he came than she had in any other single month in her life. She preferred to talk with him when I wasn't around and made up errands on which to send me when she wanted me out of the way. She was jealous of me. I became indignant with her.

Father appreciated what Jacob could do for the flocks so much that he asked him to talk with his sons about various aspects of animal husbandry. They regarded this as an affront and not only took offense at what they considered an interloper from Canaan, but felt their father didn't value their judgment and experience properly.

There had been strife and envy in our family before, but now it intensified. Within the first month definite opinions had been formed about him, polarizing the family. Father liked what he could do for the flocks; my brothers felt threatened by him. Leah liked him very much—possibly loved him. But I had loved him before she did, and I loved him more than she did, and I planned to love him forever! And I almost considered her a rival.

Father was going on an extensive trip to buy sheep and goats. Jacob was going with him because Father already had come to rely on his nephew's judgment about livestock. Jacob considered it a compliment to be asked to go with him. I hoped he wouldn't be gone very long.

When they returned, Jacob rushed to where I was keeping my sheep. He literally was breathless from running. He didn't like "stupid questions" any better than "dull conversations," so I stifled the trite "What has happened?" and waited for him to tell me.

"Rachel!" He took my hands in his strong, gentle ones and held them tightly. "My beloved Rachel, I have great news!"

He was more excited than I had ever seen him before, so excited that he groped for words. He led me over to the large stone where we had sat many times as we talked the hours away.

"Good news?"

"Good news . . . yes. But with it, some sadness. The good news is for all time; the sad part is for a short while."

"Please, Jacob, don't talk in riddles."

"Today, on our way back from buying sheep and goats,

Laban and I had a long talk. He began by telling me again how much he appreciated the help I've been to him. He said my work was so valuable that he wanted to pay me. He said that just because I was part of his family, I should not feel I had to work for nothing. He asked me to name my wages.

"Then I told him what he must have known for a long time, what you must have known, too, Rachel. I came to Haran to get a wife, and I want you to be my wife.

"I also told him I have no dowry to give for you. I have never fully explained to him or to you the circumstances of my departure from Beersheba, but they were unusual. I was not given gold or jewels to make up the gift Laban had a right to expect.

"Your father seemed embarrassed for me that I had nothing to bring him. But he was wrong. I had something to give—my service as a shepherd! It will be as good as gold and jewels to him, for under my care I promised that his flocks will increase, making him more wealthy. I have told him I will serve him seven years for you."

"You would work seven years . . . for me?"

"I would work twice that for you."

"It's my dearest dream to be your wife, but . . . oh, Jacob . . . at such a price! What did my father say about substituting that much service for the dowry?"

Jacob folded his arms across his chest and imitated father's gruff voice. " 'It is better that I give her to you than that I should give her to another man; stay here with me.' And that seems to settle it, Rachel."

It was the most thrilling moment of my life, yet the words "seven years" hung in the air around me, and my joy was diluted with quickly rising tears.

"Jacob, seven years before we can marry?"

"Your father thinks you are too young to marry now anyway."

"I am not too young."

"Nor will you be too old in seven years. We will wait, Rachel, we will wait. My work will be in Laban's distant pasturelands, so I won't be able to see you often, but I will see you in my mind every day. I'll remember the delight of being near you—and after the seven years are over, we never will be separated again."

I could not adjust to the bittersweet news. "Jacob, you should have driven a better bargain!"

"Seven years is the customary time of service to offer here in Haran. I made it a point to find out such things. And it was an offer your father thought fair. I have given him my pledge."

Jacob's kiss was sweet, and his arms were strong.

15

So Jacob served seven years to get Rachel, but they seemed like only a few days to him because of his love for her.   *Genesis 29:20*

Jacob's shepherding in the far pasturelands would be in sharp contrast to the situation I enjoyed—leading my small flock to nearby pasture then back home in the evening. In the meadows where my father sent him, the grass would be thin and cropped short. Usually flocks grazed from morning until night—the day's journey being decided by the distance to a well.

Jacob would encounter jackals, wolves, foxes, and maybe even lions. But what I feared most for him were the adders and the other darting snakes that sprang from nowhere into one's path. Attacks from wild animals were rare, but because of the possibility the shepherd lived in constant tension.

It was bad enough being on guard every minute of the day, but the nighttime called for special watchfulness, since many of the animals used the dark hours for prowling. Laban had given Jacob two fierce watchdogs. They were large, long-haired animals with bad tempers. They were so fierce that they could become a problem themselves.

In addition to the dangers from animals, there were thieves who swooped in, and the shepherd who tried to drive them off risked his life. When my brothers worked as shepherds before taking their places at the bazaar, they used to frighten me with exaggerated stories of the hazards they faced. I knew they enlarged on their experiences, but I knew also that there was real danger.

Jacob was not new to shepherding; he had told me of his years in Canaan with his father's flocks. He was experienced in handling dangerous situations, but that didn't lessen my anxiety about him.

Anxiety was a new emotion for me. I had never worried about anyone before. My mother died while I was too young to have been concerned about her ill health and impending death. When my brothers were shepherds, I was still young enough to think that most dangers were make-believe or directed to someone other than our family. My dear Jacob meant only to bring to my life a new happiness; he never intended to introduce into it the grating uneasiness of anxiety.

He had been gone several months when my father told Leah and me that he would be coming home in three days for a report on how things were going for him and his flock. Rhesa, one of my father's new hirelings, was sent to relieve him temporarily.

For three days Leah spent longer hours at marketing, instructing servants about the food to prepare, and directing that Jacob's room be furnished with a new bed mat and embroidered floor cushions. I appreciated her concern for Jacob's comfort during the short time he would be home.

Kept busy through the days with my sheep, I could not make much preparation, except to grow more excited as the time for his coming grew closer. My excitement turned to dismay when Father spoke to me the morning Jacob was to arrive.

"You know the time of betrothal has been set, Rachel; you will be guided by its terms. It is not acceptable now for you and Jacob to spend time alone with each other as you did when he first came here and helped with your flock."

"But Father, seven years never to see Jacob alone? It is not possible you would require that!"

"It is possible."

I would find a way to see Jacob alone. I would! Father caught my defiant attitude and, without further words, pounded the table with his fist. I lifted my chin, turned and left the room.

I went out to the courtyard and paced back and forth, angrier with each turn. Then, determined to stop such a waste of time and energy, I sat on a bench to think of a plan. After what had just happened, Father would be on guard when Jacob came home. All right, let him! I would be no trouble. I would get him to trust me completely so that he would relax his vigil the next time Jacob came home.

When Jacob arrived, he sensed the importance of not attempting to meet me alone. It was difficult at first, but it became a private game we played—looking lovingly at each other when we were certain our glance would not be intercepted, but being careful not even to ask each other direct questions. By the time he left to go back to the grasslands, we loved each other more.

It was the same the second time he came home for a few days. Father kept him busy, and we saw each other only when other family members were present. He also saw to it that Jacob and Leah had no time together without a chaperon. I was happy about that, because I would have been even more frustrated had I known she could talk to him alone while I could not. I thought it unusually kind of father to eliminate that source of unhappiness for me.

My brothers and their wives came to festive meals when Jacob was home. They urged him to talk about his work with Laban's flocks. "The worst thing about it for me is the endless solitude—no one to share the beauty or the danger of any hour."

Laban chided him, "I thought God's people like solitude so they can pray and wait for Him to speak to them. I have heard Abraham spent much time this way."

"I am not Abraham. I do pray and am glad to have time for it, but it does not take hours and hours for me. And I do long for the Lord God to appear to me again, but He has not—not since I left Canaan, where he appeared at a place I named Bethel."

"Are you saying that the house of God is only in Canaan and that he won't speak to you here?"

"No. I am not saying He won't, just that He hasn't—so far."

"Maybe He can't see you out in those fields." My brother Seva had never believed that the one God had talked with Abraham or Isaac—and certainly not Jacob!

"Seva, if God could appear to me on a remote hill near an

obscure village called Luz, He can find me anywhere!"

"Maybe He comes while you are asleep."

Jacob tried to ease the tension by not seeming to sense the intended insult. "He can appear to me when I am sleeping. He did at Bethel."

"You were sleeping when you saw God?"

"He came to me in a dream."

"You are only a dreamer then!"

My other brothers joined in Seva's derisive laughter. Even Father looked amused.

Jacob looked directly at Seva and spoke sharply, "I will not mention again my boredom with the sheep. And I will not try to tell how a dream can be more than a dream. Either you know, or you don't. These things—different as they are—must be experienced; they never can be explained."

They were stunned by his volatile response, and the moment of quiet that followed served to reinforce what Jacob had just said.

Then he resorted to what he really despised—trite talk about things people expected to hear. "We must turn to lighter things. We are here to enjoy each other's company and this elegant fare Laban has provided for us. I am only a guest in his house, a servant who cares for flocks. Let me be quiet now, and let us hear everything he would like to say to us."

My father never missed an opportunity like this. He deluged Jacob and my brothers with complaints of how bad business was, how herdsmen from whom he purchased animals had cheated him, how much he feared there would be no rain in time to save the pasturelands.

The food was good, but the conversation made me ill. Jacob and I were hopelessly outnumbered by the eyes on us. I left the table early.

Alone in my room I thought of Jacob, and I knew that while he talked with my family, he thought of me.

He came home every few months. Only a few times did we manage to meet alone for even a short while, and then we were so afraid we might be discovered that we were not at ease. I remember one precious conversation.

"I worry about you, Jacob."

"The Lord God promised He would take me back safely to Canaan. I'm not foolhardy in the face of danger, yet neither do I fear it. His word is sure. I'll return to Canaan—and you will be with me."

"I'm lonely—and as bored with my sheep as you are with yours."

"Lonely hours are hurting times, but try to think of each one that passes as being one less we have to face before we can be together for all time."

"That helps—but not enough."

"Rachel! We love each other! Do you know what a rare thing that is? It's a glorious thing most people never know, and it's stronger than time or distance."

"I thought you didn't like platitudes."

"These are not platitudes; they are the truth."

"I know. I just don't have your patience or your perspective on things. To me, Jacob, a minute is important—and seven years seem like seven lifetimes."

"It's no longer seven years. The first one is gone."

"Don't try to cheer me up when we do not have a cheerful situation."

"You're right. It's not a cheerful situation, but we can make it easier or more difficult—for ourselves and for each other."

"What does that mean?"

"Knowing you are unhappy makes it harder for me to leave you. I take the feeling of your sadness with me."

"Jacob, would you like another platitude? I will smile— every day. Think of me smiling." I tried to smile then, to give him an example to remember. It was forced, but it would have to do.

I did try to be happier in the days after he left—a sort of token thing I wanted to do for him. It seemed rather foolish when he could never really know. But another time when he was home we had time for a sentence or two in the courtyard, and he said, "Rachel, you have been keeping your word— smiling every day!"

"How do you know? Because I am so honest that you know I keep my word?"

"No. Because it has made you more beautiful."

By the time we were half way through the seven years, Father was the happiest person in our house.

"Jacob is my best shepherd. He has learned of prime places to graze the flocks, knows where the wells are, keeps alert to stamp out poisonous weeds, and has no fear of dangers that others run from. The flocks he tends have increased more than any other of my flocks."

"He works too hard." I said it with so much feeling that it angered Father.

"You think he made a bad bargain? If he thinks so, he can stop any time. The marriage does not have to take place."

"I think he made a very difficult bargain. If you wanted to, you could soften the terms and not require that he work the entire seven years, since he has worked so well."

"A bargain is a bargain. He has no dowry! If he had brought gold, he would not have had to do this. It's his fault—or Isaac's—not mine."

"Hasn't Jacob enriched you more than a dowry already?"

"Enough, Rachel!"

I couldn't sleep that night, so I thought about Jacob. He probably had herded the sheep into a stone den for shelter during the night. I hoped he had found brush to close off the mouth of the den so he wouldn't have to stay awake to be sure no wild animal got in—or no sheep wandered out. Maybe he hadn't found a den. He might have found only a corner section of a stone wall to partially protect him and his flock.

I worried that a wolf might attack him or his flock. I could almost see some sheep being killed and the rest being scattered. Sheep ran in such blind terror in all directions that it was sometimes impossible to find them all again. Shepherds weren't accountable for the loss of animals in such cases, but Jacob felt responsible anyway.

As I thought about the price he was paying for my dowry, it made me always angrier at my father. I couldn't enjoy the pleasant, nearby pasture I had for my flock, and I couldn't enjoy my comfortable home when I pictured Jacob in his loneliness and his hardship. I was not used to the melancholy of missing someone—of trying to share another's sadness.

But as the first three and a half years of our separation

passed, so did the second three and a half years. My father had robbed me of seven of the best years of my life, but now it was over! Jacob would be home in three days. Preparations for the wedding were underway. There would be a week of feasting, dancing and celebrating with friends and family. Then there would be a lifetime for Jacob and me—together.

It was difficult to sleep and impossible to eat. I watched the road occasionally, although it was too early for him to be coming. By the end of the second day I watched constantly.

I walked past the large rooms Father had added to our house. The new addition had a tiled roof like the rest of the house; its own door opened onto the central courtyard. There was lattice work across its windows and shutters that could be opened to let in the morning sun or closed to keep out the heat of the day.

I walked back to the old part of the house and up the stairs to the rooms Leah and I shared for so many years. I wondered if she would be lonely when I moved to the new quarters. I was pleased at the interest she took in working out the plans for the wedding celebration. She seemed to be happy for me, never mentioning how she must feel as an older sister watching a younger sister marry a man she loved herself. I felt sad for her, but too happy for myself to dwell long on dreary thoughts.

With a great sign of satisfaction I picked up the pale blue tunic, gently smoothed its folds, and thought of how soon I would be wearing it for the first time!

Then it was the day—*the day!* Jacob had arrived! I was not allowed to see him. Stupid customs! But I could put up with them because Jacob could now claim me as his wife. He had paid the dowry in full.

16

So Jacob said to Laban, "What is this you have done to me? I served you for Rachel, didn't I? Why have you deceived me?"   *Genesis 29:25*

*t*here's sorrow that can't be put into words—hope smothered by despair, joy crushed by helpless rage.

The day after Jacob returned, the wedding celebration began at our house. Our courtyard was filled with those who came to share in the festive occasion. There were many kinds of food and abundant wine. I could hear laughing and singing from my room—where I was under orders to stay—but I laughed and sang along with the guests for sheer joy. Leah was busy somewhere in the house, supervising servants who kept food and wine streaming out to the happy crowd. The merriment lasted until many hours after sundown. It began again the next afternoon and continued until late that night.

I hadn't minded losing sleep the first night. I was too excited to sleep even if it had been quiet. But this second night I was tired and feared that losing two night's sleep would make me look less than my best. I had to be refreshed and beautiful for Jacob.

One never knew how long these celebrations might last— sometimes a week, sometimes two weeks. The taking of a wife occurred when her father decided it was time to present her to the groom. I didn't know when Father would send for me. That second night I slept soundly. In the morning when I awakened, Leah was not there. She had not been there when I went to sleep either. Didn't she think the celebration could go on without her? Didn't she think the servants could manage to get the day underway without her supervision?

I was the only one in the house who didn't know. Kerah came in, apparently to awaken me. I thought it was so right to see her first on my special day. I scarcely remembered my mother, but Kerah had been a mother to me—my nurse since I was born, my teacher, my friend and confidant in these last long years. Her face was sad; her eyes were red.

"Kerah, why are you unhappy on this beautiful, wonderful day? This must be the day I am to be given to Jacob, so it can't be a day for tears. Are you crying because you think I'm leaving you? What's wrong?"

She answered my questions with a new flood of tears that she tried to wipe aside before I saw them.

"Kerah!" My voice held a mixture of authority and fear. "Tell me what is wrong!"

"The marriage is done. The bride has been given to Jacob."

"No! You are mad! Don't you see me sitting here?"

"The marriage feast was . . . late last night. The bride . . . has been given . . . by your father . . . to Jacob."

"Bride?"

"Leah."

The wild scream I felt inside could not get out. It was choked up by tears and an inability to believe what Kerah said.

Kerah, pretending to be busy around the room, was keeping loving watch over me. I didn't want to be watched! She dipped a cloth into the wash basin, made it into a cool compress and laid it against my forehead. I managed to thank her, then told her I didn't need anything more and asked to be left alone. When she was gone, I threw the cloth on the floor. I sobbed until there were no tears left—until I could not make another sound. And then I kept on crying inside.

Later in the morning Kerah came in softly and left a plate of fresh fruit. I wasn't hungry, but her thoughtfulness fed my heart.

Grief gradually gave way to anger. Anger grew into hatred—toward my father, toward Leah—toward Jacob! I let my mind wallow in bitter thoughts of the past seven years—useless, desolate years. I thought of the meaninglessness of all the future years. This was to have been my wedding day! That was the dart my mind used to punctuate all other thoughts.

I saw my father enter the courtyard below. He looked up to my window, and I slammed the shutters—hard.

Then in a moment I heard a once-beloved—still-beloved—voice raised in bitter anger. Jacob had run out to the courtyard and was shouting at my father. I opened the shutters slightly to see and to hear better. Jacob towered over a cringing Laban.

"What is this you have done to me? I slaved for you seven years for Rachel! Why have you tricked me?"

Jacob's rage made my own seem weak by comparison. I feared for Father's life. Jacob had taken hold of his tunic with such force that Father nearly lost his balance.

If he was afraid, he didn't let Jacob know it. He jerked himself loose from his grasp, took several steps back, and spoke as if to an unlearned stranger. "It's not our custom to marry off a younger daughter ahead of her sister."

Jacob lunged at him again. Father stepped back further. He would avoid physical confrontation with his strong shepherd. He tried instead to bargain. "Wait until the bridal week is over, and you can have Rachel, too—if you promise to work for me another seven years."

I clapped my hand over my mouth for fear my heart would jump through it. Their conversation was past understanding. Another seven years? Two wives? What would that solve? But what else could be done now?

Jacob turned abruptly from my father and stood looking at the ground, then up to unresponsive skies. When he spoke again, his voice was lower, his shoulders drooped, his anger was spent. "Seven more years?"

"Seven. This time, Jacob, my son, you won't have to go to those far pastures." He grinned and made a wide sweep with his right arm as if making a grand concession. "You may stay here, take the flocks out to nearby fields, and come home each evening. You will be given undershepherds to help."

"But . . . seven more years . . . with no pay?"

"Rachel is reward enough! And besides, you will not need to concern yourself with your needs or the needs of your wives—I will provide for you all."

"From the profits of my flock, Laban?"

"*My* flock, Jacob—you are merely the shepherd."

Jacob's face mirrored the strong emotions with which he struggled.

"Jacob, decide now! Another seven years and you can have Rachel at the end of the week."

"Agreed."

And so it was done.

The wedding festivities for Jacob and Leah resumed that evening and continued each evening until the week was over. When Jacob didn't look happy enough, the guests plied him with more wine and laughed heartily in futile attempts to encourage the bridegroom to be joyful. These seven days of the bridal week were as long to me as the previous seven years had been.

There was no celebration when I was given to Jacob. It was, to my father, a routine business transaction.

Father gave Leah the quarters she and I had shared, and he presented her with Zilpah to be her maid. The rooms for Jacob and me were in the new addition that had been built onto the house. Father gave me Bilhah as my maid, and of course Kerah was to remain with me. Jacob and I were husband and wife, but our joy was devastated by bitterness and fury.

As days passed, our torment diminished to a lingering melancholy. I was Jacob's wife, but not his only wife. I was his beloved wife, but not his first wife. Leah had, for all time, invaded our lives and our thoughts. Jacob tried to console me. He became more considerate than he might otherwise ever have been. He spent as much time with me as he could, and when we were together I almost believed things were as they should be—almost.

Leah complained that Jacob slighted her. He was not used to the idea of more than one wife, even though Esau had married two women. To Jacob, I was his wife; it took time for him to accept Leah as such.

Leah and I avoided each other as long as possible—each not knowing what to say to the other, not wanting to say anything at all. Jacob had a divided household, and it made things still more difficult for him.

It was late summer when Leah came to my door one morning after Jacob had gone to his flocks. "I have some news for you."

I was surprised she had taken the initiative to come to me. "It must be important if it makes you break the silence of these many weeks."

"It is important news . . . wonderfully important."

From the expression on her face I knew before she told me what it was. "You are going to have a child!"

"Jacob's first child." Her look of triumph was appropriate. I would have looked the same way if I had been in her position. She waited for my response, but I made none.

"Rachel, surely this means God has noticed my sorrow at having a husband who does not love me, and He has rewarded me with this child. Now maybe Jacob will love me a little. If it is a boy, I will name him Reuben—'See, a son.' "

Their baby was a boy. My husband was thrilled with Reuben, and I tried not to allow my frustration to spoil his joy.

I increasingly hoped for a child of my own, but the next baby was Leah's also. She named the new child Simeon, "God heard," because of her certainty that God had answered her prayers and knew of her loneliness. Jacob was proud of his two sons and had a growing respect for Leah, but his deep love was for me.

Father had to provide additional quarters for Jacob's family. He worried at times that he was not getting enough work out of Jacob this second term of seven years to merit all the expenses. He mentioned this to Jacob one time too many.

"You have said this before, Laban. And I can answer only that it is part of our bargain that you supply all the needs of my family. If you believe you are the loser in this, then shorten my term of slavery to you! I will gladly provide for my own family by working for someone who will pay me wages, not just supply a roof for our heads, food for our stomachs, and clothes for our backs."

"Jacob, my son, a bargain is a bargain. Finish out your seven years with me. I will say no more about the expense of your family. Have even more children!"

I hoped Jacob would have more children and that they would be mine. Meanwhile, I spent my time seeing to our part of Laban's rambling house and took pride in preparing fine meals. Daily I packed bread, olives, cheese, dried grapes and figs into Jacob's kidskin scrip for his noon meal.

I learned to weave goat hair and made him a waterproof cloak. It seldom rained in Haran, but when it came, it was torrential. Inside the cloak was a pouch large enough for a newborn lamb to be carried if it was injured or sick.

Jacob almost never took the cloak with him. It was heavy, and he already had to carry the scrip, the water skin, the sling and rod, and his staff.

"That's a lot to carry, Jacob." I made a casual comment as he was leaving one morning, and got a surprising response.

He must have been waiting to talk about what was bothering him. He turned back, looked at me a moment, and then began. "It's not the things I carry, but the load in my heart that's the burdensome thing. I don't know how I could have blundered into this situation. It's not right for you, not fair to Leah, and certainly not what I wanted."

"Do you think the Lord God is not watching over you, no longer guiding you?"

"That's the heaviest part of my load—the longing for affirmation from the Lord God. I can't say He is not with me, for He said He would be. But neither can I say I haven't suffered since coming to Haran.

"My prayers are not of praise but in agony of soul. If I'm displeasing Him, I want to be shown my wrongs. If I am pleasing Him, then I want to know why my life has been so difficult.

"I'm enraged at the injustice, the prolonged estrangement from my family, the years of servitude to Laban, the deception that resulted in marriage to Leah! I'm pressed to the limit!"

"So it seems, so it seems, Jacob, my dearest." I had listened to my beloved pour out his anguish but was not able to comfort him. I shared his grief and his questionings and, like him, would not pretend to be cheered by easy, sentimental words or wishful thinking about what could not be changed.

He put down the cumbersome shepherd's gear he had been holding all through his despairing speech, and, although none of his problems were solved, he smiled as if they were. He put

his emptied arms around me and sighed with a contentment
that would have seemed impossible moments before.

It was not dramatic; no one watching would have thought
he was doing anything heroic. But when I saw Jacob go over to
pick up his rod and staff and the other belongings and walk out
to his day's work, I felt he had passed a definite test and had
overcome a despair that could have been utterly devastating.
He was not shutting his eyes or his mind to our situation, but
in beautiful practicality he dealt with his next hour's responsibility. There is a certain inherent healing in doing what is
possible. It keeps your mind from a morbid dwelling on the
impossible.

The second term of seven years continued; the flocks Jacob
tended fared well; the number of Jacob's children increased. In
addition to Reuben and Simeon, Leah had borne Levi, then
Judah. She chose Levi's name, meaning "attachment," to
signify her hope that with his birth Jacob would feel more
affection toward her. She chose Judah's name, meaning
"praise," because she did praise the Lord God for the way He
blessed her with healthy, handsome sons since she could not
have the happiness of being truly loved by her husband.

Leah may have been filled with praise, but I was filled with
envy. I kept my feelings in check until the birth of Judah. Then
I could stifle them no longer. Instead of being glad for Jacob—
or at least allowing him the good pleasure of being happy
about a fourth fine son—I screamed at him for the first time in
my life.

"Jacob! Give me children, or else I shall die!"

Jacob, shocked by my outburst, answered in rage, "Am I in
the place of God? It is He who has withheld children from
you!"

I had hurt him; he responded in kind. We stood looking at
each other across the gulf we had made between us.

"Jacob, I must have children." My voice was calmer, but the
calmness was a sham. "You already have taken two wives. I
would not mind a third . . . if the third would be my handmaid,
Bilhah. As the law of our land declares, her children would be
considered mine."

"Do you know what you're saying, Rachel?"

"Yes!" I had practiced a good argument to convince Jacob, but now the words wouldn't come. I only confirmed my decision—with difficulty. "Yes, I do most surely mean it."

Neither of us moved. I wanted to run to him for the embrace of his arms, but I could not. I felt like a woman of stone.

"Rachel, Rachel, I could not love you more if you gave me 10 sons and 10 daughters."

' "I know."

"I have four sons, and that is a good family—twice as many sons as my father had."

' *You* have four sons; I do not. I want children of my own—or of my own handmaiden."

As long as I confronted him, he was unmoved. But having said what was necessary, I relaxed my rigid attitude and took the short steps to his arms—steps I couldn't have taken earlier lest I not finish what I had to say. In that snug haven I wept and said, "Please, Jacob, go in to Bilhah—that I may have children."

Bilhah conceived and bore Jacob a son. I was thrilled that the baby was a boy and named him Dan, "vindicated," for surely the Lord God had vindicated me for the inequality of things and allowed me a son, at least in this manner. The next year Bilhah presented another son, and I called him Naphtali, "struggle," for I had struggled in envy with my sister. Jacob now had six sons!

The second term of seven years was at an end. Jacob was free from servitude—but penniless. Laban felt assured of his further service.

17

Then God remembered Rachel . . . . She became pregnant and gave birth to a son . . . . She named him Joseph.   *Genesis 30:22-24*

Jacob hadn't eaten a bite of supper. He was too busy talking. "Yes, I am a free man—no more time to serve out to pay for dowries! But what can I do? I have nothing except my family, and I can hardly sell a son to pay for a starter flock of sheep and goats. I know no trade except shepherding.

"There has been no word in all this time from my family—or from the Lord God—about my returning to Canaan.

"Rachel, you've married a failure. I'm 54 years old, and I'm only now trying to begin something for myself. Until now I have spent my working years helping Father or Laban. I increased their holdings considerably, but I have nothing to show for it except experience."

"I could sell my earrings and chains. Would that bring enough for starter flocks?"

"Don't even think of that! I can't buy you jewelry, but I won't have you sell what you already have!"

"Look at this chain, Jacob. Father gave it to me years ago; it belonged to his mother—Rebekah's mother. Abraham's Eliezer gave it to her when he took Rebekah back to Canaan to marry your father."

Jacob looked at it, tracing its elaborate carvings with his fingers. "My mother left for Canaan in proper style; I want you to leave that way when we go. I want to earn enough money to outfit a caravan and go back home in so grand a manner that my family could not guess I have been nothing more than a slave for all these years."

"Will you look for work with another sheep owner now?"

"Yes! I've had enough of your father's deceit and high-handed ways."

"And so have I, Jacob. I know you will find work. Meanwhile, eat your supper."

Jacob had not quite finished his meal when Father came to our door and called him out into the courtyard. He was so polite that I worried about what sort of plan he had in mind for Jacob. I knew he would have one.

Laban sat on a bench near our door; Jacob remained standing to indicate he did not intend this to be a long conversation.

Laban drew the corners of his mouth into a grin and held it so long he looked foolish. "I would like to have a great celebration feast for you, Jacob, my son, to celebrate your completion of 14 years of excellent service to me."

He was doing his best to put Jacob in an agreeable frame of mind, but Jacob was not to be manipulated. "I remember the last great feast you had for me. It lasted a week, and it took me 14 years to pay for it!"

"Ah, Jacob, that is past. You have a fine family—beautiful wives and strong, healthy sons. You have fared well in my house."

"And you have fared very, very well, Laban! Your own sons would not have worked as hard as I have for you, and surely they would not have worked for no pay!"

"No pay? Think of the mouths I've fed . . . the clothing . . ."

"Laban, what do you want?"

"Merely to know your plans. I care about my daughters. What will become of them and their households when I no longer provide for them?"

"Don't worry. I intend to provide for them."

"How?"

"I know other sheep owners; I'll get employment with one of them."

"I hoped you might want to stay here. I will be glad to employ you for as long as you want to stay. Part of your pay will be my continued provision for your large family. But besides that you will get a worthwhile wage, Jacob. We can discuss the terms now if you are interested."

"I am not interested. I prefer to work with a man I can trust. You made an agreement with me before, only to break it."

"As I said, that is past. Maybe what I did was wrong, but I knew Leah would be a fine wife for you. Are you not happy with the sons she has borne you?"

"Yes, I am happy with Reuben, Simeon, Levi and Judah, but that has nothing to do with how I feel toward you. I distrust any promise you make."

"Don't be harsh with me, Jacob!" Laban looked offended, and his voice was full of anger.

"Then don't badger me to work any longer for you."

My father got up from the bench, his face quite red. He shook his fist at Jacob and said, "Then be out of my house— you and all your family—by tomorrow night. I owe you not one more night's lodging."

He stormed out of the courtyard and into his quarters.

Jacob, a free man, stood like a wounded animal caught in a trap; my father was a skillful trapper.

Jacob walked through our front door, shaking with rage and crushed in spirit. "Did you hear that?"

"I heard."

"He knows it's impossible to find a place for my wives, six children and all our belongings by tomorrow night—or even in the near future. It takes time to find a position such as I need and can command."

"Where is the Lord God, Jacob?"

"That's it!"

"What kind of an answer is that? I asked you where your Lord God is now that Laban is about to push you into another trap."

"And I told you. That is what I needed to hear—that's my answer. Where is the Lord God? He is with me. That is really all I do know for certain. I don't know why such difficult things keep happening; I don't know how much longer I have to wait before hearing His voice again. I could go insane thinking about things I don't understand.

"But I have His word; I have the memory of the actual

sound of His voice saying He would be with me wherever I went and would bring me back home.

"Rachel, I have God Himself as my certainty! I'll go to Laban and make as good a deal with him as I can. Let him scheme and plot; let him take advantage of me again. There will be a day when my God will say that I've suffered enough in my exile."

Jacob's face glowed. He was happy—in a different way than I had ever seen him.

"Why do I keep forgetting the central thrust of my life? I treasure His words in my heart, but I don't bring them out to lean on them! His words are support and strength for living. O Rachel, I have told you often about Bethel; you probably can say the Lord God's words along with me by now. I want to say them again—to affirm for both of us that we are not afraid of Laban because the Lord God, in His own time, will lead us to Canaan."

Jacob closed his eyes to remember the vision better. When he spoke, his voice held a reverence and a sound of joy that ran deeper than his surface frustrations could reach.

I am the Lord, the God of your father Abraham and the God of Isaac. I will give you and your descendants the land on which you are lying. Your descendants will be like the dust of the earth, and you will spread out to the west and to the east, to the north and to the south. All peoples on earth will be blessed through you and your offspring. I am with you and will watch over you wherever you go, and I will bring you back to this land. I will not leave you until I have done what I have promised you.

We were quiet for some time after Jacob spoke the words of God's message, given so long ago. Then my husband got up and went out to my father's door to talk about terms of employment.

He returned from their meeting in high spirits. He had found his father-in-law generous in his offer, and this time they had parted friends.

"Do you think he will keep his word this time, Jacob?"

"If he doesn't, he will have to answer to the Lord God Himself!"

I had lost respect for my father and felt uncomfortable

when he was around, but I had an affection for our old house and found it reassuring to go on living there. I never had faced change and thought it would be a rather frightening thing. I didn't want to cope with it until the inevitable move to Canaan. We would still be somewhat intimidated by Father, but now Jacob was not under a long-term obligation. We could leave at any time with reasonable notice, and that in itself was a freedom.

When Jacob received his first six months' wages, he went to the Haran bazaar and stayed all afternoon. He came home in the early evening, riding a camel borrowed from Father. He dismounted and took from a cumbersome pack on the animal's back two items he had selected as a surprise for me. There was a small carved cedar table inlaid with seashells and a length of scarlet material laced with gold threads.

"Presents for my bride—my wife. Oh, how long I have wanted to be able to buy you something beautiful! I hope you like the table and the material."

"Oh, I do! They were both made especially for me. I can't think of them belonging to anyone else. They are perfect."

"And here is one more thing." He reached into his money pouch and took out a ring—a slender spiral of gold designed to encircle the finger twice. He put it on me, and I never took it off.

Life was better than it ever had been. We loved each other more and learned to live with our unusual family situation.

Leah and I had times of sharp conflict, but for the most part we managed to keep Jacob's household peaceful. She and Zilpah cared for her four sons; Bilhah and I cared for Dan and Naphtali.

I didn't mention to her the gifts Jacob bought for me. He had no money left to buy anything for her—or for anyone else, not even himself. Dear Jacob—the first pay in his life spent on me! I had started to scold him for his extravagance, then decided to enjoy what he had so carefully and lovingly selected, allowing him the dignity of deciding how his money should be spent.

Each time Bilhah and I went to the river to do the washing,

we passed the temple of the moon god and goddess. She worshiped these deities, and one day she asked why I did not.

"Oh, we have a mixture of beliefs about the gods at Laban's house. We have a family tradition of believing in a God who made the heavens and the earth—and created everyone."

"You believe He created even the people who don't believe in Him?"

"Jacob does. Jacob heard Him speak."

"Do you believe your God can talk, Rachel?"

"Jacob's father also heard Him speak; so did his grandfather."

"Gods don't speak."

"Not your gods made of clay, but ours is a living God."

"And you worship that One, of course. I would worship that One also if I heard Him speak."

"As I told you, we have a mixture of beliefs at our house. Jacob totally believes in the one God and no other. But my father—and his father before him—although they believe in the Lord God, also appease whatever other gods there might be. So they divide their worship between the God of Abraham and the gods of Haran. My father has small statues of the moon god and goddess that Leah and I were taught to respect."

"You told me what your father believes and what your husband believes. What do you believe?"

"Oh, I never forced myself to make a choice. I am appalled at some of the rituals that go on in the temple of the moon god! Jacob's God is pure and holy; I am drawn to Him. But I haven't decided . . . I suppose I am superstitious enough not to want to offend any god."

"That sounds like a good idea—don't decide. Then you will have no gods angry with you."

"Jacob says that is a wrong idea. He says if one worships his God, then any worship—or even respect—of any other god is forbidden. He says I will have to choose to worship the one God and Him alone—or the other gods."

My conversation with Bilhah made me think more deeply than I had before about the one God. From the names Leah chose for her children it was apparent she had thought more about Him than I had—prayed to Him more and praised Him more. Had she had the courage to totally reject all the local gods? I would ask her.

The noise of Reuben and Simeon playing in the courtyard was a happy sound. They were growing fast, learning how to play and how to persuade their father to play with them. Their busy, busy father took time now and then to toss a bag stuffed with beans to them or carry them on his shoulders. He loved the younger children, too, but would wait until they were a bit older to pay them much attention.

My sister was no longer having children—a great disappointment to her since they were her happiness. Knowing it had become acceptable to Jacob to have children by my maid, Bilhah, she persuaded him to take her handmaiden, Zilpah, to provide more children for her side of the house.

Within the next year Zilpah bore Gad, meaning "troop." He was so named because Leah had found renewed hope of many more children by Jacob. The next year Zilpah's second baby was born—a boy whom Leah named Asher, "happy," because she was truly happy. She was content in the joy her children gave her and in the respect Jacob had for her.

She became even happier; she discovered she was pregnant again. Another sturdy son was born to Leah, and she named him Issachar, "reward," believing God had given her a reward for allowing her maid to increase Jacob's household. Then the next year she amazed everyone, including herself, by bearing her sixth and last son, whom she named Zebulun, "gifts," as she thanked the Lord God for giving Jacob such good gifts through her.

Zebulun was her last son, but she did have one more child, a girl she named Dinah, "judgment." I thought it a poorly chosen name for so lovely an infant.

I had stopped praying for a baby after my handmaiden bore two sons, but exquisite little Dinah stirred the old longing inside me again, and I wanted—more desperately than ever—to have my own child. A love as perfect as Jacob's and mine would surely produce a child. I prayed again to the God of Abraham and Isaac. It never occurred to me to pray to the moon god. My decision about God had been made without my being conscious of it. I prayed only to the living God—the God of Sarah, who waited so very long for a son, the God of Rebekah, who waited many years before having her twins. I prayed to the one God.

It was then that God remembered me. He heard me and opened my womb. I conceived a son who was born out of great love for my husband and great faith in his God. I named him Joseph, "he adds," to attest that I believed He would give yet another son to me. I was free of the curse of barrenness; that reproach had been lifted.

Joseph was Jacob's eleventh son. From the moment of his birth he was especially dear to his father. Jacob found time each day to watch him; he responded quickly to Joseph's cries. He was devoted to this child as he was to none of his other children. Part of his devotion to little Joseph was a reflection of his love for me. Our child was, in a special way, his first son!

18

In breeding season I once had a dream in which I looked up and saw that
the male goats mating with the flock were streaked, speckled or spotted.
The angel of God said to me in the dream, "Jacob." I answered, "Here I
am." And He said, "Look up and see that all the male goats mating with the
flock are streaked, speckled or spotted, for I have seen all that Laban has
been doing to you. I am the God of Bethel, where you anointed a pillar and
where you made a vow to me. Now leave this land at once and go back to
your native land." *Genesis 31:10-13*

Soon after Joseph was born, Jacob sensed that a
new chapter in his life had begun; he felt an increasing urge to
return to Canaan. He still had no word from his family—or
from his God—that the time was right to go back, but after his
many years of relative patience in the strained situations with
my father, he was becoming more and more restless.

"You'll like Canaan, Rachel. It's a land like no other in all
the world. There are beautiful, towering mountains. One
mountain called Hermon is so high it always has snow at its
top! And Canaan has the deepest valley known to anyone. It
has lakes as large as small seas, and the Great Sea itself serves
as part of its border. There is a mighty river that runs through
the land, providing water for fields that produce abundant
grain, fruit and vegetables.

"Rachel, Canaan's skies are the very bluest, and in its clear
air fly more different kinds of birds than in any other place
seven times the size of Canaan. And in springtime the earth is
inundated by a flood of wild flowers and blossoming trees.
Have you ever seen a grove of almond trees in bloom? Have
you seen the pink color of the tamarisk?"

"No . . . I've seen few trees of any kind, and I don't even
know what a tamarisk is. Is it a flower or a shrub or a tree?"

"Oh, it's a small tree with feathery clusters of pink on slender branches. We will have them planted everywhere around our dwellings. You will treasure them. And let me tell you about the ancient olive trees . . ."

"Jacob! You exaggerate Canaan's beauty because you are homesick for it."

"No, if anything I understate its beauty because it has been dimmed in memory through these long years away from it. I will show all of it to you, and you can try to find your own words to describe it."

"I believe you about its beauty, but tell me now about the houses in Beersheba, near where your father has his tents. Describe what a house might be like . . . a house such as my father would own."

"I've seen them only from the outside, but they appear quite beautiful. As in Haran, they are built with large wings at right angles to the front of the house so they provide secluded courtyards and gardens. They have wide balconies on the second floor overlooking the courtyard and gardens. They are made of dressed stone—made to last for many generations."

"Will we live in a house such as that?"

Jacob laughed as if I had just said something amusing. "That seems an impossible luxury to me, Rachel. And besides, our family lives in tents; we aren't settled landowners yet."

"Tents? Us?"

"Of course. You know I've always lived in tent dwellings."

"But . . . I thought . . . after being here and seeing how it's possible to live in town and hire shepherds to tend the animals . . . you might not want to go back to . . . tents."

"Oh, but I do! Houses are too confining. They demand too much attention to keep them in good repair. Tent living is easier; you don't have room for unnecessary articles, so you have fewer things to care for. Tent living is a way of simplicity and freedom."

I made no comment, but Jacob continued, and his voice had a new sound—finality. "Yes! We will live in tents."

"Tents." As I said it, I thought of the stark reality the word implied. Until that moment I had not pictured myself living in one.

"Don't look so anxious, Beloved." Jacob caressed my fore-head to ease the worry lines. "You will get used to living in tents while we are on caravan back to Canaan, and by the time we get there you will want no other way of life. I know it, Rachel! Rebekah left Haran and took up tent living—and loves it to this day. Sarah left the grand house Terah built in Ur and came to live contentedly in the tents of Canaan—and you will, too."

"I'm not sure . . ."

"Don't try to convince yourself now. Just promise to let yourself be convinced when the time comes."

"What will convince me?"

"Canaan itself. Tent living makes you feel closer to the land, and to be close to that God-chosen land is to be home in the fullest sense of that word."

"My poor Jacob, loving your land so much and being away from it so long . . . I hope, for your sake, that we will be on our way there soon."

We ended the conversation but not our individual thoughts about Canaan—and tents!

Jacob's thoughts of Canaan and of his home there increasingly filled his mind. The more he thought of it, the more he talked of it.

"How can I ever save enough on the wages Laban pays me to outfit a caravan to take us home?"

"I don't ask about your dealings with my father . . . but from the lovely things you bought me from your first six month's pay, I would think you could have saved something for our necessary provisions by now."

"You don't ask about my dealings with Laban, and I don't tell you. It's not a pleasant subject. My first wages were generous, and I thought he would pay that much or more every six months. He knows I'm gullible, and he still takes advantage of me."

"How?"

"My pay has never been as high since that first time. And I never know until I'm paid what my wages will be. He changes our terms to suit himself. I have no control over what he decides to allow me."

"Then Canaan is far away, both in miles and in years?"

"Perhaps."

"How could it be otherwise?"

"It depends—not on Laban, but on the God of Bethel!"

It was again the day for Jacob to discuss his next six month's term with Laban. Usually he approached these meetings with disgust—knowing whatever was decided would be undecided at Laban's whim. But on this day he seemed eager for the talk.

"Jacob, you look unusually happy, considering this is the day to talk with Father about our next months."

"I am exactly that—most unusually happy."

"Any special reason?"

"I have a plan to present to him, and it is one that won't go wrong for me—can't go wrong!"

"A plan to make things work for our good instead of Laban's?"

"Yes."

"Well, tell me. What is it?"

"It's difficult to explain—difficult to believe. And it's not my idea . . . I didn't think of it."

"Then who did?"

"The One who appeared to me at Bethel."

"The one God spoke to you?"

Jacob's delight diminished at my question, but only slightly. "No, He didn't exactly speak to me, but as at Bethel He came in a deep dream—with the force of reality itself. This is no fuzzy, half-remembered wisp of thought. I recognized the Voice, and His words were plain . . . but I understood more than the words themselves said. When I hear the Voice, there is an accompanying refreshing of my mind and senses. He speaks to my mind with messages beyond words.

"Rachel . . . it's impossible to explain, yet it's so real I can't tolerate any questioning about whether or not the Lord God actually speaks to me."

"Jacob, tell me your dream—the vision—and if I can't believe with all my heart and mind, please know that I want to believe it."

His need to share his experience with someone was so great that even though I could not unconditionally promise to believe it, he accepted my wanting to believe as good enough for the present.

He took in a deep breath and began, very slowly, "Well . . . as you know . . . thoughts of going back to Canaan have been strong in my mind. I've been trying to think of how I could afford all the things needed to move my household there— with enough flocks to be well established once we are back in the land."

"Yes, I know! You've talked of little else lately. But unless Father changes his way of doing things, he never will be fair to you. You can't change Laban, so you can't manage the cost of a move to Canaan. Jacob, it's impossible!"

"Yes, that's right. There's no way I can make it happen."

"Then why are you so happy? Have you decided to be Laban's servant for life and just make the best of it?"

"Never! And I think my recent discontent has been God's way of preparing me to make the break—to face my brother and take my rightful place.

"Anyway, I had been thinking of getting away from Haran most of the time during my waking hours, and I was beginning to dream about it at night. Last night I dreamed that at the beginning of this breeding season I looked up and saw that all the males that were mating with the flock were streaked, speckled or spotted. It seemed a curious thing, and I watched with amazement.

"And then the Voice broke into my dream. Rachel, listen with your heart, for I'm clumsy at explaining. The blessed Voice said, 'Look up and see that all the male goats mating with the flock are streaked, speckled or spotted, for I have seen all that Laban has been doing to you. I am the God of Bethel, where you anointed a pillar and where you made a vow to me. Now leave this land at once and go back to your native land.'"

Jacob stopped speaking, and while there were a dozen questions I wanted to ask, the look on his face told me to be still. He had, for the moment, forgotten I was there. Saying the words of his God, remembering the sound of His Voice, Jacob wanted no intrusion. He sat silently for what seemed to me a long time, then he shook his head slightly as if to bring his mind back to the present and to what he wanted to tell me.

"Rachel, I've been wasting energy and robbing myself of peace of mind by trying to think of how to make a fortune. My times are in God's hands. When I run ahead of Him in matters of any kind, I'm like one of my sheep who won't graze where I lead the flock but wanders off to eat poisonous weeds to satisfy its hunger. Oh, Rachel, remind me always to wait on the Lord God!

"I will today offer to work for another term for Laban at no wages—except his streaked, spotted, speckled and dark-colored sheep and goats." Jacob smiled at the thought of this divinely interpreted dream—and of the surprise his uncle Laban would get when the next kids and lambs were born. I smiled with him.

"Rachel, there is no more time for talking now. Laban is waiting for me. While I am gone, you stay here and give praise and thanks to our Lord God that He is giving me the provision to take my family home!"

I like to think of how Jacob looked when he said "take my family home!" Each word was louder than the one before it; the wonderful smile on his face grew broader.

When he returned from his meeting he was jubilant. "I know Laban likes to bargain, so I began with an offer he would flatly refuse. I said, 'Give me my wives and children, for whom I have served you, and I will be on my way. You know how much work I've done for you.'

"Rachel, I knew he would reject that, but I was surprised at the reason he gave. I thought he would again say something about my inability to provide for my family—and the necessity to keep depending on him. But he never mentioned that at all. He said, 'If I have found favor in your eyes, please stay. I have learned by divination that the Lord has blessed me because of you. Name your wages, and I will pay them.'

"I don't know what messages he has received by divination, but perhaps without his knowing it the Lord God Himself has spoken to him, confronting him with the way he has cheated me. Anyway, he next offered his familiar words, 'Name your wages and I will pay them.'

"I didn't tell him my terms right away but took advantage of what seemed a more open attitude than he had before. I said to him, 'You know how I have worked for you and how your livestock has fared under my care. The little you had before I came has increased greatly, and the Lord has blessed you wherever I have been. But now, when may I do something for my own household?'

"You should have seen his expression! I think he noticed I had new confidence, and I know that the joy I've felt since I heard God's precious Voice again has shown on my face. Laban couldn't understand the reason for the change, and he looked almost frightened as he said, 'What shall I give you?'

"I think at that moment he would have agreed to any offer I made, but, knowing him, he would have retracted it once he thought it over. Anyway, I said, 'Don't give me anything. But if you will do this one thing for me, I will go on tending your flocks and watching over them: Let me go through all your flocks today and remove from them every speckled or spotted sheep, every dark-colored lamb and every speckled or spotted goat. They will be my wages. And my honesty will testify for me in the future, whenever you check on the wages you have paid me. Any goat in my possession that is not speckled or spotted, or any lamb that is not dark-colored will be considered stolen.'

"I'm certain Laban thought I had taken leave of my senses, because the number of parti-colored animals is a minimal percentage of his flocks. He jumped to his feet and shouted, 'Agreed! Let it be as you have said!' "

It was good, listening to my husband tell of his long-awaited chance to get favorable terms from Laban.

"So now, when the flocks are gathered at their watering places and at their folds tonight, I'll take several shepherds to help, and we will take out all the animals that, by Laban's own agreement, belong to me. Rachel! I will have a flock of my own! All the variegated animals are mine now! And when the young are born to Laban's flocks, to his great surprise they all will be the kind he has allotted to me! While I tend his dwindling flocks, mine will be increasing so fast I'll need extra help."

Jacob looked at me with eyes that asked the question he

didn't put into words. I answered his question. "Maybe you remember, Jacob, I've had experience as a shepherdess. I would enjoy tending a flock of sheep again. This time I can take Joseph out with me, and I'll teach him how to care for them. And there is Leah, Zilpah and Bilhah—and all their sons; they can do the same. You will have plenty of help."

I was too excited to be surprised at my own impulsive eagerness to go back to the work I once thought boring. I suppose the thought of getting even with my father, even in this small measure, was an incentive.

"Rachel, I was thinking of your helping. I'm glad you want to do it. . . . You do . . . want to . . . don't you?"

"Of course! Let me have the first ones you separate. But do you have to start yet today and work through the night to do this separating? Couldn't you at least get a night's sleep?"

"I must go right away. I don't trust Laban not to sell off my stock before I get to it. Besides, I wouldn't be able to sleep anyway. I'm too eager to see my flocks assembled."

Jacob hurriedly ate some bread and cheese while I packed a scrip with provisions, filled the waterskin, and rolled up a blanket. We were enjoying the idea of his going to claim a flock of his own, instead of just going out to put in another day of servitude at uncertain wages.

After he left, I used the remaining daylight hours and also worked into the night preparing extra bread, weaving some of the cloth for Joseph's new tunic, and doing all I could before the first days when I would be out in the fields with the sheep.

Jacob came back when the new morning was lightening the horizon. He had a quizzical look on his face and in response to my greeting said not a word.

"I expected you to come in with excitement, bursting to tell me how many animals you own."

"I am bursting with excitement, but of a different kind than you expected. I do not own one animal!"

"You found no parti-colored animals? There had to be many of them!"

"There were none. Laban sent men to scout the flocks before I could get to them. They removed every streaked, spotted and speckled animal from every one of the flocks. My 'wages' are on the way to join the flocks your brothers are responsible for—a three-day's-journey from his all-white sheep and his all-black goats that I bargained to care for.

"With the variegated animals away at a safe distance and no animals of that kind left here, he thinks he has robbed me of any chance to succeed in raising flocks for my own profit. I underestimated Laban again. I never would have guessed he would do that—at least that he could do it so quickly."

Jacob shook his head, more in wonderment than in dismay or anger.

"Aren't you angry or troubled?" I shouted at him because I could not understand—or relate to—his calmness.

"Oh," Jacob breathed a long sigh and answered softly, "I suppose I am somewhat angry and disappointed, but I am so used to Laban's cheating schemes that I have come to expect another each time he makes a promise. One thing that is keeping me calmer this time is that by doing this, Laban has proved, surely even to himself, how evil his intent is toward me. But more important, the mating has been done; the young born into the flocks he hired me to tend will startle him with their speckles and spots! These parti-colored animals will be my wages, and I will separate them into a new flock as soon as they are weaned.

"Laban will learn that all the flocks belong first to the Lord God. He created them; they are the work of His hands. He will determine how large my flocks will become and how fast the increase will come.

"And, Rachel, another cause of my even temper this time is that in God's own words, our leaving of this place is to be done as soon as possible."

As Jacob said, it was not long before there were beautifully marked young lambs and goats born among Laban's flocks. Laban was astonished. When they were old enough for grazing, the wives and sons of Jacob led them daily to pastures Jacob selected for us.

Jacob trusted in the Lord God to increase his flocks. We tended them carefully. He bred them wisely. He even used the ingenious means of placing peeled branches in the watering troughs when the ewes were in heat and came to drink. They mated in front of the branches with the speckled and striped branches in front of their eyes. Laban and others laughed at this and at his meticulous care of each animal in Laban's flock, but they did not laugh at the results. Our flocks increased rapidly!

In panic Laban suggested that they reword their bargain so that only the speckled ones would be Jacob's wages. Jacob agreed, and the Lord God caused all the young to be speckled. Then Laban reversed the terms, stating that only the streaked ones would be Jacob's wages. Again Jacob agreed, and the Lord God caused all the young to be streaked.

Our flocks provided abundant wool, which was sold to buy choice stock to improve our flocks—to provide even better wool. Each day was exciting, and Jacob's hard work was having, at long last, very rich rewards. The Lord God was bringing great prosperity to the household of Jacob.

On the morning that would change the course of the rest of our lives, all the women and sons had led their flocks to their assigned pasturelands. At midmorning Jacob sent messengers to Leah and to me, telling us to return from the fields at once. The messengers would watch the flocks in our absence.

When we got back to our home, we found Jacob pacing the courtyard. He began to speak, not attempting to come to the point gradually but pouring out all he had to tell us.

"Rachel! Leah! This time it was not a dream! This time the Lord God spoke to me—as He did to Abraham and to Isaac before me! He said, 'Go back to the land of your fathers and to your relatives, and I will be with you.' He spoke . . . to me!"

Jacob paused so that the words of the Lord God would stand out in prominence—separate from his own, which then followed in an emotional torrent.

"I've just this morning learned that your brothers are saying, 'Jacob has taken everything our father owned and has gained all this wealth from what belonged to our father.'

"It's not just their lying that concerns me, but I've noticed that Laban's attitude toward me is not what it was before. I'm used to his taking advantage of me and ridiculing me for being naive, but now it's beyond greed and ridicule. I've seen actual hatred for me grow . . . as rapidly as my flocks have increased.

"Now that the Lord God has taken control of the situation between Laban and me, Laban is confronted with One he cannot control. He must know God has taken away from his livestock and added to mine . . . according to the dream I told you about before.

"I've called you to say it's time to leave this place—time to move to Canaan."

Leah and I had known such a day would come, and at times had longed for it, but now that it faced us, we were shaken and with one accord we looked toward the sprawling house whose wings now seemed like arms that embraced the courtyard where we sat with Jacob.

But our love for our old house was overshadowed by our attitudes toward our father. For all we knew, he might remarry, have children by his new wife, and disinherit any of us he wished to—it would be like him! I thought of that as I broke the short span of silence. "Do we still have any share in the inheritance of our father's estate?"

Leah was of the same mind and she said, "Does he not regard us as foreigners already? Not only has he sold us, but he has used up that part of the dowry that we, as Jacob's brides, might have expected to receive."

I was thinking again of the lies my brothers were telling and I spoke to that. "Surely all the wealth God took away from our father belongs to us and our children. The Lord God cannot do wrong!"

Our loyalties were with our husband, not with our father who had proved over and over to be unworthy of respect or trust or affection. Leah and I said, almost as one voice, "So do whatever God has told you."

After a brief search in Haran Jacob found a young man named Lahal, experienced in outfitting caravans, who would be able to assemble one quickly for our departure to Canaan.

Jacob was enthusiastic about Lahal's capabilities. "I liked him the moment I saw him. He is knowledgeable about what we need. I have every confidence in him.

"I impressed on him the importance of secrecy in assembling the caravan. I told him everything must be ready on a moment's notice, no later than when the first sheepshearing of the season is begun.

"He appeared worried at that, not because he couldn't have it ready, but because he thought secrecy implied something illegal. I assured him it was far from that. I told him he was part of a plan made by the one God—and would be blessed for helping me. He knew nothing of our God or His blessing, but something in my manner convinced him . . . or . . . perhaps the Lord God spoke directly to his heart. Anyway, he was convinced it would be well with him if he helped."

"Jacob, I'm so excited that I'm trembling. Do you think we can get away without actual violence from my father?"

"I don't want violence. That's why I decided to leave at sheepshearing time. Laban will go to supervise the shearing of the sheep that belong to him and your brothers, a three-day journey in the far pasturelands. When he leaves, we will leave. By the time a messenger could get to him to report on us, we will be three days on the way. By the time Laban returns here, we will be three days further. It would take him a day or two to organize a group to come in pursuit. We should be at least eight days ahead of him.

"And more important, the Lord God promises that we will go to Canaan.

"You look worried, Rachel. Don't you trust the Lord God, or are you still convinced tents will be an uncomfortable way of life?"

"I trust God, but possibly not as much as you do. As for the tents, I've lost my ill feelings about them. I will wait, as you suggested, until I see how it will be.

"My serious face is because there's something I must do before we leave my father's house. Please don't ask about it. It's . . . just a . . . a sentimental thing you wouldn't understand."

Jacob smiled indulgently, and I took it as his permission for me to do what I would not talk about. But if he had known, he would not have allowed it.

Jacob obviously was amused that he had been able to plan so well, carry out the plan, and keep Laban from knowing what he was doing. "Laban told me I was foolish to shear my sheep so soon. He said if I waited another two or three weeks the wool would have been better. He's convinced I've reached the turning point in my business success and with such ill-timed actions as shearing sheep early I'll be back to depending on him again."

"Did you lose much profit by shearing the sheep early?"

"Not enough to think about—compared to the time it will save. Our flocks are ready now to move out in caravan. In another week the wool will be marketed and the proceeds invested in additional maidservants, menservants, camels, donkeys, and provisions for our trip. Lahal is doing a fine job. We will be ready to leave as soon as Laban unwittingly gives the signal."

"Joseph will hardly remember Haran; he has spent only a few years in his native land."

"Native land?"

"Yes, Joseph was born in Haran, in Mesopotamia."

"But his native land is Canaan! He belongs to Canaan!"

My dear Jacob had spent 20 of the prime years of his life in Mesopotamia but never really left Canaan, for so much of it was in his heart.

19

Then Jacob put his children and his wives on camels, and he drove all his livestock ahead of him, along with all the goods he accumulated in Paddan Aram, to go to his father Isaac in the land of Canaan.   *Genesis 31:17-18*

Rachel! Pack your things. We leave today—by midafternoon if possible! I'm going into town to have Lahal bring the camels and donkeys here to load our people and their things. Alert the other women. Tell our servants. Send word to our people in the fields to lead their flocks to the appointed place. Laban left early this morning for his pasturelands!

"And Rachel, remind everyone to make their preparations unobservable for as long as possible. We don't want a messenger starting out to tell Laban too early. We need all the head start we can get. We want the messenger to have to go the whole three-day-journey before being able to tell his news to your father.

"Rachel! Did you hear?"

"Yes, I heard. We have rehearsed the procedure so many times that I can do my part almost without thinking. Don't worry, Jacob, your household will be ready by midafternoon. All of our things have been packed since you began the sheepshearing. I hope Lahal is as ready as we are!"

"Oh, Rachel, I have no need to be anxious about anything you're responsible for—whether it's overseeing our household and having everything ready to move, tending our flocks, or raising our precious son. Everything you do is perfect in my eyes. Beyond being my love and my joy, you are like another right hand."

And then, as though we didn't have a thousand things to do, Jacob took me in his arms, and for a few moments we forgot the tenseness of our circumstances and the hard journey ahead.

With his arms around me I even forgot what I had decided to do the minute Father left to go to the sheepshearing. But when Jacob went to find Lahal, and I had carried out the feverish tasks of alerting our people and warning them to be as subtle as possible in their preparations, it came back to my mind.

I walked across the courtyard to the door into the main room of Father's house and pushed it open. I walked toward the family altar, staring at the ugly idols that sat on it. The silver teraphim, in spite of their lustruous, shining metal, were hideous. How could I ever have worshiped them or believed that they were more than something a silversmith made for a handsome profit? And yet, standing in front of them and remembering Father's insistence that we pay them respect, I felt an old superstition sweep over me. I did not want to offend them, whatever they were or whatever they represented.

But there was more than worship or superstition involved. Whoever held these idols held the privilege of primogeniture. I smiled at them without feeling happy. All I had to do was take them, and Jacob, as son-in-law of Laban, would have claim to the inheritance of the major share of Laban's estate. Since Jacob had invested years in developing Laban's wealth, it seemed only right. And it was easy to do; there was not a servant in sight.

I had never touched them before. They were cold and heavy and looked frightening. Their heads were large, their bodies dwarfish in comparison. Their eyes were narrow and empty. I dropped them in the leather bucket I had brought for their first hiding place and ran across the courtyard to our door. Then I stopped. I felt ill. Jacob would not want them under our roof. I thought of returning them, but I looked back over my shoulder just in time to see Laban's servants carrying water into the house to fill the pitchers and waterskins. It was too late to take them back without being seen.

What if the servants noticed that the gods were gone from the altar? What if they began a search and found that in the rooms of Jacob's household everything was packed, ready to be loaded onto carts and pack animals? After all our careful planning, why had I taken such a chance?

I went inside our quarters and emptied the idols onto a heavy wool cloth, wrapped them carefully in it, and placed the bundle among my tunics in a wicker chest. I wondered if the servant who loaded the chest would notice its surprising heaviness. What if Jacob himself loaded that chest? Surely he would ask what made it so heavy. What would I tell him?

I was torn with doubts about the wisdom of taking the gods and oppressed by guilt, but I decided to consider the matter settled. I slammed the lid of the chest closed and tried to put the entire matter out of my mind. I fixed lunch for Joseph and me, then waited for Jacob to return so we could begin what seemed to me an impossible journey.

Shortly after midday Jacob, Lahal, and a few of our menservants rode up to Laban's estate. Lahal was first, riding a donkey. Behind the donkey were several camels. Each camel was tied to the one in front of it, and the first camel was tied to a ring fastened to leather straps on Lahal's donkey. The third camel from the lead had large wicker chair baskets slung on each side, fastened to a ring that fit over the saddle. Those chairs, padded with a quilt and pillows and covered with a sunshade of white material, were for Leah and me.

Immediately ahead of the basket-laden camel were two other camels, each holding a heavy plank of wood across its back. The planks stuck out on each side of the animals, and from the ends of the planks ropes were stretched over posts fixed above the saddle, supporting bright red and orange awnings under which Bilhah and Zilpah would sit on large cushions.

There were handsomely saddled camels for Jacob's older sons and donkeys and carts for the younger children and the maidservants who attended them.

In addition to these animals and travel gear Lahal had stationed large herds of sheep, goats and cattle, several strings of camels, a hundred donkeys, and appropriate herdsmen and servants to care for them all outside the city gate. Those shepherding our newly shorn animals and lambs drove them to the appointed place to meet Lahal's group.

As soon as we could load our household things and personal belongings on the pack train, we would join the rest. Our actions now seemed like those in a dream, not having substance or reality. But when the last chest and the last child had been loaded, and I was in the basket that hung from the side of the kneeling camel, reality struck with the force of a sharp knife. The forward and backward lunging as the camel awkwardly stood up made my stomach ill.

I would not see Haran or the house that had sheltered me again. I would miss that great house and Haran and the nearby pasturelands and the large well near the city gate. It was sadly strange—that I'd miss inanimate things but had no regret about leaving my father or brothers.

There were no farewells. All the people I loved were going with me. The adults in our group were quiet and thoughtful as we rode through the narrow streets and out the gate, and we were thankful for the chatter and the laughter of our children, excited with this wonderful adventure.

Swaying back and forth in that basket kept my stomach uneasy. I was especially uncomfortable because I had taken those wretched teraphim out of the chest at the last moment and put them in the folds of the quilt in the basket seat. I would be aware of their annoying presence all the way to our destination, which was weeks away! I couldn't risk moving them again, for if Jacob knew what I had done, he would be furious. There had been a few times in our life when he was impatient or disappointed with me, but he never had been really angry. I could not have that happen now.

Many times I wished that the idols were back at Laban's altar; then at other times I was glad I had them along. These were old, familiar things, and we had been carefully taught to revere them because they protected our family. I didn't worship them; I just felt better to have them with me. Thoughts about them could not be shut up in a chest or folded into a blanket.

I didn't see Jacob as we traveled because he had taken his place on the lead donkey. I missed him. I needed to talk with someone but no one was near; even Leah, sharing the same camel, was out of conversation range in her basket on the other side of the huge animal that carried us.

We followed a larger caravan headed for Egypt. It was safer traveling near others through bandit-infested areas, and the experienced caravaneers led us to good watering places.

I thought of Sarah, who had gone over this same route many years ago, and of Rebekah, who also traveled it. I looked forward to seeing Rebekah. My father and Jacob both said I looked very much like her.

Our road wound along the twisting Kara River, past the point where it lost its identity as it flowed into the Balikh and then came to the Euphrates. I had dreaded trying to ford it, but it was more exciting than dangerous. The caravan trail crossed at the most shallow place, but even so the water was deep enough that our wicker chairs touched it slightly. Small children and servants who couldn't swim or wade across rode over on rafts supported by inflated animal stomachs. I had no idea that crossing a river would be so strenuous. I remembered Jacob telling me how, on his way from Beersheba, he helped get his caravan's animals across to safety. Just as he described it, most of the animals swam over in fine style, but a few were swept away with the current, and herdsmen who got to the other side first ran along the far bank and often out into the river again, rescuing the confused animals by grabbing them with their crooks.

The scenery changed gradually from the near treelessness of Haran to wooded landscapes that made me gasp with delight.

We came to a place of chalk cliffs and deep valleys—dramatically beautiful. Jacob halted our caravan early to encamp. His eyes drank in the splendor. He breathed deeply of the air of his native land.

Jacob called the place Gilead. As with every place we came to in Canaan, Jacob was eager to tell me all he knew about it—from personal experience or from what Abraham and Isaac had told him.

"Did you see the large flocks of goats, Rachel? They cover many hillsides here like a mantle of wavy brown hair on a giant head! Soon we will see not only hills, but mountains. Snowcapped Mount Hermon is not far from this place. This is a region for spices—spikenard, calamus and cinnamon."

I thought he had finished speaking, and I nodded agreement to what he had said, then closed my eyes—too sleepy to think further of goats or mountains. He had only paused to catch his breath and to decide which wonder to speak of next.

"From Gilead's mountains comes the stream that finally widens into the Abana and waters the land around Damascus."

I heard him say "Damascus" when I was more asleep than awake. Damascus—I dreamily remembered our stop there overnight, near the city wall. Jacob sent servants into the marketplace to buy bread, cheese and fresh fruit. I had looked for a long time at the city wall with the enormous ziggurat to the moon god towering above it. I had thought of the wall and the moon god temple of Haran that by comparison were so much smaller that I felt defensive for my familiar places and instantly disliked Damascus.

Damascus and now Canaan—rivers, cliffs, trees, and grasslands—flowers and orchards—Jacob was still talking, and I knew I should try to listen. No wonder Jacob had thought Haran was bleak and brown. It was, but I had never known it.

"Did you hear me, Rachel? I said we will see more of the hill country of Gilead tomorrow."

"What? Oh . . . yes, Jacob, I heard you. But I was half asleep and my mind is a jumble of snow and spices . . . and rivers and cities and . . . trees and city . . . walls . . . and ziggurats . . . and more of Canaan tomorrow . . . and . . ."

20

Then God came to Laban the Aramean in a dream at night and said to him, "Be careful not to say anything to Jacob, either good or bad."

Genesis 31:24

Jacob told me the next morning that I never finished my sentence. I was tired; sleep closed my eyes and my lips.

I wakened to find the sun high in the skies and no activity around the camp to indicate we were getting ready to move. Jacob was sitting at the door of the tent as though all he had to do was watch the sun climb even higher.

"Jacob! What has happened? Aren't we late in breaking camp?"

"We will rest here today, then move again tomorrow."

"Why?"

"Because we are all tired. We have been pushing the flocks and the people at a pace that is hard to maintain. Everyone is exhausted."

"You're stopping because I'm too tired. I'm holding you back."

"No, I told you—we are all tired. Rachel, my dearest, the rest will be good for the children, for the flocks, for everyone. And besides, we are home! We are in Canaan! Don't you think the air is fresher? Can't you smell the spices of Gilead?"

Jacob looked so happy that I couldn't disappoint him by saying I noticed no difference in the air and could not smell anything except the usual camp odors. "Already I know Canaan is as you said it would be, my husband; it's a garden decorated by mountains and lakes. I'm eager to see the rest of it."

"And so am I, but we stay here today. I want our herdsmen to check the flocks to see that all is well with them. I want to take my sons to the top of one of these cliffs and tell them about the land they have entered—their land!"

"Will you take little Joseph with you?"

"I will especially take Joseph with me, and you are not to worry about him because I won't let him out of my sight."

Jacob left, and I fell back on the cushions of my bed mat. I had never felt so tired in my life. I scarcely left my tent all day—partly because I really needed the rest and partly because I was afraid someone—even one of the children—might come in and find those silver idols in my chair basket.

As I became rested, I also became aware of the danger we were in by halting our caravan for this whole day. We lost our caravan escort, and, even worse, Laban might overtake us. So far we had outdistanced him with our head start, even though he could travel much faster with a small group of riders than we could at the pace of our large flocks. Was he coming after us? If he caught us, he would be looking for his teraphim, for he would not have left home without going to the altar to invoke their blessing. When he found them gone, he would suspect they were in our belongings. I looked at the chair basket in the corner of my tent. The soft quilt the idols were wrapped in was folded in such a way that no one could guess it covered bigheaded gods.

The servants had prepared supper by the time Jacob returned with his sons. Everyone ate a hearty meal and was ordered to retire early in order to be rested by morning and ready to go on toward the lake called Huleh and the Jordan River.

Sleep was sweet again that night, but before it settled over me, I thought of the delight of seeing the sun come up over the white cliffs of Gilead in the morning.

I awoke, not to gentle stirrings of people busy with morning chores and breakfast, but to voices raised in sharp anger. One of the voices was Jacob's—and one was Laban's!

"I've been chasing you—you with your sneaking start on me! I and my men have hardly stopped to eat or sleep. We have ridden hard, but it has been worth it. I have things to say to you!"

"Say on. What accusation do you have? What grievance? Think carefully before you speak, or your own words will trip you up."

"Indeed I will say on! You keep your tongue still and your ears open, Jacob. I laid awake all night on that hill over there, knowing in the morning I would face you. I've shown great patience in holding my peace until this morning. I could have stormed in on you in the middle of the night!

"Now—what are you trying to do to me, stealing my daughters away as though you are taking them captive? Why did you run off secretly and deceive me?"

"I was afraid because I thought you would take your daughters away from me by force."

I had heard enough to make me feel ill, and I walked to the door of my tent. Father saw me and immediately changed his tone and forced an imitation of a smile.

Continuing now in almost a whine he said, "Why didn't you tell me, so I could send you away with joy and singing to the music of tambourines and harps?"

Then he noticed that Leah, Zilpah and Bilhah had come out of their tents, and all the children were gathering around to see what the commotion was about.

Laban loved an audience, and his whine became a loud whimper. "You didn't even let me kiss my grandchildren and my daughters good-bye. You have done a foolish thing."

When he tired of playing to the crowd, he turned back on Jacob. "I have the power to harm you, but last night the God of your father said to me, 'Be careful not to say anything to Jacob, either good or bad.' Now you have gone off because you longed to return to your father's house. But why did you steal my gods?"

Jacob could have called his servants to chase Father and his escorts off as the intruders they were. Instead, he stood to answer Laban.

"If you find anyone who has your gods, he shall not live! In the presence of our relatives, see for yourself whether there is anything of yours here with me; and if so, take it."

Jacob had pronounced my death sentence! Father was not the kind of person to conduct a superficial search. He wanted those gods, and he wanted revenge on the one who took them.

My mouth and throat went dry; there was a churning heaviness in the pit of my stomach. I went back into the tent, desperately trying to think of what to do and much relieved that the search was beginning in Jacob's tent and not in mine.

After finding nothing in the first tent, Laban, accompanied by a smug-looking Jacob, searched the tents of Leah, Zilpah and Bilhah. Nothing was found.

By the time they came to my tent, Father was seething with anger. He thought Jacob had hidden the idols very well if he couldn't find them in his ransacking rampage. Without a word to me he emptied my three small chests then proceeded to shake the mat and cushions.

My panic had fled. I was almost entertained by my frustrated father. I enjoyed this opportunity to trick him. I sat serenely in my basket chair. "Don't be angry, my lord, that I cannot stand up in your presence, but the manner of women is upon me."

Laban didn't dare question that excuse; it would have violated even his sense of propriety. I hardly could keep from laughing as he continued hunting but could not find the idols.

Jacob watched the indignity of the search, knowing nothing of my having the missing gods. He felt he had at last suffered too much from Laban. He put one large hand on the old man's shoulder and propelled him out of the tent, but not out of the range of my hearing.

"Now, Laban, it's my turn to speak! You have invaded my tents. You have brought charges against me that you could not substantiate. You were told by the Lord God not to bother me. But now that you have bothered me, you will listen to me until I am through saying what I want you and all the rest of the family to hear!

"Now that you have searched through all my goods, what have you found that belongs to your household? Put it in front of your relatives and mine and let them judge between the two of us."

Laban drew his robe around him in a gesture of disdain and

turned to leave. Jacob put his hand back on Laban's shoulder and wheeled him around.

"I am not finished! I have been with you for 20 years now. Your sheep and goats have not miscarried, nor have I eaten rams from your flocks. I did not bring you animals torn by wild beats; I bore the loss myself. And you demanded payment from me for whatever was stolen by day or night. This was my situation: The heat consumed me in the daytime and the cold at night, and sleep fled from my eyes. It was like this for the 20 years I was in your household. I worked for you 14 years for your two daughters and six years for your flocks, and you changed my wages 10 times. If the God of my father, the God of Abraham and of Isaac, had not been with me, you would surely have sent me away empty-handed. But God has seen my hardship and the toil of my hands, and last night He rebuked you."

Jacob thundered out only a tenth of what he might have said, but it was enough to vent his emotions and to impress his children. And it was enough to make me proud of my husband.

Laban made no reference to Jacob's tirade. He had no defense, so he changed the subject, directing attention from the hardships and faithful service of his son-in-law to what he still felt was his great loss. His affectionate tone of voice was almost convincing. "The women are my daughters, the children are my children, and the flocks are my flocks. All you see is mine. Yet what can I do today about these daughters of mine or about the children they have borne? Come now, let's make a covenant, you and I, and let it serve as a witness between us."

From the look on Jacob's face I thought he was going to shout something like, "These are my wives, *my* children, and *my* flocks!" But he only clenched his fists and raised his strong arms toward heaven, muffled a groan, and let his arms drop to his sides. He shrugged his shoulders as if to say that Laban was not worthy of any more notice. Jacob meekly took a large stone and set it up as a pillar, and he called to his sons, "Gather some stones." So they took stones and piled them in a heap, and later they ate a ritual meal by that heap of stones. Tempers had cooled, the men ate in silence.

Laban called the place Jegar Sahadutha, meaning in Aramaic, "witness heap." Jacob called it Galeed, which means the same in Hebrew.

Laban looked at the high pile of stones and said, "This heap is a witness between you and me today. May the Lord keep watch between you and me when we are away from each other. If you mistreat my daughters or if you take any wives besides my daughters, even though no one is with us, remember that God is a witness between you and me."

"I will not go past this heap to your side to harm you, and you will not go past this heap and pillar to my side to harm me. May the God of Abraham and the God of Nahor, the God of their father, judge between us."

Jacob took the oath in the name of the Fear of his father Isaac. Then he offered a sacrifice there on the hill.

In gracious hospitality Jacob invited all in our camp, Laban and all who traveled with him, to come to a great meal in the evening. Early the next morning Laban kissed his grandchildren and his daughters and blessed them. Then he left us and returned home.

I watched him go with a sudden sentiment I had not known was in my heart for that wretched, greedy man. Part of it was pity, but mixed with the pity was a certain inherent love of daughter for father that is as natural as breathing.

The servants had packed our things, and the tents were folded. We, too, were ready to leave Gilead.

Jacob and I walked over to the heap of stones, and he called the place Mizpah, which means "watchtower." I repeated the words my father had spoken, words harshly warning that God would watch to see if either Jacob or he broke their covenant. But I said them like a prayer, "May the Lord keep watch between us, when we are away from each other."

Part Four

Return to Canaan

Jacob—
coming home to Canaan,
his God-given inheritance.
Jacob—
attended by angels,
overshadowed by the Lord God,
renamed ISRAEL.

Jacob . . . God's plain man

> Realizing His protection
> —at Mahanaim.

Jacob . . . God's quiet man

> Accepting God's blessing
> —at Peniel

Jacob . . . God's chosen man

> Given a new name—
> Prince with God!

21

Jacob also went on his way, and the angels of God met him. When Jacob saw them, he said, "This is the camp of God!" So he named that place Mahanaim. *Genesis 32:1-2*

Jacob was occupied with his own thoughts after Laban left. He had no affection for the man, but he felt a surprising sense of loss in those first hours of final separation from him. Laban had been a central part of his life for so long that now he could not imagine making plans or decisions without regard for him. Several times he looked toward the watchtower, Galeed-Mizpah, as he supervised the packing of the camp on the morning he led his caravan out toward Laish.

He tried to evaluate this last encounter with Laban and decided it had been good. He could proceed now with a feeling of full independence. His fear of Laban was gone, and he smiled as he remembered how he had shouted his grievances in defiance of his father-in-law. The smile widened and twisted a bit as he assessed the likelihood of Laban's finding anyone else to take advantage of for another 20 years. Even Laban's household gods seemed to have deserted him. Jacob wondered if his father-in-law really cared about those teraphim—and if they really were missing.

The trek southward was thrilling for Jacob. With each step he repossessed land that was dear to him. He looked at the cloudless blue sky and thought his heart would burst with sheer joy. He had been so caught up with Laban's difficult assignments, with his large family, and with the arrangements for preparing to move that now, traveling alone at the head of his people, he treasured the luxury of the comparative quiet.

They proceeded easily down the Jordan valley as the caravan route took them through increasingly desirable land. They encamped a few days in pleasant grassland near Lake Huleh, then made a longer stay east of the lovely Sea of Kinnereth just north of the Yarmuk River. Jacob and his family enjoyed Canaan's bright sunshine and the breezes that animated leaves and bent tall grasses.

The younger children of the camp played tag and caught butterflies; the older boys went fishing with servants—and the fish made fine eating. Maidservants washed clothes in the fastflowing Yarmuk.

"Isn't the land beautiful—as I said it was, Rachel?"

"It is. I wonder that you ever could have stayed in Haran so long."

"You were there; that helped make it possible. But now—with you here in Canaan—my cup of joy is filled and overflowing!"

"Couldn't we stay here, in this very place, for a long time—perhaps for always? Is there a certain area where we must live in Canaan?"

"The Lord God will tell us in His time where we should go. Meanwhile, I want to see my father and mother . . . and Esau. It seems I'll see my brother first. I heard news of him from men in the caravan we traveled with out of Haran. He has become a powerful chieftan and controls vast lands in the south. The men told me that at this time of year he travels into this area, purchasing animals to add to his flocks and arranging to lease pasturelands to supplement his, which are located in more arid places. I hadn't thought of meeting him first—and alone—away from the tents of Isaac."

"You never told me about the trouble you had with him—or the real reason you left your home so suddenly and stayed away so long."

"And there is no need to tell it now. It happened long ago."

"Are you still afraid of him?"

"Well . . . not actually afraid, but I don't look forward to seeing him, and I won't be comfortable around him."

"Did you do something wrong to him back then?"

"He thought so."

"Did you?"

"It was . . . it was the wrong thing—for the right reason."

"Is that possible? One seems to cancel the other."

"It appeared to me to be right then . . . or . . . nearly right. Anyway, it is done. Don't speak to me about it again or ask any more questions. . . .

"Rachel, forgive me for being abrupt with you, but recalling bitter parts of the past helps no one, and in retelling them they are relived in a way that gives them new power to hurt."

He smiled to ease the tensions their serious talk had built up and said, "And Rachel, my dearest . . . when you meet Esau, be at your charming best."

Jacob thought with a tinge of bitterness that he merely had traded the hazards of life with Laban for possibly greater danger from Esau. And yet Elohim had called him home to Canaan and would protect him, so he called his mind back from anxiety again and again, wanting only to share the beauty of Canaan with Rachel, but gnawing at his thoughts persistently was his dread of the imminent meeting with Esau.

At least he would be in no hurry for that meeting to take place. The pastureland was good, and he decided to move just a few miles south each day.

The further into the land he went, the more constantly his mind focused on the one God. Truly, truly, the Lord God had blessed him abundantly—above all he could have imagined. He had left 20 years earlier alone, with not enough money for the meager expenses of his trip. He was returning as head of a great household of 11 sons and a beautiful daughter; husband of two wives and two concubines; owner of large strings of camels and herds of sheep, cattle and goats—and his servants numbered nearly 200! Because of the way it had happened, Jacob felt no sense of personal achievement. Rather, he had a deep, deep awe for the Lord God who, in spite of the misfortunes he suffered in Haran, could bring him out with all this wealth.

Jacob looked forward to the more important part of God's pledge to him at Bethel. All the families of the whole earth would be blessed in his seed—and his descendants would spread over the earth to the west and the east, the north and the south!

Jacob thought for a long time on each of his sons and wondered through which of them the earth would be blessed. All of them? One of them? Would it be Reuben, the eldest? Or would it be another of Leah's sons—Simeon, Levi, or Judah? Surely the choice would not be the child of a concubine. Would the Lord God work through the pride of his and Rachel's life, Joseph? Joseph—the slightest thought of him or the mention of his name made Jacob smile as though everything in the world already were blessed. Thoughts of his sons—their potentials and their varied personalities—kept their father's interest through the long hours of midmorning travel.

Suddenly his attention was on a brightness in front of him. Within the brightness were the same marvelous creatures he had seen in his dream years ago at Bethel just before the Lord God spoke to him. As before, they were lustrous—the essence of calm strength and profound wisdom. He had not told anyone about the angels he saw at Bethel for want of words to describe them and because he doubted that anyone would have believed him. Yet here they were—in daylight on the road in front of him. Now others would see for themselves and share the glory of the sight.

He instantly halted the caravan and sat transfixed in wordless wonder as they came nearer. He continued to watch with awe as they assembled on either side, in back of, and in front of his company—his honor guard and his strong protection. The Lord God allowed him the vision of attending angels not only before he left Canaan many years before, but now again close to the heart of the land as he returned.

Jacob's eyes were filled with the radiant reality of the hosts of God as he dismounted and ran back to Rachel and Leah to help them dismount. He called a servant to assist Zilpah and Bilhah in dismounting and he ran to get his sons himself.

When they were together in one place, Jacob could not find words to begin his speech and stood looking at one, then another, of the members of his household. All he saw in their eyes was blank wonderment—and in a few a look of fear at his unexplained behavior. From their expressions he could tell they had seen nothing wonderful, nothing unusual. He could not believe he alone had seen the heavenly messengers. He turned back toward the angels, but now, like the rest of his family, he saw nothing wonderful, nothing unusual—just the caravan trail and the wide valley stretching out on either side of it.

But they had been there. They still were there. Jacob knew it!

Looking back at his family, who were watching him in confusion and even impatience, he simply said, "The Lord God has given me new assurance that His hosts are with us. I will name this place Mahanaim, 'Two Camps,' for there are two camps here—our own, weak at our best strength, and God's camp, completely encircling ours with divine protection.

"Reuben and Simeon, help me select a tall stone to put up as a marker for this place."

When the marker was erected, Jacob decided to encamp at Mahanaim. With new courage because of the invisible host around him, he now felt ready to consider his meeting with Esau, but he would not move again until he had a plan.

After thinking over the possible courses of action, he decided on one and called for his swiftest runners.

"I want you to hasten south along this highway until you come to the camp of my brother, Esau. This is what you are to say to him: 'Your servant Jacob says, I have been staying with Laban and have remained there till now. I have cattle and donkeys, sheep and goats, menservants and maidservants. Now I am sending this message to my lord, that I may find favor in your eyes.' "

After the runners left the next morning at daybreak, Jacob rallied his servants to move the caravan southward. When, in leisurely time, they came to the banks of the Jabbok River, Jacob set up camp there to wait for the return of his messengers.

Only a few hours after they were settled in at the river-bank site, his breathless, excited delegation returned and ran directly to Jacob's tent.

"We went to your brother, Esau, and now he is coming to meet you—with 400 men!"

Jacob commended them for their speed in completing their mission, then dismissed them so they could get some badly needed rest.

There was no rest for Jacob. He tossed on his bed most of the night, unable to sleep. Then he got up and paced the floor of his tent. Finally he went outside and walked to the edge of the Jabbok. His mind raced faster than the swirling stream that reflected the first pale light of the new day.

Four hundred men—and Esau! Esau alone was a problem! His brother's attitude toward him had not changed, or else his father would have sent for him to return. Four hundred men seemed like 4,000 to Jacob as he thought of his smaller band of servants, only a few of them armed and none of them expert in battle. Esau's army, still as invisible to him as the angelic one had become, captured Jacob's full attention. The hosts of the Lord God surely stood in wonder at the way God's man had forgotten them so quickly—and at the way he struggled for a plan, a strategy to outthink or outfight 400 men!

In the early morning Jacob aroused the camp. His face and his voice registered distress and fear. He ordered the people divided into two groups, and the flocks and herds and camels as well. His desperate plan was to have one group be a decoy if necessary, letting the other group escape.

This done, he thought to talk it over with the Lord God. Without first waiting in His presence, Jacob plunged into a heartfelt prayer—a prayer that revealed even to the one who prayed it that it was a confession not only of inadequate power for battle, but of spiritual immaturity as well.

O God of my father Abraham, God of my father Isaac, O Lord, who said to me, "Go back to your country and your relatives, and I will make you prosper," I am unworthy of all the kindness and faithfulness you have shown your servant. I had only my staff when I crossed this Jordan, but now I have become two groups. Save me, I pray, from the hand of my brother Esau, for I am afraid he will come and attack me, and also the mothers with their children. But you have said, "I will surely make you prosper and will make your descendants like the sand of the sea, which cannot be counted."

After this prayer Jacob decided to send a peace offering to his brother. He ordered his herdsmen to separate the following:

200 female goats
20 male goats
200 ewes
20 rams
30 female camels and their young
40 cows
10 bulls
20 female donkeys
10 male donkeys

He put them in the care of his servants, each herd by itself, and said to them, "Go on ahead of me, and keep some space between the herds."

To the one in the lead he gave these instructions: "When my brother Esau meets you and asks, 'To whom do you belong, and where are you going, and who owns these animals?' you are to say, 'They belong to your servant Jacob. They are a gift sent to my lord Esau, and he is coming behind us.' "

He instructed the second and the third, and all the others who followed the herds: "You are to say the same thing to Esau when you meet him. And be sure to say, 'Your servant Jacob is coming behind us.' "

Dividing the people and possessions into two camps, the time of prayer, and the assembling and dispatching of the large gift for Esau had taken all day, but now everything was done. In the early evening Jacob led his caravan across the Jabbok and stayed with them until he was certain all was as secure and comfortable for the women and children as possible. Then he left them and made his way to the river, wanting to cross back to spend the night alone—to think and to pray. He had reached the water's edge when he heard her call. She was running toward him across a moonlit field.

"Jacob, my husband, let me go back with you, and let's take some servants. It's not good to be alone after dark in this place. There are wild animals—I've seen a few from the road—and there always is danger from robbers if one is alone."

Jacob saw the anxiety on Rachel's beloved, beautiful face, and he reached to touch her cheek, brushing back a wisp of dark hair that had fallen across it.

"You sound like your aunt Rebekah. I will be all right. I need some time alone before I face my brother tomorrow. You go back and be with Joseph; dress him in his best tomorrow . . . for he will meet his uncle Esau.

"And Rachel . . . remember the assurance God gave me at Mahanaim? We have nothing to fear. I'll see you in the morning."

After taking gentle leave of Rachel, he stepped out into the cool, shallow turbulence of the rushing Jabbok and walked toward its northern bank, reminding himself—as he had reminded Rachel—of the dependability of the God of Abraham and Isaac.

22

Then the man said, "Your name will no longer be Jacob, but Israel, because you have struggled with God and with men and have overcome."

Genesis 32:28

Jacob stepped from the Jabbok onto the stony bank and walked with determined step. He went directly to the top of a small hill from which he could see his camp and beyond it the road Esau would travel with his approaching army. It was an excellent vantage point. He intended to watch through the night. The full moon would enable him to catch an early glimpse of any group of men who might choose to invade the camp under cover of darkness. If they did, he would shout a quick, loud warning and then recross the narrow Jabbok to his people.

He sat on a robe he had thrown over the dewy grass. He had never been more alone—no one to talk with—no sheep to tend—no one—nothing.

It was the ideal time to pray; the combination of approching danger and unique solitude demanded it. But he found no words to express the inner turmoil of his fears as they assaulted his faith, nor could he find words for an honest appraisal of what he was in contrast to all that the Lord God meant him to be. Who can describe another's bitter night of spiritual struggle?

Jacob wrestled to be free from self-pity and pride, fears and doubts, everything that kept him from consistent, close fellowship with the Lord God. But at the same time he clung to ill thoughts about his family who had sent him off to Haran and then ignored him, confidence in his own strength and intelligence, the fear that caused him to dedicate to Esau much that

God had allowed him to bring back to Canaan, and a compulsion to add his own work to the security God provided for him and his household.

His strenuous wrestling with these spiritual facets of his life became a physical wrestling, for the One who promised always to be with him *was* with him, and Jacob's struggle against what that One permitted and ordained in his life was, in reality, a struggle against that One.

The struggling increased. Jacob, exhausted by it, wondered why he still fought so hard to defeat the One who could free him from all he detested in himself. But he fought on.

Then, as a loving parent disciplining a child who will not give up a dangerous plaything, the One who wrestled with him touched the socket of Jacob's hip so that his hip was wrenched. It was the necessary symbolic lesson. As Jacob felt the strength in his leg break, he felt his stubborn inner man break also.

Jacob had no strength left to contend with the past—regretting its wrong or resting in its right. He had no strength to spend in trying to take from the future its trouble or its joy. He had strength only to cling to the present moment, to accept from it all God had to give to His waiting child. And Jacob clung in that moment to that marvelous One.

Then the man said, "Let me go, for it is daybreak."

But Jacob replied, "I will not let you go unless you bless me."

The man asked, "What is your name?"

" *Ya'aqeb*," he answered. "Heel."

Then the man said, "Your name will no longer be *Ya'aqeb*, but Israel, because you have struggled with God and with men and have overcome."

"Struggled with God . . ." Jacob recognized his Opponent, but in the spirit of awe that overshadowed him he could not let himself fully accept that Elohim, El Shaddai—the One who embodied those Names and more—had not only come to him in a dream, not only communicated with him by a Voice, but now had descended from the heavens, had taken the form of a man, had touched him!

Choked with mystery, reverence and a profound humility Jacob replied, "Please tell me your name."

But He replied, "Why do you ask my name?"

Jacob, who had long disliked what he called "stupid questions," smiled at what he had asked of the One who stood before him in perfect love and power. In the presence of that One he relinquished the guarding of his camp to His hosts. In the presence of that One, he made as full a surrender of *Ya'aqeb* as it was possible for him to make at that time. Then that One blessed him there.

Israel knelt in wordless praise and wonder long after his God withdrew His physical presence from that little mound on which Jacob had staked his sentry post. Then, ready to face the day he no longer dreaded, with strength supplied by God alone, Israel prepared to rejoin his people. But first he consecrated the place where he had tarried as Peniel—Face of God— saying, "It is because I saw God face to face, and yet my life was spared."

The sun rose above him as he passed Peniel, and he was limping because of his hip. He bore in his body the physical marks of his spiritual struggle. He walked slowly with the aid of his shepherd's staff—and with the aid of his Shepherd.

23

God has been gracious to me and I have all I need.   *Genesis 33:11*

as Jacob looked once again toward the road beyond his encamped people, there was Esau coming with his 400 men. He hastened his pace, almost unmindful of the sharp pain in his leg.

Once back with his household he quickly divided them, putting the children with their mothers. Then he assembled them in order, the maidservants and their children in front, Leah and her children next, Rachel and Joseph in the rear.

Each of the women noticed that he walked with a limp, obviously in pain, and each noticed that he also moved with assurance instead of his former apprehension—but there was no time to ask the reason for the enigmatic changes.

He went on ahead of them all, walking out alone to meet his brother. Facing Esau, he was silent, but he bowed to the ground seven times in an exaggerated show of traditional greeting. No one except Jacob knew the pain it caused him— physically and emotionally. Only the day before he had planned to overcome Esau by appearing too powerful and wealthy to know fear, but now he was humbling himself before the brother who had always intimidated him. The repeated bowing inflicted intense pain on his injured leg.

In a burst of emotion Esau ran the few steps that still separated him from Jacob. He embraced him. In the watchful presence of their astounded followers—and the unseen hosts of God—the brothers clung to each other and wept. Their mingled tears were more eloquent than any words they might have rehearsed in their minds.

Jacob led Esau back toward his camp, to a small tent he had

instructed his servants to put up for their meeting. In the tent rich carpets had been laid on the ground, and there were leather mats for seating the two brothers who had many things to discuss.

They were exchanging superficial remarks, customary for even important conversations, when the procession of women and children began approaching them. Esau looked up and saw the women and children. "Who are these with you?"

"They are the children God has graciously given your servant." Jacob nodded toward his family, and they began to present themselves to Esau. Zilpah came first with Gad and Asher; next were Bilhah with Dan and Naphtali; then Leah with Reuben, Simeon, Levi, Judah, Issachar, Zebulun and Dinah; last of all, in her place of honor, came Rachel with Joseph.

Jacob watched his children with pride as one by one they bowed before their uncle. They were handsome—a wealth that outweighed all the flocks, herds and strings of camels.

Esau accepted their homage but made no comment to them or to his brother about them. Instead, he turned to ask what was uppermost in his mind. "What do you mean by all the droves I met?"

Jacob was offended at Esau's disregard of his family, but he answered his brother's ill-timed question. "To find favor in your eyes, my Lord."

Esau drew himself up in the manner of a man who wants it understood he needs no one's gifts. "I already have plenty, my brother. Keep what you have for yourself."

"No, please! If I have found favor in your eyes, accept the present that was brought to you, for God has been gracious to me, and I have all I need."

They were behaving not so much like brothers as like two chieftans making the traditional speeches expected of them. When a large gift was offered, it was to be rejected at first. Then, seemingly only at the great insistence of the donor, it was reluctantly accepted. And so in the end Esau took the very large gift. Jacob realized he had paid dearly to impress and appease Esau.

Jacob felt an inner uneasiness because of the great loss of

his possessions, and even more because he was aware he had not overcome his deep-rooted fear of Esau—not even after Mahanaim—not even after Peniel.

Esau, exuberant with his new wealth and another victory over his naive brother, was eager to move now. But unwilling to seem ungrateful, he said, "Let's be on our way; I'll accompany you."

Jacob had no intention of beginning a partnership with Esau. He had been unequally yoked to Laban long enough to be wary of another entanglement with a self-seeking associate. He answered, "My lord knows that the children are tender and that I must care for the ewes and cows that are nursing their young. If they are driven hard just one day, all the animals will die. So let my lord go on ahead of his servant, while I move along slowly at the pace of the droves before me and that of the children, until I come to my lord in Seir."

"Seir? How did you know I was going there?"

"I learned from a caravaneer we traveled with out of Haran that you had recently come from there to lease pastureland in this area."

"The information he gave is correct."

"If the pastureland is not good year-round, why did you choose that place?"

"There's more to that area than pasturelands! Its terraced hills produce fruit and vegetables. Its cities are famous for excellent woven material and dyed garments. It's a major trading center.

"And . . . there is more." Esau's eyes squinted as his smile became wider. "The caravan route winds through the hills and up into the mountains, through passes between sandstone cliffs so close together that men and animals must go through in single file. It is a route that can be controlled very profitably by those who control the land!

"And, Jacob, you must see those mountains! They are variegated shades of rose reds. Great palaces have been carved into the face of them."

"Do you live in Seir?"

"No, but I have holdings there. After I have finished this business here, I'll return to Hebron where my wives and children are, and where I still supervise the flocks of our father . . . from time to time.

"Father! We have talked of many things, Esau, but I have been wondering about Father. I was afraid to ask. He was not well . . . 20 years ago . . . and in all that time I've not heard from him nor from our mother. Is Father well?"

"He is not well, but better than when you saw him last. He recovered from what we thought would be a sickness ending in death and, although he has not resumed full activity nor regained complete eyesight, he's busy enough for a man of his years and is content to live each day as it comes."

Jacob shook his head in disbelief—and in puzzlement over why his father had not sent for him to return long before this. Then he voiced one remaining question, "And our mother— how is she?"

Esau's expression answered the question. He no longer looked at Jacob, his shoulders drooped, and his face was void of animation. "After you left, she gradually lost interest in things. . . . She had no appetite, gradually became weak. She complained of pain in her arms and legs. Our active, vibrant mother became quiet and placid—withdrawn. Then 12 years ago she . . . Jacob, she is dead."

Esau's last word hung heavily in the air. Jacob refrained from useless questions about why he had not been sent word of his mother's death. Esau refrained from inadequate apologies.

In an effort to lessen the tension rising between them, Esau steered the conversation from the painful topic of their mother's death to the timely one of their next move. "Let me leave some of my men with you, Jacob—to protect you and to guide you."

Jacob, remembering the hosts of Mahanaim and the closeness of the Lord God at Peniel, smiled as he answered, "That is not necessary. Just let me find favor in the eyes of my lord."

As they parted company, Jacob struggled to suppress a scream of anger and sorrow. Rebekah was dead. And when, he wondered, if the Lord God had not ordered him home, would Isaac or Esau ever have sent for him?

24

There he set up an altar and called it El Elohe Israel.   *Genesis 33:20*

Jacob moved his family and flocks to Succoth. The highland pleased Jacob. Although they were still in the wide Jordan valley, Succoth's rolling slopes made one forget that. On one of the highest plateaus Jacob pitched his tents over-looking vineyards and fields.

They had been at Succoth for three days, and Jacob had scarcely left his tent. He had instructed his servant that he was not to be disturbed.

Rachel worried about him. He was a man of action, and it wasn't like him to stay in his tent like this. She smiled as she remembered the strong young stranger who had been so impatient to get her flock of sheep watered that he lifted the large stone off the well by himself. Her smile was erased by tears as she thought of the way he limped now, leaning on his staff. He had not told her what happened that night at the Jabbok, and she knew he would not welcome any questions, at least not for a while.

The mystery of it fascinated her. What could have dealt him such a blow and yet given him so much more courage? She was proud of the way he had faced Esau, of the way he controlled grief on learning of his mother's death, and his general restraint in the reconciliation attempt. But that kind of courage was in sharp contrast to his withdrawal from everyone for the past few days.

"Rachel."

She heard his voice say her name, and she looked up from her weaving. Never had her lover looked so enchanting to her as did the mature, handsome man he had become. She wanted him to speak further, but at first he only sat down beside her and took one of her hands in his.

After some moments of silence he spoke slowly, as though trying to recall a prepared speech, but unsure of the order of the lines.

"I know you wonder why I haven't spoken to you—or to anyone else—these past days. There are many reasons—the shock of learning of my mother's death, the strain of meeting my brother, the need to think deeply of the revelation the Lord God gave to me at Mahanaim—and then there has been this pain. I was too exhausted to attempt conversation. So much has happened . . . so quickly."

"I've tried to understand as much about all these things as I can, Jacob. I ached to offer you comfort and sympathy, but you turned away from me, and I was not able to help."

"I sensed your feelings, my dearest, and that gave me comfort." He looked at Rachel with the delight of one who had just met a lovely young shepherdess.

In a moment he continued. "But I have had an even more awesome experience than those I have mentioned, and this is what has occupied my thought most of all during my days of solitude. It happened the night I spent on the other side of the Jabbok—alone, but not alone."

"Someone else was there?"

"Elohim was there!" Jacob reverently spoke some of His names: "El Shaddai, the Almighty God; El Elyon, the Most High God; El Olam, the Everlasting God!"

Rachel saw her husband's face become radiant, and she quietly waited for him to be able to say more.

"I met Him. I struggled with Him. I've been thinking of the meaning of it . . . the consequences of it."

"Consequences? You mean your lameness?" Rachel became pale with the shock. Had the Lord God crippled Jacob? Why? Why?

"My lameness is just the physical consequence—given, I suppose, as a reminder of the greater thing that happened in my heart, in my mind, and in my will . . . when He . . . in the form of a man . . . came to me . . . to *me* . . . and He touched me."

He continued as if he had forgotten Rachel was beside him,

as if he were still alone in his tent. "How could His glory and power have been contained within the form of a man for even those few hours?"

Rachel was quieter than ever, almost holding her breath. What Jacob was saying was far beyond her understanding, but she could share in his reverent wonder of it.

"I . . . can't speak of it any more now, except to say that what He did for my grandfather, He has done for me. He has given me a new name. It is Israel. I have a new name!"

"Israel." Rachel said it gently, savoring its sound.

That name, some years before, would have filled young Jacob with pride; now it evoked an awe and a humility that scarcely would allow him to say its definition aloud. "It means . . . prince with God."

Jacob got to his feet and paced around the room in thoughtful agitation. "Rachel, after this unique meeting with the Lord God, after accepting my new name, I thought I'd be different instantly, far different from what I was before. But I'm not."

"You are different! Not only I, but the other women noticed your calmness as you carried out that difficult meeting with Esau; we were impressed with your control in that stressful situation."

"I'm glad for that, but I still know how it is in my heart. I deluged Esau with gifts and courtesy that was, in large part, bribery and formality. I held back my true feelings from him. I even let him think I planned to go immediately to Seir. It will be a long time before I go there—if ever! I can't explain the strange, lingering fear I have of offending him when I know that as a 'prince with God' I should fear no man."

"Jacob . . . Israel . . . you demand too much of yourself, too soon, perhaps."

Jacob answered in firm seriousness. "Don't encourage me to be anything less than all I should be, Rachel."

Not only Jacob, but also his household needed a prolonged rest after the difficult journey from Haran. Succoth was a pleasant place, and Jacob decided to stay there indefintely. He ordered shelters built for his livestock where the animals could be driven at night after pasturing in open fields. Then he had simple houses built for his family.

Jacob's younger children were free to roam the fields and to fish in nearby streams. The older boys hunted small game with bow and arrow. Jacob watched them, gladdened to see them enjoy themselves in their land.

He knew he must spend more time with them now, teaching them of their heritage. They not only must love this splendid land, but must also be aware of the tremendous privilege and responsibility of being God's own people. He thought of the urgency of teaching them to read and to write—as Abraham had taught Isaac and as they both had taught him. He would have a more difficult task than his father or grandfather—they did not have so many sons!

Three months passed, and Jacob experienced healing in body and spirit. His leg mended, and his mind became more settled about his immediate future. Since he had no further leading from the Lord God, other than to return to the land of his kindred, he would be in no hurry to move further. For a while he and his family would remain at Succoth.

He would have liked to have gone to Hebron, at least for a visit, but with his father's disinterest in him and with Esau still active in overseeing business affairs there, he decided against it. He did send a delegation of servants with a gift for his father—a small flock of choice lambs and three elegantly harnessed camels. He charged his messengers to give Isaac his loving salutations and to explain that his son was busy getting the camp at Succoth organized but wanted to see him soon. He hoped his father would send for him, or even come to visit if he were well enough.

When the messengers returned from Mamre, they told Jacob that his gifts were well received. In return Isaac had sent a unique gift—Deborah, Rebekah's nurse, who had come with her from Haran and faithfully served her mistress all the days of Rebekah's life. Deborah was aged, and her years of working were over, but Isaac could not have sent a finer treasure. Jacob always had loved Deborah; she was part of his earliest memories. She walked slower now, but still with the dignity of a royal lady. No person outside of his own immediate family ever meant more to him.

Jacob embraced Deborah, made her feel welcome, and provided her with the best his camp could offer. She was a supportive, easygoing person and she infused a special kind of joy into the household of Jacob.

These were some of the happiest years of Jacob's life. His family thrived, and his herds increased. He felt at peace with all the world and with his God.

Months became years before Jacob decided to move to larger grasslands. He chose to go to the area dominated by the great Oak of Moreh across the Jordan. Abraham had built his first altar there after entering Canaan. If that was a proper place for Abraham to have chosen for an altar, it would be a good place for Jacob and his family to be.

He announced his plans, and his family received them in high spirits; they all were ready for a change. It had been six years since they began living in houses that had been built for temporary use.

The Jordan crossing was made easily. They looked forward to the west side of the river being as pleasant as the east side.

Shechem was the city nearest to the place Jacob planned to go, and he followed the main caravan trail to it, eager to arrange for grazing lands and a site where he could erect his many tents.

Shechem was a fortified city controlling the valley between the formidable mountains of Gerizim and Ebal. It was subject to Egypt, and the culture of that nation influenced it. The Hivites who inhabited Shechem worshipped Egyptian gods and imitated the sophisticated Egyptian way of life as well as they could.

The ruler of the town was a man called Hamor. He had named his son Shechem in honor of the town that he was in line to govern when Hamor died.

Jacob walked to the city gates of Shechem whole and sound, his limp scarcely noticeable. He arranged for pasture rights and for a campground not far from the town. The work of setting up camp went well, and by nightfall of the fourth day after they had crossed the Jordan they were settling into their new home.

Jacob spent the first days at Shechem alloting flocks to his many herdsmen. His older sons were given flocks to tend, and the younger ones were given work to do around the tents. Dinah was assigned to help the women grind grain each morning—a job that bored her terribly. Even the youngest, Joseph, was given some lambs to watch for a few hours each day, assisted by his mother.

After the camp was organized, Jacob took two servants and walked over the surrounding fields, visiting his shepherd sons. Then he went into Shechem, taking with him porters to carry his purchases. He bought quantities of olive oil, honey and spices, and he bought flutes for each of his sons. Later his servants would attend to the shopping, but Jacob wanted to know what manner of town Shechem was. After his marketing he sent the porters back to camp. Then he continued with two menservants to walk along the narrow, winding, stone-paved streets.

He saw potters, tentmakers and carpenters; he saw men standing in the marketplace waiting to be hired as day laborers; and he saw beggars. There were unattractive one-room houses with flat roofs. Most of them were made of dried mud bricks or rough sandstones with wide, irregular openings between them. There were a few fine houses made of hewn stones, built two stories high with spacious ells to form enclosed courtyard gardens.

Jacob looked at the pagan temple, grotesquely ornate, being readied for a festival that would last for a week. He would make certain none of his people entered the town during that time of debauchery.

While Shechem celebrated a festival to their gods, he decided he would set a day aside to worship Elohim. He would call his family together at the place where Abraham had knelt in worship long ago. He hurried home, his mind filled with plans for this special occasion. He sent word to all his sons that they should be ready to go with him early the next morning. They were to see that servants took their places with their flocks or in their other assigned duties.

Jacob took his sons to the place he determined was the Oak of Moreh. There was an old altar under its wide branches. It was a time of closeness with his sons, and he used it to tell them again about Abraham and God's call to him; about their grandfather, Isaac; and about the great line of which they were a part—a people to whom this land would be given forever, a people through whom God would work for the good of all nations in time to come.

As he spoke, he regretted he had devoted so few hours like this to his children. The demands on him in Haran precluded it, and the rigors of the trip to Canaan prevented it. The time at Succoth had lent itself more to family worship and to periods of teaching, but Jacob knew that more should have been done. In Shechem he would attend to it—he was certain he would.

He ended the session at the altar under the oak by saying, "We must be at our best. We are the family who represents the Lord God in a land where people don't know Him—and His law of holiness."

The boys listened to their father, and even if they didn't understand all he said, they enjoyed the attention he had given them. It was a good day.

After they had camped at Shechem for nearly a year Jacob came to Rachel with exciting news. "I've decided to stay here indefintely. This will be home! There is plenty of good pasture, abundant water from mountain streams flowing into the valley—springs and wells besides—and a city nearby for provisions. What more could we want?

"I went to see Hamor, father of the man who bears the name of the town, and I asked to buy some land. For a hundred pieces of silver I have bought the ground where our tents are pitched."

"You bought the land? For a hundred pieces of silver?"

"Yes."

"I thought Canaan was yours—a gift from God."

"Rachel, you know that promise is to be fulfilled in the future. I need land now. I trust the Lord God to enable our family to have the land when it's His time. Meanwhile, it would be wrong to attempt to take it from those who claim it presently. I want nothing but peace from the people of Shechem—from all the people among whom we live. Rachel, the Lord God has given us the land in the sense that He provided me with the means to have the hundred pieces of silver to give to Hamor.

"And now I will build an altar for our family to the Lord God. We will respect the altar made by Abraham, but we will use our own for our sacrifices and our worship."

When Jacob finished building the rough stone altar, he called his family around for the sacrificial offering of an unblemished lamb. As he readied the knife for the throat of the lamb, he marveled at his grandfather's love of God, evidenced in his willingness to sacrifice his beloved son at Moriah. He looked around at his boys as he raised his hand for the plunge of death. When his eyes fell on Joseph, his only son by Rachel, he was blinded by tears, and as the knife fell, he thanked his God that he had not been put to such a test with any of his boys, especially Joseph.

The name he gave the altar he built at Shechem confirmed the name the Lord God had given him. He called the it El Elohe Israel—God, the God of Israel!

25

Now as the Shechemites were keeping a festival, Dinah, who was the only daughter of Jacob, went into the city to see the finery of the women of that country.   Josephus, *Antiquities of the Jews*, I, xxi, 1

It had been six years since Jacob moved to Shechem. Leah's older sons—Reuben, Simeon, Levi and Judah—had the responsibility of overseeing much of the grazing lands and at times were put in charge of taking animals to the marketplace in Shechem. Jacob's younger sons helped with the flocks under the supervision of carefully chosen shepherds, who would train them well and protect them in case of danger.

Jacob felt Joseph still was too young for any responsibility other than helping tend a small flock of lambs in a pasture bordering the campsite. Rachel accompanied her son. They usually spent only a few hours a day with the flock; servants took over by midday.

Jacob was more at ease than he had ever been before. He was pleased with his choice for a home. His sons were a great help in the necessary work. His sacrifices to the Lord were in praise of a bountiful life. In less than two months a priceless new treasure would be added to his family; his beloved Rachel was that near to the time for her second child. Jacob's heart sang.

Dinah was the unhappiest member of the family. Her brothers were company for each other, but she had no sister and had to rely on the companionship of a few maidservants. She had soon become restless with the monotonous task of grinding grain for the daily bread and had been allowed to take up weaving as her principal work. She became quite skillful at it, designing bold patterns with brightly colored yarn. Material that came from her loom was as beautiful as any found in the marketplace in Shechem. Jacob told her that nothing finer could be found even in the bazaar at Damascus.

Dinah did find a measure of fulfillment in the fabric she wove. She liked unusual colors and original designs. Her family believed she had found a way to forget her loneliness, but it still was very much a part of her.

Several times a year Leah took Dinah into the city on shopping trips, and the girl found it fascinating. She delighted in the booths that sold linen and wool fabric; she could have spent hours watching the potter design pitchers and bowls if she had not been hurried along by her mother. She thrilled at the sight of glittering earrings, bracelets, rings and chains brought in from Egypt, Damascus and Babylon.

Leah wondered if she should take Dinah to the city more often because she liked it so much—or if she never should take her again because she liked it too much!

Dinah, at 15 years of age, was beautiful, winsome and artistic. All the family loved her fondly. She was Leah's delight. Leah's sons often reminded the other boys that she was their full sister; they guarded this distinction jealously and were her self-appointed protectors. None of the other boys dared tease her. Leah took pride in the closeness of her children. She encouraged their special love for each other—a family within a family.

It was time for the great festival at Shechem, and Dinah could think of nothing else. She had never been allowed to go to the city at festival time, but her four older brothers had gone the year before—long enough to see the sights and come back to tell her about some of them. The city was filled with the din of loud chanting and jarring music from different groups who paraded with tambourines, flutes and cymbals. There were fierce wrestling matches between slaves. There was dancing and rich food and much, much wine. Dinah thought it sounded perfectly thrilling. Her brothers told her only of the lighter things. They thought she had no need to know the sordid part—immorality indulged in for exhibition, animalistic expressions on celebrants' faces, vulgar talk.

Dinah put away her work on a scarlet, blue and purple cloth and walked to her private tent. No one saw the bright flush on her cheeks; no one noticed how she tilted her head and swung her shoulders as she thought of what the day might bring.

As 15-year-old girls do, Dinah often thought of running away. Just thinking of it had been enough of a release for her until this day. Now she would do it. Not for long—just long enough to go to Shechem, see the festive fashions of the women her brothers told her about, and hear the music! It was not far to the city. She knew the way, and she had a plan that would get her there.

"Mother, I'll take some things to Simeon and Levi. They're tending sheep in the north pasture fields, and it would be fun to surprise them with a fresh lunch from home. I feel like riding out to see them; weaving doesn't interest me today."

"This is a good day for a ride over green fields. I'll get the basket lunch ready. Take Kihan and Baka with you."

"Can't I go alone—just out to the pasture lands?"

"You can't go alone, especially now. It's festival time in Shechem, and the roads are crowded with pilgrims coming in to celebrate . . . . Some of them might wander off the road and into our fields. Kihan and Baka will go with you."

Dinah had not counted on that, but since it had to be, she would try to enjoy them. If they bored her, she would simply send them back to the city gate to wait until she was ready to return home.

Before midmorning the three girls, riding their plodding donkeys, took a sumptuous lunch for themselves and for Simeon and Levi and left the tents. Leah watched them start out; they were laughing, sharing some exciting, girlish secret. She was glad her daughter would have a happy day.

Dinah, Kihan and Baka ate lunch a short distance from the city. They packed what they didn't eat into their saddle bags, planning to enjoy it on the way home. They really weren't hungry at the moment because of their impatience to see what a Shechem festival was like. They felt daring, and if they had any apprehension about what they were doing—or about any disciplining they would face when they went home—they didn't speak of it. It was a day to be young and free—a day to thrill to new experiences.

They could hear raucous noise from where they ate their late lunch—the carnival sound of competing groups of noise-makers. Soon they would be part of it.

"I wish we had different clothes to wear. We'll look out of place." Kihan smoothed her tunic as if by pressing her hands over it she could make it a different shade or style. It remained brown and plain.

"If only we had some coins, we could buy garments and dress like the women of Shechem." Baka hoped Dinah had some coins and would take her suggestion.

"We aren't here to be part of this place or to imitate its people. We would be different from the Hivite women even if we dressed like them. Why should we care what they think of us? We are here for something to do to pass an otherwise boring day—just to watch the festival for a while.

"Walk with your heads high. The foolish women in their fancy clothes will wish they had tunics as fine as ours!"

Dinah demonstrated how to walk like a proud princess, overacting so that all three girls burst into laughter. Then they pranced and strutted as if they had invented a new game.

Dinah could have looked no lovlier if she had been given her choice of any garment in Shechem. Her long-fringed white tunic complemented her olive skin, her magnificent dark hair, and her long-lashed brown eyes. Her natural beauty sparkled when she smiled. She knew that, so she smiled often, not that she was particularly happy, but because she knew it enhanced her appearance.

When the girls came to the city, they almost decided to turn back. It was too noisy, too big. They hesitated at the gate and looked at each other, each waiting for another to be the first to move.

Dinah became impatient with herself and her maids. "By now we're in trouble at home even if we don't go in. Since we've come this far, we will stay a while at least! We want to see a festival. We want to see what Hivite girls wear to festivals, and we want to see the processions. Come on!"

She looked back at the three donkeys tied to a hitching rail.

Should she lead the girls back to them—or through the gate?

What would her brothers think? Wait until she told them where she had been! She laughed out loud just thinking of them and stepped through the gate.

"We'll go right to the temple area, the center of all the festivities."

Shechem's narrow streets were filled with merrymakers. The girls were jostled and pushed.

"Dinah, I'm scared! Let's go home." Baka was not enjoying her first impression of festival. Neither was Kihan.

Dinah called over her shoulder to the lagging girls. "As soon as we see the temple and what's going on around it."

She was so used to the rough play of her older brothers that she naturally gave an unladylike push to a young man who purposely blocked her path. He didn't move, and she pushed him harder. Just because he was handsome and dressed up like a king, did he think he owned the street? The young man still did not budge. Her hard shoves only amused him.

He grabbed her by the shoulders, laughing wildly. She shouted to Baka and Kihan for help, but the frightened girls were running down the street toward the city gate.

Dinah was thrown down on the rough stone pavement. She fought in outrage as she felt her tunic being torn. She was sick with fear and helpless in the strong hands that held her. Onlookers called out encouragements to her attacker—and obscene taunts at her.

The young man's eyes were glazed from too much wine and from the excitement of what he was doing.

When Dinah could struggle no more, she screamed. When she could scream no more, she closed her eyes tightly to shut out as much of the savage ordeal as possible.

Then there was a closing in of heavy blackness.

26

His heart was drawn to Dinah daughter of Jacob, and he loved the girl and
spoke tenderly to her.   *Genesis 34:3*

*W*hen Dinah awoke, she was in a large bedroom of a
pretentious house. She looked around, moving only her eyes;
her head was too bruised to turn. At first it was difficult to
focus on objects, but her vision cleared in a few minutes.

A maidservant offered her a drink of water. She didn't
know where she was. She didn't care. It was too much effort to
sip the water. She slept again.

When she awoke hours later, she desperately tried to
move, to get up, to run. Her attacker was at her bedside! As
she began to stir and tried to scream, he reached over and
touched her, but this time with gentle hands; the restraint he
used was protective. "You are Dinah?"

She didn't answer; she never would speak to this man. But
some of her initial terror subsided as she heard his voice, now
soft and soothing. The face she would not look at was showing
concern. Again he asked, "You are Dinah?"

She nodded her head slightly, then closed her eyes and said
her name, "Dinah." At the sound of her own voice she burst
into tears.

Young Shechem looked at her helplessly, then beckoned
the maidservant who had been sitting beside her all through
the night. "See if she will drink water or eat something."

The maidservant, without even looking at Shechem,
walked past him to comfort the girl, who had become
hysterical.

Shechem left the room and went to his father. "She is
Dinah, daughter of Jacob, as I told you last night when I

brought her here. I've seen her in town before with her family. She's awake now. Perhaps she will take some food."

Hamor looked at his son with disdain mixed with sympathy. He sensed the torment Shechem was feeling because of his despicable behavior. He didn't respond to his son's information about the young woman, except to order a servant to saddle his camel.

"Where are you going, Father?"

"To see Jacob and tell him where his daughter is . . . and to try to make a settlement of some kind with him."

"Father," Shechem's voice trembled a little, "when you talk to her father and her brothers, tell them I love Dinah. I can't make up for what I've done to her, but with all my heart I want to marry her."

"Love? Marry? The Hebrew?"

"Yes! Love . . . marry . . . with their permission . . . Dinah!"

Hamor shook his head as he looked at his son with bitter disgust. "I don't believe—and Dinah's family will not believe—that you know the meaning of the word *love*."

"In these past hours I've known a young woman of courage and beauty; I do love her. If I convince her of that, I will be one fortunate man. I will speak tenderly to her. I will overcome her fear and hatred of me. I will comfort her . . . even if she never loves me.

"Father, will you offer Jacob a dowry for Dinah?"

"Yes, if that's what you want."

"That's what I want. Make the dowry a large one—a very large one!"

Hamor saw tears in his son's eyes as he turned to run back to his vigil at Dinah's bedside.

Hamor didn't prod his camel. He needed as much time as possible before the confrontation with Jacob. The meeting was impossible to plan; emotions would run roughshod over reason when Dinah's family learned what had happened. He couldn't blame them!

Hamor decided it would be best to keep the details to a minimum. He would state the matter bluntly: Shechem had lain with Dinah, and now he wanted to marry her. Then he would offer an irresistably large dowry. It was a regrettable situation, but there was no need for the families to make it worse by resorting to strife of any kind. Shechem and Dinah would make a fine couple. Hamor allowed his thoughts to escape to a possibly pleasant future instead of dwelling on the traumatic present.

By the time he arrived at Jacob's tent, he was in a fairly optimistic mood, ready to be generous. He hoped Jacob would be understanding of youthful passions at festival time. He hoped he might even be appreciative of the large dowry he was prepared to offer—and of the prestigious family Dinah would join when she became Shechem's wife.

The previous afternoon when Kihan and Baka fled from the city, they came home as fast as their deliberate donkeys would bring them. Once at the campsite they rushed to tell Leah that her daughter was in great trouble in Shechem.

Their panic and concern for Dinah were genuine, but they were of little help to the distraught mother. They didn't know exactly what had happened to Dinah; they had run away too quickly. They didn't know who her attacker was. They hadn't any idea where she would be by then.

Leah ran to Jacob and told the story—even more incoherently than the maidservants. He dispatched 10 men into Shechem. They were to search for Dinah and bring her home. At the very least, they were to learn all they could about where she was and what had happened.

Jacob tried to comfort Leah, and together they waited out the long night. At times they hoped that their fears were unfounded and that the servants would bring their daughter home safely by morning; at times they imagined things that broke their hearts and made them ill!

It was almost daybreak when Leah asked a question that added to Jacob's heartache. "Is it harder to believe in the God of Bethel today than it was yesterday, . . . when all was well with our family?"

Israel answered after giving careful thought to the difficult question. "Circumstances are always in a state of change. What seems reasonable or unreasonable to me does not change the fact that the God of Bethel has said He is with me wherever I go—in all things.

"When trouble and sorrow come, He doesn't expect me to refuse to see things the way they are. Leah, if I didn't grieve and suffer, I would not be a better person—I would be less than human.

"I've thought many times of His precious words to me. He said He would be with me, watch over me. He did not say there would be no trials or testings. He never promised I would not have heartaches and difficulties."

His words did nothing to check Leah's tears, and from a devastated heart she cried out, "What good is it if He stays with you . . . watches over you . . . and yet lets troubles come?" Her voice was not that of a skeptic; it held the longing of a woman trying to find refuge in her personal storm.

"I can't fully answer . . . and it's better to be in silent awe of what I don't understand than to rebel in useless frustration. But I know this: I seek His face more consistently when I'm in sorrow, and I'm always humbled by trouble that I can't control. And so even the harshest things in life have drawn me closer to El Elohe Israel in a lowly spirit.

"My greatest comfort, Leah, has not come from controlling situations or from prosperity or even from my family; it has come from knowing beyond all doubt that He is with me— beyond and above and around everything!"

Leah was quiet for a time, thinking of what her husband had said. Then turning her tear-streaked face toward him in the first light of morning, she attempted to respond. "I'm beginning to understand what you mean. Having the Lord God's presence . . . in time of trouble is like my wanting to be here with you through this long, terrible night. . . . Even though my sorrow remains, being with you, . . . knowing you share my grief and . . . concern about Dinah—I'm strengthened to face what I must, Jacob."

"You have said it well, Leah. The Lord God can use any situation that arises to bring us into a closer relationship with Himself."

Jacob and Leah continued their silent vigil until long after it was daylight. Each one, as fully as possible, kept aware of the strengthening, comforting presence of the God of Bethel.

The messengers returned from town in the late morning. They came to Jacob's tent and with bowed heads reported to the anxious father and mother.

Jacob and Leah listened in stunned silence to their description of brutal immorality; they remained silent when they learned that the molester was Shechem, son of Hamor. When the servants finished their story, Jacob dismissed them with one scarcely audible word, "Go."

The parents thought they had been prepared for any news that would come, but now they sat numbed by grief too deep for tears, unable even to cry out to the Lord God.

A servant arrived at Jacob's tent in a short while, saying that Dinah's brothers, who had been summoned the previous evening, waited to meet with him. Leah arose and walked from the place of long vigil. Jacob saw Rachel waiting to meet her; she put her arm around her weeping sister and walked with her back to her tent.

The brothers had learned from the servants what had happened. As soon as Jacob gave them permission to see him, they rushed to his tent with no thought for his crushed feelings, filled with their own fury. Jacob scarcely looked up as they came in, shouting at each other and at him.

"Dinah and Shechem will be the talk of the whole city—and beyond!"

"It's the right of brothers to avenge a sister!"

"It's more than a right—it's a duty!"

"Death to Shechem and Hamor and all who were in the city—all who could have prevented this outrage! They are guilty—every one of them!"

"Revenge!"

Jacob endured their tirades for a few moments, then stood with his right arm held high in authority. "Be still!"

The young men became quiet but were still shaking with rage. Jacob began to speak, then stopped as he saw they had a visitor. Hamor had arrived and had been listening to the furious brothers' talk of vengeance. Jacob acknowledged him and asked him to enter.

Looking uneasily at the brothers seething with anger and brandishing clenched fists, he turned to Jacob. "I will get right to the point. Things are not as bad as they may seem to you. My son, Shechem, has set his heart on your daughter. Please give her to him as his wife. Their marriage can be profitable for both of us. Take what land you want; it's all open to you."

Before Jacob could reply, a haggard, serious-looking young man ran in and knelt before him. It was Shechem. He had followed his father from town to present his own case to Dinah's family.

"Let me find favor in your eyes, and I will give you whatever you ask." Shechem had rehearsed his speech many times, but now he delivered it with more emotion than ever. "Make the price for the bride and the gift I am to bring as great as you like, and I'll pay whatever you ask me. Only give me the girl as my wife."

Although he had addressed Jacob, Dinah's brothers made the reply. They reminded him that they had a responsibility to avenge their sister; then they withdrew from the tent to talk over their answer.

Jacob, Hamor and Shechem awaited their return in uneasy silence that grew steadily more oppressive. Shechem was fearful and ashamed, and yet his expression at times evidenced a faint hope that all might go well with him now.

When the brothers came back, they solemnly told Shechem that they would give Dinah to him only if he would honor the requirement of their God that all males be circumcised—every male in the city of Shechem.

Jacob was aghast. He never would permit Dinah to marry into a Hivite family. And there was no reason for the entire male population of a pagan city to be circumcised.

If Jacob was shocked speechless, Hamor and Shechem were not. The offer seemed good to them. They hurriedly left Jacob's tent, assuring Dinah's family that what they required would be done at once.

Hamor and Shechem went to the city and immediately ordered the townsmen to assemble for a special meeting. The men came reluctantly because it took time away from their celebrating, which was still in full sway. They quieted down at

Hamor's command and listened as he persuaded them to comply with the unusual demand of Jacob's family.

His speech was a long one. He reminded the men of the friendly relations the city had with the large house of Jacob and of how intermarriage would benefit everyone. His concluding remarks contained an exciting question: "Won't their livestock, their property, and all their animals be ours?" It lacked logic, but Hamor made it sound appealing to the men of Shechem. He ended his speech with a loud, dramatic call for immediate action. "Let's give our consent to them, and they will settle among us."

Hamor knew how to handle a crowd, and after a few days of riotous celebration they were exceptionally easy to influence. They were in no condition for intelligent discussion. They shouted approval of Hamor's decision to appease the house of Jacob, although many of them did not even know what they were shouting for. And so every male in the city was circumcised.

Three days later the incapacitated men were in the worst period of their pain; many of them had a high fever. The town was quiet. Debris from the festival lay in the streets.

Into the city's stillness rode a band of men led by Simeon and Levi. They rode fast, screaming war cries. At the temple site they dismounted and went through the town, putting every male to the sword.

They purposely left Hamor's house until the last. Simeon and Levi personally stormed it and killed both Hamor and Shechem. Then they found their sister and carried her away from there.

Later they led their men through the city, ransacking houses, taking women and children captive, and seizing livestock.

They convinced themselves they were heroic. They anticipated accolades from their father and gratitude from Dinah. They had been the mighty avengers!

27

God said to Jacob, "Go up to Bethel and settle there, and build an altar there to God, who appeared to you when you were fleeing from your brother Esau." *Genesis 35:1*

Clan war was common in Canaan; revenge was a way of life—but not for Jacob, who was a quiet man of peace. He would have been hard pressed to wage a war as Abraham had against Kederlaomer; he even avoided confrontations over wells.

Simeon and Levi took full responsibility for the massacre and the looting. "The city is ours, Father! We can live in its fine houses and be protected by its fortifications. From it we can control the caravan route between the twin mountains . . . as Esau told you he controls the road through the mountains of Seir."

Their talk of safety, profits and power did not impress the patriarch. In agony of spirit he upbraided his sons with a voice so shaken that they had to listen carefully to hear his words. The acclamation they hoped for did not come.

"You used the guise of religion to satisfy your anger and your greed! You dishonored your word!"

His sons were startled by his reprimand; they were dismayed that he showed no intention of occupying the city they had taken.

"You have brought trouble on me by making me a stench to the Hivites and to others living in this land. We are few in number, and if they join forces against me and attack, we will all be destroyed."

Simeon and Levi answered as with one voice, "But he should not have treated our sister like a prostitute!"

Jacob knew there was no use to speak further to them; he ordered them to leave his tent.

Jacob was overwhelmed by the passions and the devastation of the past few days. He was relieved to have Dinah home again, but the camp had an atmosphere akin to mourning. He would not move into the walled city and set himself up as any kind of ruler. He would not even go there for protection against neighboring tribes that might well attack him in revenge for what had been done in Shechem.

"I see no way out . . . I see no way out." He spoke aloud to himself. "What I've built up here is gone. My family name is a reproach because of something I had nothing to do with. I've wronged no one. I've lived at peace with all my neighbors, but surely they will bring reprisals on me for what my sons have done."

He walked over to his bed, hoping his exhaustion was great enough that it would give way to sleep. It was.

The sleep was healing, and he awoke to face his desolate circumstances comparatively unperplexed. He would deal with his problems as positively as he could and not dwell on what might happen in the next days. He would take the widows and orphans of Shechem into his household and care for them. The ownerless flocks and herds would be added to his own.

Then he would prepare to leave the portion of homeland he had purchased and move to another place. In so doing he would leave a part of himself. No matter how horrible the last week had been, it would not cancel out his good memories of this haven between the mountains.

But even after coming to these conclusions, great surges of despair overwhelmed him from time to time, and his tears flowed. His family and servants often saw him with arms lifted high toward the heavens, as if reaching for the God who promised always to be with him.

He shut himself away from the rest of the family, as had become his custom when he had serious thinking to do or when his mood of melancholy was heaviest. He left his quarters infrequently and then only to comfort Leah or to encourage Dinah to resume her weaving as her strength permitted. When talking with them he was gentle and calm, but in moments alone he agonized over what to do, where to go, and when.

Rachel decided it was time to break in on his solitude and went to his tent one morning just after Joseph had left with a servant companion to lead his little flock of lambs out to the pasture where his overseer waited for him. Jacob saw her approaching; he hoped she was not going to offer trite, sympathetic phrases.

He should have known his Rachel better than to think she would be thoughtlessly superficial. She simply smiled at him, then said, "Joseph has just left with his flock. I don't go with him now but send a servant in my place. I am busy resting and waiting for our next beautiful child."

She changed the atmosphere of his tent with her warm, loving presence. She turned his thoughts to his favorite son and to the unborn child he awaited with a joy that all his problems couldn't quench.

He managed to smile. That delighted him, for he had convinced himself he could never smile again.

"Rachel, my love . . . my helper . . . my right hand. You always know what is needed. Whatever would my life have been without you . . . or without our son, Joseph?"

"Let's talk about Joseph! He's doing well with his lambs and seems content enough, but I wonder if he should become a shepherd."

"What's wrong with being a shepherd?"

"Nothing. But some men are suited to that and others to something else."

"And you think Joseph would not make a good shepherd?"

"I think he is better at studying the things Abraham and Isaac have taught you—the legacy of learning brought from Ur."

"But all my sons have learned to read and write; they know the arithmetic procedures—addition, subtraction, multiplication and division. And Joseph is already learning all that."

"Does it seem to you, Jacob, that our son is a more eager

student than his half brothers? Isn't he more responsive to your teaching?"

"I suppose so. I thought it might have been because I've had more time to spend with him since his older brothers have taken over much of my work."

"I'm glad you have more time for Joseph. When I see how you two enjoy your hours of study together, I'm reminded of what you told me about the time you spent with Abraham, learning not only knowledge brought from Ur, but also the story of your people back to the beginning of time—traced through the records he kept so zealously."

When Rachel mentioned the family records, Jacob suddenly sat up and jerked his head back as if someone had splashed him with cold water. She was afraid she had diverted her husband's thoughts from Joseph and his studies. His next words seemed to confirm her fears.

"Now you have reminded me of another thing—the family records! My father has added to them, and I must make certain entries also. Some of it I will not want to write, as I'm sure there were things he didn't want to record. But the things written down are of the Lord God's own choosing, not any man's. When we finally go to Hebron, I will attend to the writing, and as the Lord God directs, I will add to what is already in the box my father has.

"But . . . getting back to what we were talking about . . . the knowledge handed down from Abraham—yes, there was much more than elementary learning that he passed along to me—astronomy, the study of medicine, and the square and cube roots of numbers. He always challenged my mind."

"And I think you should set up more study times for Joseph. His mind is keen and needs similar challenges."

"I'll think it over, Rachel. I needed your reminder that Joseph is growing up fast . . . and will be the baby of the family for only a few more weeks!"

Rachel left Jacob's tent feeling pleased with her mission. She had diverted her husband's attention from the morbid things he had been dwelling on for too many days, and she had started him thinking seriously about Joseph's education. She wanted more than a shepherd's life for her son. She never wanted to think of him out in the fields—lonely, beset by hostile weather, confronted with wild animals or robbers. She wanted only the best for her firstborn. In her own mind the matter was settled; Joseph would be the student of the family. They had enough shepherds.

Several days later Joseph was still taking his small flock to the pasture. He had not told Rachel of any new study sessions planned with his father, so she mentioned this to Jacob one evening after Joseph had gone to bed.

"I can't think of beginning the studies now, Rachel! There is the immediate problem of where to move. I have to concentrate on that until it's settled. Each day we stay here, I wonder if we will be attacked by tribes who would gladly use revenge for Shechem as an excuse. And I will not move behind the walls of that city!"

"There is no need to move behind walls—or to fear. You still have the hosts of Mahanaim, have you not?"

Rachel thought her mentioning the glorious host that her husband had seen at Mahanaim would comfort him, but he looked even more distraught and sighed heavily. "Yes, the hosts of God . . . and the Lord God Himself! To know they are with me and yet not be able to throw off this depression . . . makes me more depressed! Rachel, why can't I live as I believe? I say I trust God; I mean to trust Him. But I'm frightened to stay and fearful to move! Why can't I grasp the wonderful fact that each day we are not attacked is proof that the host of God surrounds us and has already instilled the fear of God into the minds of our enemies?

"How patient the Lord God is to stay with one so unable to cope, even with His help." Jacob's voice had become softer—with a hint of tears barely held back.

"Should we just stay here, since they guard us so well?" Rachel's suggestion came from her desire to avoid travel until after her child was born.

"I want to move because there is a cloud of sorrow over this place now, and I feel a great restlessness. The peace we've known before will never be ours again until we are away from here.

"We might go to Mamre. The children should meet their grandfather, and I want him to know them. And I would like to see Mamre, Hebron, Gerar and Beersheba. It has been so long since I was there. But I won't move until I have definite instructions from the Lord God. I chose Succoth and then Shechem, but I will not choose my next move."

Rachel had been thinking of the many miles between Shechem and Mamre. It seemed inappropriate even to think of such a journey at such a time! "That would be a long way for me to travel just now, my husband. I'd like to stay here until after our child is born. . . . It will be only a few more weeks."

"Rachel, I've told you I don't plan to rush to Mamre or anywhere else before the Lord God directs me, nor will I stay here a day longer than necessary after He gives me an understanding of the place I should go."

Rachel never doubted her place in Jacob's heart. She knew she meant more to him than anyone else, with the possible exception of Joseph. She also knew that neither she nor her son could come between Jacob and El Elohe Israel.

She longed for the next weeks to end. Life seemed to be in suspension, without reality. She had felt so secure, so established; now she didn't know where "home" really was—except that it was no longer near the vacant town of Shechem.

Her pregnancy had been an easy one even though she was past the best years for childbearing. Only in the last few weeks had she felt the weakness that made her dread the actual time of giving birth. She decided her weakness had to be the result of the emotional trauma that the family had experienced in varying degrees over Dinah—and the violent aftermath Leah's sons had been responsible for. She would rest and regain her strength—and hope the child soon to be born would bring new joy to the house of Jacob.

She thanked the God of Abraham, Isaac and Jacob for the blessing of continuing life. Possibly she would give her child a name that meant new life.

The dizzying weakness passed over her again, and she lay down to rest and to think about her child until she fell asleep.

28

God said to him, "I am God Almighty; be fruitful and increase in number. A nation and a community of nations will come from you, and kings will come from your body. The land I gave to Abraham and Isaac I also give to you, and I will give this land to your descendants after you."

Genesis 35:11-12

Jacob spent all that night at the altar he had built in a happier time when he first moved to Shechem. In the morning he went over to the old altar of Abraham under the Oak of Moreh. That evening he went back to the altar of El Elohe Israel. He determined to fast and pray as long as necessary— until he received guidance for himself and for his greatly enlarged household. If they were to move before the birth of Rachel's child, it must be at once.

Without dazzling light, without the sound of cascading water, without the vision of heavenly hosts there came a still, small voice within Jacob that rang as clear and strong as the loudest sound he ever heard. God said to Jacob, "Go up to Bethel and settle there, and build an altar there to God, who appeared to you when you were fleeing from your brother Esau."

Against the background of weeks of fear and disgrace, of indecision and despair that Voice spoke out in dazzling contrast. At the sound of it new strength flooded into Jacob's tired body, and new elation spread through his mind. His God was directing his way!

Now with divine direction Jacob's organizational ability and determination resurfaced, and he immediately began planning the move to Bethel. He called together his chief servants, the overseers of his flocks, and his sons.

"Prepare to move quickly. We will not leave a single person, animal or possession behind. Report to me tomorrow morning how your preparations are going and how soon we will be ready to begin our journey. Time never has been more valuable for, as you know, a new heir is to be born to the house of Jacob, and it's urgent Rachel doesn't have to travel many miles a day—yet that we arrive at our destination in as few days from now as possible.

"And there will be a unique requirement for everyone to meet before we begin the first mile. Each person—not only the Hivite women and children who have just joined us, but all the servants who have been with us before, even everyone in my own family—must be told there will be no images or teraphim—or even a talisman earring—permitted in the caravan! Tell it over and over again to everyone—no foreign gods!

"Each idol must be brought to the field beside my tent, and from there they will be carted away and buried near the Oak of Moreh. The altar built by Abraham will tower over them, proclaiming to all of Canaan who the God of this land is—El Elyon!"

Jacob spoke with great emotion so his hearers would know he meant what he said. If only they could have seen his God and heard Him speak, they could more easily have identified with Jacob's intense feeling.

He had known for a long time that the camp had to be cleansed of foreign gods. It weighed on his mind especially since the Hivite remnant had joined them. They naturally would try to keep their idols as tangible ties with their old home. He would have none of it! He thought perhaps even some of his sons might have acquired an image of a foreign god in their looting of Shechem. His own family, especially, must not possess anything pertaining to idolatry!

His command was passed along to the people, and the people obeyed. Before the end of the day there was a mound of monstrous statues in the field beside Jacob's tent. Some were carelessly thrown down; others were laid lovingly in their place. Many of the images were made of copper, and a few were bronze, but most of them were wood or earthenware. All of them were grotesque. Earrings, which had been worn as charms to bring good fortune, were of silver and gold. Each item represented a sacrifice on the part of its owner, a sense of loss. Jacob's eyes were moist as he pondered how to place in the hearts of his people a love for the one God, whom to know made all these things dross by comparison.

He called for servants to load the miscellaneous collection into a wagon and take it to the place of burial near the altar at the Oak of Moreh. He was eager to get them out of his sight—out of his camp. He mounted his camel and led the strange procession. On the way he met two of Rachel's servants who seemed embarrassed to be seen by him. Jacob puzzled over their uneasiness, until he came to the great tree. There, exactly where he had told his people that the gods would be entombed, lay silver teraphim—images such as were worshiped in Haran, such as Laban had searched for in Jacob's tents in Gilead!

Jacob was incensed that Rachel had these in her possession all these years without his knowing it. Surely . . . surely she had not worshipped them! How had she hidden them from Laban the day he searched her tent? And where had she kept them all this time? He would have a talk with her at the first opportunity.

He smiled in spite of his anger and shook his head in bewildered amusement at the way she had turned them in without any confrontation. Since she had hidden them so successfully up until now, she could have continued hiding them. He was content that she had decided to give them up—glad she wanted them gone now. As he personally covered them with the idols of lesser material value, he had a marvelous feeling of elation. An important link with Haran had been severed; his bond with Rachel was stronger.

All was in order for their move. Jacob called his people to him for final instructions. They were to begin the journey in personal cleanliness and in freshly washed garments, for they were going to holy ground.

"In the morning we leave for Bethel. When we arrive, I'll build an altar to God, who answered me in the day of my distress so many years ago and was with me on the way on which I traveled."

The house of Jacob moved from Shechem unmolested through the countryside. Jacob knew they were safe because the hosts of heaven that surrounded them miraculously filled all those who would harm him with terror of Jacob's God.

Moving directly south, traveling slowly and stopping often because of Rachel, they came to their destination, the village of Luz, or Bethel. As they were nearing the town, Jacob thought of his old friend Rekem, the potter. Rekem would be surprised that the poor, frightened young man he had helped did manage to get to Haran—and now had returned as a man of immense wealth. He hoped Rekem was still alive; he would find him and introduce him to the wife—the wives—from Haran. And he would answer the old man's request to speak to him of his God, the God who went with him.

While servants set up camp and shepherds settled the flocks, and while Kerah and Deborah ministered to Rachel, Jacob went on alone to the hill where he first heard the voice of God. Would He speak again? Jacob thought so, for He had called him to come to this place of remembrance. Jacob's heart pounded as he climbed the hill, more from anticipation of hearing the Voice than from the exertion of getting to the top of the hill.

With joy and reverence Jacob built a huge stone altar near the place of his former one. He called the new one El Bethel, meaning God of the House of God. He sacrificed a perfect lamb without spot or blemish.

Jacob's excitement mounted. All through his being he was thrilled to be kneeling on that well-remembered hilltop. He thought now that he should have come here in the first place, as soon as he returned from Haran. But he did not dwell on the past with its regrettable errors of judgment. He was at that precious moment exactly where God had called him to be, and he had given instant obedience to that divine summons. He now need only wait until the Lord God spoke to him.

Waiting time was necessary. Jacob's mind must be at rest and quietly trusting—not denying problems or sorrows, yet not letting them dominate. It was a time to center his thoughts around El Shaddai.

Jacob stayed to watch and wait through the night, the

following day, and through the second night. There had been only silence around him except for the calling of birds and the soft rustling in the carob, olive and almond trees.

His offering had been made, and to it had been added the sacrament of silent waiting in God's presence. It was enough for this time. He would go back to his family, then return in a few days to continue waiting on the Lord.

Jacob was walking down the path leading from the hilltop when he heard high-pitched shrieks that cut through the atmosphere and into his heart. The disturbance came from his camp! After the shrieks came a continuous wail from many, many people. Jacob was filled with terror. Those were the sounds that traditionally announced a death had just occurred. Rachel! Rachel! He ran the rest of the way down the hill. His servants, stationed at the foot of the hill, had his camel ready, and with the greatest haste they headed back to the encampment.

The lamenting increased in volume as additional voices joined in the persistent mourning. When he neared the tents, terrifying words assaulted his ears over and over again: "O dear woman" and "Alas, she was our mother" and just "Oh! Ah! Oh!" It was the customary dirge for the dead, but to Jacob they seemed to be the most wrenching cries he had ever heard. Rachel! Rachel! Was it Rachel?

Reuben and Judah had saddled their camels to summon their father. When they saw him approaching, they halted but waited to be the first to tell him the news.

"Deborah is dead." Reuben spoke evenly, without drama.

"Deborah!" If ever true sorrow mingled with true joy, it was in that word of Jacob.

Judah added details to Reuben's curt announcement. "She was walking back to her tent after having spent most of the day waiting on Rachel and . . . she just fell . . . and was dead. She didn't even get back to her own tent."

"And Rachel—how is she?"

"She stays in her bed, grieving for Deborah, feeling responsible for her death."

Jacob hadn't heard the last words of Judah's sentence. He had dismounted and was running to Rachel. He knelt beside her and embraced her, feeling a luxuriant joyfulness in the knowledge that the funeral wails were not for her. He did experience a poignant sorrow in the loss of Deborah, but the death of the aged brings a different kind of heartache from the death of the young.

Rachel was comforted by Jacob's coming to her, but at the sight of him she burst into tears again. "Deborah never told me she wasn't feeling well. Jacob, she shouldn't have been here waiting on me; someone should have been caring for her! Dear Deborah!"

Jacob tried to quiet her, but she tossed restlessly and continued to express her grief: "Why did she spend her last hours waiting on me? Kerah was here, and others could have helped. But . . . Deborah insisted.

"O Jacob, she is gone! . . . None of the other women has her gentle strength. She had a way of making everything seem right; she absorbed the tensions around her and never caused uneasiness to anyone. I . . . loved her so . . . even though I'd known her only these last few years. Even more than my Kerah, she seemed like a mother to me. And she was good at caring for Joseph . . . and would have devoted herself to our new baby. Jacob! Deborah is gone!"

His own grief caught up with him now, and he wept unashamedly with Rachel. Deborah! Jacob could not imagine a world without her in it somewhere, helping someone.

They chose a place for her burial under an oak, strong and beautiful, like the character of Deborah. They named the oak Allon Bacuth, the Oak of Weeping.

When the burial was accomplished and the initial time of mourning over, Jacob's thoughts turned to Rekem again. He sent a messenger into Luz to inquire about him. In a short while the servant returned with information that Rekem the potter had died several years ago.

A chill spread over Jacob as he thought of the inappropriate news of his old friend's death and the inopportune death of Deborah. This was to have been a time for great, blessed joy—the anticipated meeting with the Lord God and the final waiting for Rachel's new child. Death should not intrude in such an untimely way on life!

When things returned to normal in camp, a more thoughtful Jacob walked back to the hilltop where stood the timeworn altar Abraham had built, the monument he had left when he was running from Esau, and the new altar he had built and used only the past week. In this place so holy to him he resumed his waiting on God and his shutting out of distracting thoughts. He prayed; he spoke his praise aloud; but most of the time he was silent in His presence.

At the moment of the Lord God's choosing, He appeared in a transcendent theophany. Jacob bowed in awe before His magnificence. In this meeting Jacob's new name of Israel, given at Peniel but not yet appropriated by Jacob, was affirmed. God said to him, "Your name is Jacob, but you will no longer be called Jacob; your name will be Israel."

And God said, "I am God Almighty; be fruitful and increase in number. A nation and a community of nations will come from you, and kings will come from your body. The land I gave to Abraham and Isaac I also give to you, and I will give this land to your descendants after you."

Then in breathless amazement Jacob watched as El Shaddai, the Lord God Almighty, went up from him, from the place where He had spoken.

Jacob set up a pillar of stone to mark the place where God had spoken to him, and he anointed it. He shouted his praise to God for the whole world to hear.

Israel left his sanctuary. As dear as his family was to him, his fellowship with the Lord God was infinitely more precious. Moments with El Shaddai had in them the essence of eternity, the strength of omnipotence, the perfection of joy and peace.

It was evening when he came down from the hill. He went directly to his tent to devote hours to reliving in his mind the shining moments of Bethel.

After another day's rest at Luz he would lead his caravan south as far as Ephrath. Then, as rapidly as Rachel could travel, they would move on down to Mamre. Rachel's child would be born at his father's home!

29

So Rachel died and was buried on the way to Ephrath .... Over her tomb
Jacob set up a pillar, and to this day that pillar marks Rachel's tomb.
Israel moved on again and pitched his tent beyond Migdal Eder.
Genesis 35:19-21

*N*o matter how many times Jacob supervised the
packing of his camp, each departure was exciting to him. He
was convinced the sun rose in special grandeur on the morning of their leaving from Bethel. He was going home!—
Beersheba, Hebron and Mamre!—Reunion with his father!

The animals, gathered into a semblance of order, were
already grazing in fields bordering the caravan highway.
Household goods and personal belongings were piled into
carts and into now bulging saddlebags.

Jacob was pleased with how expertly everything had been
done; an early start such as this pleased him especially. His
sons and his servants had taken their places of responsibility—
some to care for the children and babies, some to help with the
animals, a few to attend Rachel, Leah, Zilpah, Bilhah and
Dinah as they rode in their wicker basket seats slung from the
camels' sides.

He smiled with no little pride at his hundreds of sheep,
goats and cattle, his folded tents and their belongings, his
many strings of camels and dozens of sturdy donkeys. His face
glowed as he looked at his servants and his family. It was a
moment of triumph as he contrasted all this to his first departure from Luz in what seemed to him now like another lifetime. It was hard to identify with the young man he saw in his
memory—apprehensive and alone, going in the opposite
direction from the one he was taking now. Exile and home-

coming were as different as night and day. He shouted his praise to the Lord God for this wonderful day!

Then he bowed his head in humility as he thought of the large retinue of the hosts of God surrounding him—and of the God of Bethel, El Elohe Israel, who had granted him all these blessings!

He had taken precious moments to enjoy his present situation. Only he and the God who went with him knew how costly it had been to reach this point of satisfaction. Its price in hard work and disappointments had been high—high enough to make him appreciate all that now enriched him.

"Rachel is calling for you!"

Jacob was startled from his pleasant thoughts by a maidservant whose tone of voice told him her message was urgent.

In long strides he hurried to Rachel seated in her large basket chair, leaning on its cushions. When he had seen her earlier that morning, she was in high spirits and seemed ready for the move; now she looked as tired as if she had not slept in many days, and her face was drawn.

"Must I travel today?"

"Rachel! Everyone is ready! We are all packed! We'll go only a very short distance—just to Ephrath. If we can go a few miles each day, we will be at Mamre before our child is born."

"It would mean very much to you . . . to have the child born at Mamre?"

"Oh, yes! It's my home! I've wanted to be back there for so long, and now that we're this close, my homesickness is . . . overwhelming!"

Rachel did not appear convinced about the importance of going to Mamre.

Jacob added another reason for getting to his planned destination. "Rachel, if we can get to Mamre before the child is born, you will want for nothing in the way of care for you and the baby."

"I already want for nothing. Kerah has seen to all I need. It's just . . . oh . . . now that I'm faced with actually beginning the tiresome move . . . it exhausts me even to think of it."

"Then try not to think of it. Close your eyes and rest." Jacob didn't know if he was being trite or practical, but in either case he deeply cared about her freedom from unnecessary anxiety or pain. "Is your basket chair comfortable?"

"Yes."

Jacob struggled with the decision that faced him. El Elohe Israel had not told him to go to Mamre. Should he stay on at Bethel? But—everything was ready to move!

Rachel spoke to him again. "How far is Ephrath? Did you tell me?"

"Only a few miles." A few miles—so few that Jacob was about to decide it was not worth the risk involved, when he heard her softly laughing to herself.

"Why am I behaving so childishly? You would think I never had a baby before! Only a few miles . . . should not be too difficult. I'll take your advice; I'll close . . . my eyes . . . until we come to Ephrath."

"All right, my dearest. Then, when we get to Ephrath, if you don't want to travel further, we'll stay there until you deliver our child."

"Thank you, Jacob . . . I may . . . accept your offer . . . to stay at Ephrath . . . for a very long time. I don't . . . at the moment . . . share your desire to travel on . . . not . . . at all."

She drifted into light sleep, and Jacob walked to the head of the caravan, mounted his donkey and began to lead the string of camels in a slow walk down the worn caravan route. He hoped Rachel would sleep most of the day. He felt years older than he had earlier that morning. His elation had given way to a haunting uneasiness that made the fields of Mamre seem hopelessly remote.

Her birth pangs began as they approached Ephrath. Kerah sent a servant to tell Jacob. She ordered a small tent to be set up for Rachel and the supplies designated for just this emergency to be taken from the pack and carried to that tent immediately.

When Jacob reached her side, she was lying on a bed mat—pale, frightened, and in hard labor. Kerah was trying to sooth her, encourage her, and assist in the desperately difficult birth. With Kerah were three maidservants trained as midwives. Three times three would not have made any difference.

The mystical moment of birth came. Rachel screamed in

fear—fear of the strange way everything looked to her—fear because of her lack of any sensation of pain—fear because Kerah's voice sounded as if she were far away, calling from a cavernous valley.

Rachel could just make out Kerah's loving words as she strained to hear. She was saying, "Don't be afraid; you have another son!"

Another son—Jacob would be pleased.

She was pleased—but her fear remained. Her surroundings looked less and less familiar. She was not certain where she was.

She felt her strength ebbing rapidly. There still was no excessive pain—except for the stabbing sensation in her heart when she heard Kerah scream "Hemorrhage!" The scream sounded unreal to Rachel, like a shouted whisper.

She felt the weight of the infant as he was placed across her body, and with a great effort she raised her hand to caress him. Then she looked to where Jacob knelt beside her.

Once she had thought of giving this child a name that signified life, but now she could not do it. From the expression on Jacob's face she knew she was dying.

"I call . . . his . . . name . . . Ben-Oni, . . . son of my . . . sorrow." She accepted death, sorrowing for the years slipping away from her, yet comforted by the thought of a new son who would live after her.

Jacob would not demean her courage by offering false consolation; he would not promise that she would be all right after she had rested. Neither would he let her die with a name of sorrow in her thoughts.

"No, Rachel! Rachel, my beloved, . . . this is not a child to be called sorrow! He is beautiful; he will remind me of you each time I see him. I will call him Benjamin, . . . son of . . . my right hand."

Rachel closed her eyes. She smiled, then took Jacob's hand. Right hand held right hand—until one of the hands could grasp the other no longer.

The infant, sprawled on his mother's lifeless form, initiated the shrill cry of the mourners. Kerah swooped him up in her arms and drowned out his cry with her own. The midwives joined in, as did those waiting outside the tent. Soon the deafening wail—like the one at Bethel only a few days before—permeated the camp of Israel.

The only one in the camp who did not join in the wailing was the one who grieved the most.

Jacob asked Reuben and Judah to see to her burial that same day. When it was done, he set a pillar of stone on her grave to mark the place for all time. It was a tall, impressive pillar. Everyone who traveled the highway would see it and would know that the mother of the household of Israel was honored and beloved!

After days of mourning—days he spent alone in his tent—Israel sent for his sons and his chief servants. He stood up when they came, towering over them all—not in stature, but in inner strength and wisdom.

"It's time to move on. I'm in no hurry now to reach Mamre. We'll go only as far as the fields beyond Eder to make our next permanent camp.

"Eder has advantages for me. It's an easy journey from there to Hebron and Mamre, so I can visit my father often and even help Esau supervise things, if he wants me to. It would be unwise for me to move to Mamre, for Esau has even more livestock than I, and there would not be enough pasture or wells to support both camps."

He had gone over his plans with the men because it helped to firm them up in his own mind. He was satisfied with them; they seemed logical. "Yes, Eder will be the place for us to stay for the next months—until I make long-range plans for the future." He needed no affirmation, except from himself.

"We will leave two days from today, very early in the morning. Be ready."

Those two days were almost interminable for the one who, when he left Ephrath, could not take . . . . Would he ever be able to say her cherished name again?

Their quiet caravan left the campsite near Ephrath on the designated day. As Israel rode the lead donkey, he raised his eyes often from the road in front of him, searching the heavens; and his eyes were filled with tears that those who rode behind him never saw.

They passed Eder with its towering fortress and settled in grasslands a few miles to the south. Israel supervised setting up the camp, checking every detail.

Late that night his sons sat around a campfire, talking of their father who had retired to his tent. They spoke of his great loss—and of how he had been so grieved and yet had attended to the many things that had to be done.

Simeon agreed that his father had reacted to his bereavement bravely, but he laughed a bit cynically and said, "He likes to preach to us so well, I thought he would speak of the God of Bethel, who is with him in everything—even this."

Joseph waited; then with innate perception he looked at Simeon and said, "He did!"

Part Five

tested and
rewarded

Israel . . .
Mourning for Rachel,
Grieved by his family,
Bereft of his son,
Stunned into helplessness,
Trusting in Lord God,
Living his faith.

Israel . . . *tam*
Israel . . . chastened

Bewildered
Burdened

Israel . . . *tam*
Israel . . . tested

Hungering and thirsting
Led from the land

Israel . . . *tam*
Israel . . . rewarded

Victory!
Peace.

30

His brothers were jealous of him, but his father kept the matter in mind.
Genesis 37:11

*T*he grazing land of Eder was a comfortable place to live, and Jacob settled into a slower pace. His sons eagerly assumed the managing of his herds and flocks. They wanted a larger share in Jacob's holdings because they looked forward to families of their own. They would stay in the clan's pasturelands but would be more independent of their father after they married.

And so Jacob had more time for Joseph. Rachel had been foresighted; she knew her son well. He was suited to the life of a scholar, and he welcomed the almost daily sessions with his father. He had an interest in every field of knowledge that his father could share with him and even asked questions Jacob couldn't answer.

"You want to know more than I ever cared about, Joseph. It would be good if there were schools in Canaan where you could learn more . . . but to send you to Mesopotamia or Egypt . . . even to Damascus . . ."

"Out of the land?"

"Yes."

"I would never leave the land, Father, and I would not leave you. You've already taught me all I need to know for life here in Canaan. I like to work with figures, so I might be a merchant some day . . . or . . . maybe I'll finance caravans."

Joseph walked away from his father, thinking large thoughts. He never intended to become a shepherd.

They had been at Eder for nearly a year, and no word had

come from Isaac. Jacob knew his father would have heard about a chieftan who had taken a large amount of land in the area bordering on Hebron and had settled there, planting crops and stocking it heavily. He would have sent messengers to learn as much about him as possible, so he would have been aware of his son's nearness. It was evident that he and Esau still did not choose to welcome him home. But he was home—any place in Canaan was home!

Except for his lessons with Joseph he had little to occupy his time. He filled it with long walks and naps. He saw little Benjamin often. But there was a campfire every evening, and Israel used these times to teach his sons and some of the servants who came with them. He told the stories he loved—about the beginning of all things and how Elohim called His creation good. He told of mankind's misuse of the good creation—of Eden lost to Adam and Eve, of a whole world lost to a depraved generation. He spoke of Noah and new beginnings.

His voice showed special excitement when he related how God had worked since those new beginnings. He instilled a pride in his sons that the Semite people were descendants of Noah's son, Shem, and that they, as direct descendants of God's called out persons—Abraham, Isaac and Jacob—were a unique family in the Lord God's plan for all time. But lest they be filled with too great a feeling of importance, he reminded them that such favor also meant responsibility. For now that responsibility was to be His people in a heathen land. This called for more than morality; it called for holiness.

His sons listened but tended to remember only the part of his teachings they liked best. Sitting around the campfire, they could think with him about honor and goodness, but these virtues seemed less appropriate when they were not in their father's company. They were adapting to the coarse life of the shepherd, and their dreams for the future included little more than trips to exciting trading centers to sell wool and animals—and one day owning their own large flocks and herds.

Joseph had little in common with his brothers. They would have been bored with his studious life; he would have been uncomfortable if he had gone with them on their merchandising trips.

"You never mention my mother." Joseph's statement came suddenly, for no apparent reason, at the end of a geometry lesson.

"That doesn't mean I don't think of her."

"What do you think . . . when you think of her?"

"That she was a shining part of my life . . . everything a man would want—loving, faithful, beautiful, practical—a part of me."

"Why don't you talk about her sometimes?"

"Because I don't have the right words to describe her or how I feel about her or to tell how much I miss her."

Joseph saw tears in his father's eyes, and he was sorry he had mentioned Rachel, but he did need to talk about his mother with someone!

"Joseph, it's good to talk of her." Jacob didn't try to hide the tears that were stinging his eyes, but he was smiling. "Tell me what you remember about your mother."

Joseph burst into an emotional description of a woman who had laughed with him, talked with him, bandaged his cuts and bruises, taught him to care for lambs and sheep. Her beauty had not been lost on Joseph, who remembered her as far more lovely than the mothers of his half brothers. She had filled her son's life with humor and song and taught him to have an interested eye for wildflowers, trees, butterflies and clouds.

As Jacob listened to his son, his still grieving heart was filled with delight, because his beloved was remembered so eloquently.

"Joseph, the Lord God has been generous with us, giving us . . . Rachel . . . as wife and mother. And now, although she has died, He has left in our minds only the brightest memories of her."

Their sharing of their love for Rachel brought them into an even closer companionship than before. They did not talk of her often, but each was sure he loved the other more because they both loved her.

Conversations with his other sons were not always that pleasant. There was jealousy among them; each wanted the best pasture for his own flocks. There was also strife between them, as a group, and Joseph. They thought he should be out in the fields as they were.

"Are Rachel's sons better than we are? Neither Joseph nor Benjamin works in the fields!" was a definite concensus of their opinions.

"Benjamin is a baby yet!" Jacob's voice thundered as it had not for a long time. He was enraged. "And Joseph is learning things to complement your work with the flocks. He is not lazy or idle. We are a family, and I am the head of that family and will decide how work is apportioned!"

Later he regretted having spoken harshly, but he had experienced so many major difficulties in his life that now he could not abide having trivial jealousies threaten the tranquility left to him. He wanted his sons to live peaceably with each other. If they had grievances, he would talk with them and try to mediate, but his authority would not be threatened rudely, and they would not speak hatefully of Joseph in his presence without reprimand.

But to his angry sons, their problems were not trivial, and to them he seemed withdrawn from every interest except Joseph.

Reuben, eldest son of the household, seethed with a strong desire to confront his father with the fact that he would not be treated as merely a quarrelsome child; he was an adult! He had major responsibility for the flocks his father no longer supervised. He saw to the selling of wool and chose the marketplace.

Reuben's self-importance was exaggerated, but he could not recognize that. Once his mind was caught up in this heady combination of pride and self-pity, it fed on itself until he believed he actually was the head of the household and his father just a disinterested spectator.

One evening Reuben came in from the fields in an extreme state of frustration. As eldest son he should have some privilege. It seemed he had more work and responsibility—but no more privileges—than the others. He would not go on in this unfair situation any longer. He would assert himself—but how?

He knew he could not win an argument with his father. Jacob was logical and quick-witted, and when those assets were not enough, he had the additional point of being head of the clan—which meant the power to be arbitrary. He could stop working and refuse to take responsibility. But then his father would probably just put Judah in charge of things, and Reuben certainly didn't want that to happen!

If he couldn't defy his father by argument or renege on responsibilities without risking his place of prestige, how would he do it? An absurd idea came into Reuben's mind, but the more he thought about it, the less absurd it seemed. Should it be Zilpah or Bilhah?

To Israel there was a great difference between sorrow and trouble. Sorrow was painful but had with it a wistful sweetness and involved deep caring for someone. Trouble was painful, too, but it had an ugliness and brought with it deep resentment. Of the two, trouble was the harder to bear.

Judah told him about Reuben and Bilhah. He had the most to gain from the telling. With Simeon and Levi already in disgrace with their father—and now Reuben—Judah was next in line as the one his father would depend on. And yet when Judah told his father what had happened, he was not self-seeking; rather, he was assuming the role of the eldest—taking responsibility for something that had to be done. His father should know.

Israel received the news in silence and dismissed Judah from his tent with a wave of his hand. Then he followed a pattern his family had come to expect from him—he withdrew into solitude for the next few days. Israel never gave the impression that he was instantly comforted by God, but he always let his family know that in his times of extremity he turned in trust only to the One who had allowed the hard thing to touch his life, the One who knew the way out of the morass of grief and difficulty. El Elohe Israel knew the man He was perfecting. He let him become bored with grieving and disgusted with his own self-pity; then He enabled him to take up his life again with strength and purpose.

Israel decided to say nothing about the scandal that had shaken his household. By saying nothing he gained a victory. Reuben had lashed out against his father's disinterest only to find himself more totally ignored. His treasured responsibilities gradually were given to others. Any hope of his being the one to receive the birthright-blessing was gone.

Isaac's prolonged silence weighed more heavily on Jacob since he had settled near Eder. He decided the time had come to end the estrangement. He would wait no longer for an invitation; he would just go home.

A small camel train was prepared to go to Mamre. He would take none of his family and as few servants as possible. Since it could not be the grand homecoming he once planned, it would be an unostentatious one.

The reunion with his father was easier than he had thought it might be—unemotional but genial. Esau welcomed him with the proper cliches. No mention was made of Esau's interests in Seir, but he and Jacob decided the present situation was satisfactory. Esau would still live at home, and Jacob would remain at Eder, near enough to see his father often, yet far enough away to pose no threat to Esau's grasslands and water supply.

In the years that followed the households of Isaac, Esau and Jacob met infrequently but on good terms, honoring the importance of strong family ties.

Isaac died at the age of 180 years—five years longer than his father, Abraham, had lived but not nearly as long as their forefathers. Jacob and Esau buried Isaac, then made a peaceful settlement of things. Esau finally made his long-discussed move to the region of Mt. Seir, where he prospered even beyond his most vivid imagination.

And Jacob dwelt in the land he loved—in the part of that land he loved the best. Beersheba, Hebron and Mamre were again his neighborhood.

Israel now had come into possession of more than a claim to the land for his children; he had the box of sacred writings.

For many days he gave himself to prayer and writing, then prayer and rewriting—as the Spirit of Elohim led.

The Spirit comforted him as struggles and sorrows were brought to mind. The same Spirit enabled his heart to soar as he relived Bethel, Mahanaim and Peniel and as he wrote of the altar called El Elohe Israel.

Joseph had learned all his father could teach him and returned to tending sheep, but he spent many of his hours in the field reviewing the things he had learned. All his life he had an insatiable desire for knowledge.

His flocks were pastured with those of Bilhah and Zilpah's sons, so he shared their company from time to time. He felt a closer kinship to Dan and Naphtali than to his other brothers since their mother was his mother's handmaiden. Bilhah had looked after Joseph since Rachel's death, and he had great affection for her.

A good comradeship developed among the boys, and gradually they had conversations they did not share with just anyone—such as the story they told Joseph one day about Reuben and Bilhah. Joseph ran home, leaving his flocks in the care of his brothers—or to be lost or eaten by wolves. It really didn't matter. His heart, only beginning to mend from the loss of his mother, was broken again.

He ran to tell Jacob and found that he already knew. To Joseph, his father's awareness of this dark thing associated him with it. The boy's face contorted with disbelief and revulsion. Bilhah! And they all had known it except him. He wished he never had learned of it at all!

He went to his tent, laid on his mat, and was overcome with sobbing. He pounded the ground with clenched fists. In his frustration with everyone he had no one to turn to. Benjamin was too young, and the others didn't matter any more than his neglected sheep.

Israel watched the anger of his son and let it run its course. He longed to have Joseph live in a world without hurts, but it was impossible. The boy would have to learn to find his own source of comfort and renewal; it was part of growing up, and sometimes it took a lifetime.

Jacob sought to cheer his son by having a special coat made for him of the colorful material that Dinah wove. The robe had long sleeves, setting its wearer apart from the servants and from shepherds who wore only simple sleeveless tunics.

Joseph wore it proudly. His brothers, who had resented him before, began to hate him. They would have nothing to do with this boy who was so indulged by their father.

Joseph had no idea of the depth of their hatred, and he made an ill-advised attempt to get their attention. He had dreamed an unusual dream, had laughed at it, and wanted them to laugh with him. At the campfire one night he decided to tell it.

"Listen to the dream I had. We were binding sheaves in the field, and suddenly my sheaf rose and stood upright, and . . . you should have seen it . . . your sheaves gathered around and bowed to my sheaf."

To young Joseph it was a ridiculous picture; to his brothers it was another evidence of his arrogance. "Do you intend to reign over us and have power over us?" They had not laughed; instead they hated him all the more.

Joseph dreamed again, and at another campfire he described it—innocently sharing something too fantastic to keep to himself. "I dreamed again. This time the sun and the moon and 11 stars bowed to me!"

Again the brothers did not laugh. This tattler! This father's pet! This boastful 17-year-old child!

Even Jacob rebuked him for the suggestion that he was putting himself not only above his brothers, but also above his father and mother. He regarded it as impertinence.

Later in his own tent Israel could not sleep. He pondered what the meaning of his son's dreams might be. He remembered his own first prophetic dream at Bethel. Sometimes God did speak in dreams. Joseph, of all his sons, was the one who would be most responsive to God's claim on his life. Should he tell Joseph that the dream could be a message from God? He thought not. When God wanted to speak to a person, He spoke clearly enough so that no interpreter was needed. If God were speaking to Joseph, Joseph would know it.

Israel thought a long time about Joseph and the dreams, and he spent much of the night in prayer.

31

Then Jacob tore his clothes, put on sackcloth and mourned for his son many days.
Genesis 37:34

The barley was reaped without anyone seeing any sheaves bow. The harvest had not been as bountiful as usual, for the expected rains had not come to bring the crops to full maturity. Grasslands were withering; animals were becoming lean.

Jacob thought of the fields around Shechem; they would be the nearest ones that might provide help. There was no use going further into the Negev; it was even drier. The drought was widespread. Jacob supposed Esau already had left Seir to scout for temporary pasture, as he had the year of their meeting of reconciliation. Esau might even think of Shechem this time.

Shechem—Jacob flinched at the memory of its name. There might be some danger in sending his sons there, but it had been a long time since . . . since they were there before. He would send only his four older sons—Reuben, Simeon, Levi and Judah—and the servants they needed.

They took the assignment readily, glad to be away from home on an extended trip. But as they left for Shechem they grumbled, too.

"We have to go on long, hard assignments—but Joseph doesn't."

"We'll leave him to his easy life; but we won't bow to him as we go, or when we come back."

"Or ever!"

The brothers were gone a long time, many weeks beyond what Jacob had thought would be necessary. The local rains still had not come, so their stay would be even longer. He had been anxious about them ever since he chanced sending them to Shechem. He decided to convince them of his concern; he would send a message, not with a servant, but with his own beloved son.

Jacob instructed Joseph about the route to take and the safety precautions necessary. He gave him money for food and lodging on the way.

Joseph began his journey with a fear he would never admit but also with an obvious excitement. He started off at a pace Jacob knew he could not keep up for long. A short distance away he stopped, turned and waved. Then he turned back and hurried away, out of his father's sight.

When he arrived at Shechem, he learned that his brothers had been there some days before, but now had moved north to Dothan—15 miles further—15 more miles for tired feet to carry a tired body—many more hours with the haunting possibility of attack from robbers or wild animals. He wavered only a moment before getting up and starting out again, determined to finish what his father sent him to do.

He even managed a smile when he thought of how surprised his brothers would be to see him. They might even be proud of the way he had traveled so far—alone—just to bring word from their father.

The brothers thought they had been getting along quite well without interference from home. Shechem had been an interesting place, and now they were enjoying Dothan. They had no desire to hear from Jacob—or Joseph. They didn't want to return to their father's house until they were ready—rain or no rain.

Simeon and Levi were watching their flocks in the fields nearest the highway leading from Shechem to Dothan. Simeon looked toward the road and jumped to his feet in startled dismay. He saw a familiar figure coming across the wide field adjoining the pasture.

"Look! Here comes the dreamer!"

"No! Where?" Levi couldn't believe it was Joseph.

"There!"

Levi nodded his head slightly in the direction of the road and then turned so Joseph wouldn't know he had been seen. "Simeon, let's kill him!"

"Kill?" Simeon paled as he whispered the word. "Kill?" He asked again, for Levi had not answered his bewildered question.

"Yes . . . kill him." Levi's voice was lower now, with a heavy seriousness that replaced the spontaneity of his first outcry.

They were so intently plotting their conspiracy in the moments before Joseph came within the sound of their voices that they didn't hear Reuben approach from the opposite direction in time to hear the last of their conversation: ". . . and when we've killed him, we'll throw his body into a pit and say some wild animal ate him."

Levi's plan was so well thought out that Simeon wondered if he might have planned it before this present opportunity came. But Simeon gave instant consent, voicing a bit of sympathy for his unsuspecting brother: "And that will be the end of his dreams."

Reuben assessed the situation immediately. He, too, had seen Joseph coming across the field. He knew the limitless anger of Levi and Simeon and remembered that they had not backed away from murder years ago—mass murder! Reasoning with them would be useless, but he made one attempt to save his brother. He had to try, for Jacob would hold him—the eldest son—responsible for anything that happened to the boy.

Reuben's voice was bold. He wanted to control the situation if at all possible. "I heard you, and I see Joseph coming. We have only seconds to talk. Listen to me. Don't kill him. Why have the blood of our brother on our hands? Just put him in that pit you were talking about . . . and leave him."

It was too late to say any more, but Simeon and Levi nodded in agreement. They both turned and rushed at Joseph. Pouncing on him together, they ripped off the colorful robe they so despised. Together they carried the screaming boy to the abandoned well. With wild shrieks of victory they threw him into the pit.

Levi and Simeon thought their own plan would actually

have been kinder. Now in continual darkness Joseph would know the chilling discomfort of the muck and mire beneath him. He would go mad with terror. Thirst and starvation would torture him until his agony ended in death.

Reuben watched the attack begin, then turned his back and walked away from the passionate cries of his brutalized brother.

His reason for having Joseph put in the well was to spare him from instant death at the hands of his brothers. He felt the boy was safe for the moment, even though hurt and frightened. He needed time to think how he might rescue him and send him home to his father.

Simeon and Levi returned to where they thought Reuben would be waiting. He was not to be seen, but Judah was coming in from his section of the pastureland since it was noontime. Undershepherds watched the flocks while Jacob's sons customarily met at midday for a hearty meal.

"Where's Reuben?" Judah called to his brothers as he walked into easy conversation range.

"Probably took a walk to settle his stomach" Simeon grinned.

"Was he ill?" Judah was surprised; Reuben never was ill.

"I think so. He looked pale when he was here a few minutes ago. He'll be back."

The three began to open their scrips to take out lunch. They were hungry after a strenuous morning.

Simeon affected concern and said, "I wonder if our little brother is hungry."

"Little brother?" Judah could make no sense of that comment, and he already was uneasy about the unsatisfactory explanation of Reuben's absence. He stopped eating, looked at his brothers and waited for an answer that would not hedge the issue.

Simeon pointed to a crumpled, colorful robe lying beside a nearby thorn bush. It was badly torn and covered with dirt.

Levi poured out a barrage of information. "Joseph came a while ago, We don't know why he came. Simeon clamped his mouth shut before he said a word. When we get home, we will find out any exciting news he was sent to tell us. We can wait. Joseph will not go back with us. He's in that abandoned well on the other side of the field, and there's no way for him to get out. . . . We haven't shed his blood; we'll just let him die."

Judah didn't finish his lunch. Now he knew why Reuben had felt ill.

Caravans were a common sight from the field where the men ate lunch; the one passing just then gave Judah an idea. He was excited but began to speak in a matter-of-fact way: "What profit is it to us if we kill our brother, even without shedding his blood? If we want him gone, we could sell him to those Ishmaelites in that fine caravan over there and send him off to wherever they are going."

Simeon and Levi looked at the caravan and Judah saw that they were considering his suggestion favorably. He made his case more convincing. "The caravaneer won't let him get away. We'll never see him again."

His brothers were silent, thinking it over.

Judah continued, "Let's not be responsible for his death; he is our brother."

Judah was persuasive. They would be . . . generous. They would get him out of the well so he could live—as a slave. No one would bow down to a slave!

Judah took it on himself to see if he could sell a good-looking, strong, healthy, well-educated boy! He began crossing the expanse between their site and the road with long strides.

Levi and Simeon ran back to the well and tossed in a rope, calling to Joseph to grab hold. They pulled him out of his dark, damp cell through the small opening at the mouth of the well. He blinked hard as he climbed out into the sunlight.

The sobbing Joseph bowed to them and thanked them for letting him live. He had never known that anguish like he had felt in the past hour was possible as he faced torment and death. His crying subsided, and he tried to give them their father's message.

"Be still, Joseph! We don't want to hear anything you have to say. You're free from the well, but do you see that caravan along the highway over there? You are going to be part of it—if they will have you."

They would have him. A full-grown man brought 30 pieces of silver, but for just a boy, even an educated one, they would pay only 20. The brothers thought it was a fair bargain; they had more than if they had not been so kind and let the boy live.

The caravan had come from Gilead, laden with spices, balm and myrrh for Egyptian markets. Now added to their merchandise was one handsome, black-haired boy whose face was covered with mud and tears.

Joseph pled with his brothers not to sell him and struggled as his owners pulled his arms behind his back and tied his wrists with strong rope. The lad, whose feet were bruised, cut and tired from his long walk from Mamre, would have more suffering and exhaustion as his traveling companions.

When the brothers returned to their campsite, Reuben was there pacing aimlessly, his face ashen. "The boy is not there! Where could he be? How could he get out of that well?" His face registered panic.

He was told what had happened. Almost in shock, he reached for his share of the 20 pieces of silver. Then he killed a young kid of a goat, and as the others watched, he dipped Joseph's wonderful coat into its blood. With that grisly evidence, they could convince their father that Joseph was killed and eaten by wild animals.

Jacob tore his clothes, put on sackcloth, and mourned for Joseph for many days. His sons tried to comfort him, but he refused to be comforted. Perhaps the hypocrisy of their sympathy only added to his agonizing desolation of spirit.

32

> When Jacob learned that there was grain in Egypt, he said to his sons, "Why do you just keep looking at each other?" He continued, "I have heard that there is grain in Egypt. Go down there and buy some for us, so that we may live and not die."
>
> *Genesis 42:1-2*

*t*wenty-two tumultuous years had passed since Jacob buried the battered, many-colored coat on a hill overlooking his campsite. Through those years he had seen his wealth—as well as sorrow and trouble—increase. Leah had died and had been laid in the tomb of Machpelah, along with Sarah and Abraham, Isaac and Rebekah. Jacob regretted that Rachel's tomb was so far away; yet it was appropriate for her to have a singular place in death to correspond to the singular place she still had in Jacob's heart. Bilhah and Zilpah also had died and were buried in an oak grove, their places designated by stone markers. Judah's sons, Er and Onan, had met untimely deaths. The sound of mourning rose often from the tents of Jacob.

Heavier than the sorrow of the deaths were the crushing burdens of trouble Jacob's family kept bringing to him. The aging patriarch was numbed by grief over Judah's marriage to the daughter of Shua the Canaanite and even more over Judah's illicit relationship with Tamar—his own daughter-in-law.

Jacob could not forget the disgrace Reuben, Simeon, Levi—and then Judah—had brought to the family. He could not free himself from almost continual despair over the loss of Joseph. But beyond all this was the gnawing apprehension that the Lord God might not find even one of his sons fit to be used as His channel of ultimate blessing. He petitioned El Shaddai, who had turned Sarah's physical barrenness into the ability to bear a son, to remake his sons into the likeness He would have them be.

In optimistic moments Jacob considered that the Lord God might choose Benjamin. His life had not yet been marked with blatant sin, and his father prayed it would never be. Benjamin's problem was his aggressive nature, lashing out at what he was afraid of, grabbing for what he wanted. But the boy was still young—he could change.

He looked for signs that Benjamin would develop a desire to read and memorize the sacred writings as Joseph had. He hoped his youngest son would want to learn all the things he had taught Joseph. He never shared the deep companionship with Benjamin that he had with Rachel's first son, but he still had spent many happy days with him. Jacob let his mind drift to times they walked the fields around their home, inspected flocks, took trips into Hebron and sometimes went as far as Beersheba to market. Benjamin was full of the zest and lightheartedness of youth. Thinking of him brought a smile to Jacob's face; the boy was Rachel's legacy of joy to him in his old age. He was the son of his right hand. If their father now favored Rachel's younger son, even the 10 remaining brothers did not censure him.

Israel had stopped hoping for a bright happy life, but his God did give him the strength to battle desperation with a marvelous degree of victory. Even the piercing heart wound of being bereft of Joseph was not without its beautiful memories that covered the hurt like a rich tapestry. No amount of distress that had come to be associated with the name of Joseph could erase the priceless memories in which the beloved son still lived.

Israel never thought it important to pretend to be happy when faced with torrents of grief. He never looked for easy answers as to why the Lord God allowed him to be deluged with desolating circumstances. His family never heard him cry out against his God, but his soul-wrenching cry for "El Elohe Israel" was familiar to them.

It had been a very long time since he had seen Him, but he continually reminisced about Bethel, Peniel and Succoth. He always was delighted that the remembrances of those meetings were as sharp and as spiritually enabling as if they had just happened. If the world wondered at the immense adversities that came to Israel, it wondered more at his source of comfort that strengthened him to take each day as it came.

He had been using his staff more often, not to lean on—for his leg had healed years ago—but as a tangible reminder that he was supported by the God who had wrestled with him at Peniel. At times the wrestling continued, as well as the blessing.

Some who knew Jacob-Israel thought he was foolish to worship a God who would allow suffering. Some thought he must be evil to have all these things happen to him. Some ridiculed him; he made no sense to them at all. He was a man to laugh at, to make jokes about.

Jacob had no one to turn to when he knew fear, depression, pain, anger or sorrow. He had no one to encourage him when he couldn't feel the inner support of faith or hope. But throughout his life he called to El Elohe Israel. The calling was believing, and the believing gave him enabling strength to call again until he was brought back into communion with the Lord God.

He had seen God! He could never be totally overcome with doubt or discouragement, no matter what things defied his human reasoning. Elohim, El Elyon, El Olam, El Shaddai—the living, ever-present One was with him as He said He would be.

To know God was with him was enough, not to dispel all the melancholy of his realistic facing of problems, but to superimpose on that melancholy the joy and peace of mind that nothing or no one—not even Jacob himself—could annihilate.

Now there was this famine! Jacob could not take it as a personal misery, for it was bringing down the entire land of Canaan into threatened starvation. This year the spring rains had not come, nor the fall rains. The dews in the mornings had been light. Canaan was not a country of large storehouses of grain. Pasture grass was fragile when moisture was scant. People went from plenty to dire need rapidly as crops failed and cattle grew lean.

Jacob had a new understanding of why his grandfather had gone to Egypt even in the absence of his God's permission to leave the land. Seeing the suffering around him—his own grandchildren without enough to eat—he thought of going there, too. He tried to push such a presumptuous action from his mind, choosing to wait on God for specific direction—or for rains. Neither came.

With all his wealth he could not buy enough food for his large household in Canaan, but there was abundant grain in Egypt. Everyone talked of that source of supply, and those who could outfit a caravan or travel along with one had already been there to purchase all they could afford. Jacob could not understand the Lord God's silence, but he would not leave Mamre without His instructions to go. He began to wonder if it would be practical to send his sons. They had made unfortunate marriages and had become entangled in immorality in Canaan. Could they fare worse in Egypt?

33

Pharaoh gave Joseph the name Zaphenath-Paneah and gave him Asenath daughter of Potiphera, priest of On, to be his wife.   *Genesis 41:45*

It had been a long time since Jacob called his 10 sons to a family council; Benjamin was not yet included in these sessions. When they arrived at his tent, they found him looking less anxious than in a long time. He didn't waste a minute in telling them why. "I'm sending you to Egypt for food!"

The 10 were silent. The four older sons cringed inwardly at the mention of Egypt. The younger ones, knowing their presence was tolerated but their opinions not requested, had instant thoughts of food, travel and the excitement of a foreign land.

Jacob had expected a response other than this silence. He roared at them, "Why do you just keep looking at each other?"

They still made no answer. Jacob could not fathom the expressions on his son's faces—but they often puzzled him. He shrugged off their reaction to the thought of food from Egypt as another of their behaviors he would never understand. He would be patient. He would explain further.

"You must have heard that anyone who has the money can buy grain in Egypt. I have enough gold and silver to buy all that our pack animals can carry. You *will go* to buy food for us, so that we may live." His plan, at first detailed in quieter tones, reached a crescendo as he ordered them to go.

As though they were still children, they were intimidated by their father when he shouted orders—and they were concerned about their hungry wives and children. They undertook the immediate work of outfitting a caravan of empty carts and saddle bags, then left for Egypt within three days of Jacob's command.

In all their preparations, Benjamin's name never was mentioned; it was mutually understood he would stay home with his father. The older sons preferred it that way. They did not want to be responsible for him. If anything happened to Benjamin while he was with them, they never could face their father.

While his sons were gone, they were seldom out of Jacob's thoughts. He prayed for them, trusting that they would be safe and successful and could return with food before the hunger pangs of their children became much more severe. There was one thing he was certain of—he would never send Benjamin to search for them, no matter how long they stayed.

While they were gone, Jacob resumed supervision of his herds and flocks. He saw to it that they were moved as little as possible to conserve their strength, and then only to areas that would make moving them most worth while. Day by day he was confronted with burnt pasture land, dying animals, discouraged servants, shepherds and overseers—and his hungry, anxious household. But he felt more fortunate than many of the others in the land; his sons were coming with sacks of grain for bread and for feeding his animals—and he had wealth enough to replace his stock when the long drought ended.

It was the shout Jacob was waiting to hear! The guard at the outpost let the camp know that the caravan had been spotted and would soon arrive at their camp. Jacob eagerly prepared to meet them; wives and children ran out along the road—each trying to be first to sight their loved one. There were warm greetings. Choice tidbits of dried grapes, cheese and olives were proudly pulled from saddle bags and given to hungry girls and boys. The excited entourage was nearly back to the campsite when above the happy voices rose a terrifying scream from the wife of Simeon, standing with her children as the caravan moved past them. Simeon was not there.

Jacob's initial joy at seeing the lifesaving caravan was cut short. Simeon! He went back to his tent without asking for an explanation. He would let his other sons enjoy their homecoming and allow Simeon's family their private grief. In due time, after his sons came to him with the story of what had happened, he would go to the tent of Simeon with such comfort as he could give.

What Jacob heard from his sons was so strange that he knew they never could have made it up, and they would have no reason to purposely tell such an incredible tale. He sent them away, then went over in his mind all they had said.

They had gone to the store city of Menofer and had found the granary. They took their place in the line of people from many countries. They arrived at the store house at the same time as the renowned Zaphenath-Paneah, second in command to Pharaoh.

They described him to their father as a younger man than they, clean-shaven like the other Egyptians, dressed in fine linen. He had a ponderous gold chain around his neck and wore a jeweled signet ring. They had seen him step from his ornate chariot and watched as he walked rapidly toward the treasury where commercial transactions were handled. As he glanced at Jacob's sons, he slowed his pace, looking at them intently. He asked them through an interpreter who they were and where they came from.

Following the customary procedure before speaking to the ruler, even through an interpreter, they bowed before him with their faces to the ground. Then they answered that they were from Canaan and had come to buy food.

The grand vizier said he did not believe them and accused them of being spies. Although it was difficult because they were not able to speak directly to him, they assured their mediator that they were part of a family of 12 sons, one of whom was at home with his father—and one was dead.

Zaphenath-Paneah listened to the interpretation and asked about their father's health and well-being. The brothers had taken it as an attempt to seem less curt and ominous than he had up until that time. They were pleased to tell him that their father was well. They hoped it would end the interview on a pleasant note.

Instead, the words of the man became more harsh. He was

still certain that they were spies. The only way he would be convinced they were not lying would be if they proved their story by bringing to him the younger brother they claimed was at home. And he was keeping Simeon hostage until they returned with Benjamin.

Jacob tried to find reality in the story. He could not, and an additional fact further unnerved him—the money for the grain had been placed inside their sacks. His sons discovered it long after they left Menofer when they opened the sacks to feed their animals. It was all utterly incomprehensible. Jacob saw no reason to send Benjamin to such a capricious man as Zaphenath-Paneah.

As his sons argued with him about returning at once with Benjamin to free Simeon and bring him back to his family, Jacob only became more defensive. "You have deprived me of my children. Joseph is no more and Simeon is no more, and now you want to take Benjamin. Everything is against me!"

They were all very tired; emotions were volatile. Jacob told his sons they would speak more about the matter in the morning. He lay awake for long hours, at times wondering how he could leave Simeon hostage—how he could ever send Benjamin into possible danger—at times being comforted by the thought of 10 sons at home and the certainty of food for his large household and his animals in the coming months. He would decide the difficult problems in the morning. It had been a long, confusing day. Sleep was finally welcome.

It had been many years since Zaphenath-Paneah had dreamed his boyhood dreams. He had watched for his brothers for a long time, knowing that as the famine continued, they would join the Canaanites who crossed the desert wilderness to fill their sacks from Egypt's abundant supplies. He felt certain they would come to the granary at Menofer; it was the first one on the direct route from Beersheba.

He was surprised that his brothers had changed so little in appearance. He might have overlooked any one or even two of them, but he could not have missed all 10 together. He didn't wonder that they had not recognized him, for there was a vast change from a 17-year-old boy to a 40-year-old man. Besides that, he dressed and spoke as an Egyptian, and he most certainly was not a slave!

He had no intention of revealing his identity until he learned what kind of men they had turned out to be—and until he had an opportunity for a mild revenge. The plan to accuse them of being spies could provide for both.

It had been difficult to keep the composure of a grand vizier as Joseph watched his brothers bow down to him, tell of their father and younger brother at home, then agree to let one of them remain in Egypt as a hostage. It had been even more difficult to keep his emotions under control when, pretending not to understand Hebrew, he heard the older brothers talking among themselves about "surely being punished because of our brother." They had discussed this at length, and for the first time Joseph knew that Reuben had prevented his instant death.

Such potent memories rushed in on him that the mighty ruler of Egypt turned from the men from Canaan to weep. Then he turned back to them and ordered Simeon bound and put in prison to await their return—with Benjamin.

Joseph had first decided to take Reuben, the eldest and therefore the most responsible, as hostage, but on hearing of Reuben's part in saving his life that terrible day, Joseph passed over him and took the next eldest, Simeon. He could still almost feel Simeon's hands as they had ripped his coat and with Levi's help had dragged him to the deep well. For months afterward when he closed his eyes to sleep, he would jump up, startled by a remembered sensation of that violent fall into the dark, clammy shaft.

Joseph was not surprised that his brothers also relived that traumatic day in their own memories now that they were in the land of his bondage—and forced to leave another brother there.

After they had begun their journey back to Canaan, Joseph wondered how soon they would return with Benjamin. He was suddenly overcome with longing to see his father; he should have ordered his father brought to Egypt, too. Possibly he would come anyway. He would be filled with curiosity about the unusual treatment his sons were receiving. Joseph smiled as he thought about the money they would find in their sacks. He didn't need their money. He had thought of putting 20 pieces of silver into each sack but decided that might give away his identity too soon. Instead, he simply ordered the full price of the grain returned by dividing it equally and placing it under the closure of each man's saddle bag.

Now he would wait for their return to work out the rest of his plan for testing them.

The morning sun wakened Jacob; Reuben was already waiting to speak with him. "Father, have you decided how soon we can go to Egypt with Benjamin?"

Receiving no immediate answer, Reuben became agitated. "You may put both of my sons to death if I don't bring him back. Trust Benjamin to me!"

Jacob's eyes flashed. Could Reuben think that killing two other boys might alleviate the grief of losing Benjamin? Reuben spoke so easily about the lives of others! When Jacob answered his son, he was more adamant than before. "My son will not go down there with you; his brother is dead, and he is the only one left of Rachel's children. If harm comes to him on the journey you are taking, you will bring my gray head down to the grave in sorrow."

His decision was based on more than choosing between sons. He did not trust the Egyptian who made wild accusations and requests and could imprison anyone at his whim. He might never release Simeon even if they took Benjamin there. He might already have executed Simeon as a spy, and next time all the brothers might be detained—or killed! Jacob flatly refused Reuben's demand. He would comfort and care for Simeon's family, but he could not compromise what he decided was best for his own family.

The famine continued to be severe. The rains did not come, and the need for Egypt's grain became more acute the following year. Jacob faced a dilemma. They could not eat, nor could their animals survive, unless they had large quantities of cereal grain from Egypt. But he could not send his sons back there unless Benjamin went along.

There were no words to convey his tangled thoughts to his

God. He knelt in silence and became more aware of His presence. Then God's plain, quiet man softly called His names—Elohim, El Shaddai, El Olam, El Elyon, El Bethel, El Elohe Israel. Jacob's inadequacy was overshadowed by Adequacy. There was power and peace in those names.

Early in the morning Jacob called for his sons. Nine men faced him, and he knew each one was ready to be off to Egypt. "Go again to Egypt and buy us food."

Judah spoke to him, gently and firmly. "You do remember the terms under which we must go back. We have to take Benjamin."

"Why did you even tell the man you had a brother at home?"

"Because he questioned us specifically about our family." Judah knew that his father was not seeking information but only trying to delay for even another minute before giving reluctant approval for the young man to go. Judah spoke again, attempting to allay a portion of his deep fears. "Entrust Benjamin to me. I'll guarantee his safety."

Jacob smiled and put his hands on Judah's shoulders. At least Judah offered himself—not his children as Reuben had done. Both he and Judah knew what he must say, but Judah summed it up for him to bring the matter to a close.

"Father, we must go. Our food supplies for our families and for our cattle and sheep and goats and camels and donkeys have never been this dangerously low. We could have made two trips by now if we had not delayed."

Jacob gave the inevitable permission. Since they had to go, he had planned how they could make as good an impression as possible on Zaphenath-Paneah. "If it must be, do this: Take the best fruits we have gleaned from the land, and give them to the man in Egypt; take some of our store of spices and myrrh, containers of pistachio nuts and almonds. And take double money with you, as payment for the grain you go to get now and as repayment for the silver you found in your sacks. We are not beggars!"

His sons did not move. They were still awaiting the expressed permission for Benjamin to go with them, and Jacob knew it. He took a deep breath, swallowed hard, and in a steady voice said, "Take your brother also. Go quickly!"

He raised his hands to heaven and prayed for the Lord God to give them mercy before Zaphenath-Paneah and to allow both Simeon and Benjamin to return with the others. Not with doubt or cynicism, but in a surrender of himself, his possessions, and his sons to whatever God would ordain, he added in a strong voice, "If I am bereaved, I am bereaved."

The brothers made the caravan ready. They loaded their gifts for the Egyptian ruler and the double silver payment into strong sacks. They left the camp of Jacob. He watched them go. He did not smile, but there were no tears.

34

[Judah said,] "Now then, please let your servant remain here as my lord's slave in place of the boy, and let the boy return with his brothers."

Genesis 44:33

*T*hey halted their caravan for a few days at Beersheba, the last city on Canaan's side of the highway through the desert. They purchased such additional supplies as they could, but found little for sale. Any merchant in Beersheba with goods to sell could name his price. With the drought spread over more of the land this year than the year before, the number of camel trains bound for Egypt seemed to have doubled. Many who had previously scrounged out an existence now resorted to banding together with others if necessary to get to the storehouses of Egypt.

Benjamin had not traveled further than to Beersheba in his life and then only in the company of his father. His thoughts of the trip ahead of him were exciting. His innate optimism and his youth kept him from thinking the fearful thoughts that beleaguered his companions.

Zaphenath-Paneah knew that the family of Jacob would return soon. Simeon was still in custody, and they would want him back. In addition, by now the grain from last year's trip would be gone. He alerted his men at various granaries to watch for them and let him know when they arrived.

The anticipated day had come. The grand vizier of Egypt was torn between a natural craving for revenge and persistent persuasion toward forgiveness.

He ordered the brothers to be brought to his house before he had sorted out his feelings—before he knew what course he would take with them. The setting would be a banquet. He instructed his chief steward to have an animal slaughtered and a grand meal prepared.

The brothers approached the palace of Zaphenath-Paneah in cold fear, certain that they would be charged with stealing the silver the year before. When the steward met them at the door of the house, they hurriedly tried to explain their situation. "Please, sir, we came down here the first time to buy food. But at the place where we stopped for the night we opened our sacks and each of us found his silver—the exact weight—in the mouth of his sack. So we have brought it back with us. We have also brought additional silver with us to buy food. We don't know who put our silver in our sacks."

The steward listened patiently to their story, then told them not to be concerned. Their God and the God of their father had given them the silver, and they had done well to return it. He was repeating the words his master had told him to say, but he was as bewildered by them as were the men who stood in front of him.

Then the brothers caught sight of Simeon being escorted to join them. He looked well. There was a brief, emotional salutation and much embracing. Then they were all taken into the house and given water to wash their feet. Servants took their donkeys away to give them fodder.

They were told Joseph would arrive at noon. Meanwhile they could rest. They shared with Simeon the experiences of the past year, and together they wondered what would happen next. They thought nothing could surprise them any more. They prepared the special gifts their father had sent for the Egyptian and looked forward to the noon hour with some apprehension.

Their host received them in the grand hall before the meal was spread. The awed men in varying degrees of fear bowed before him. One sheaf stood tall, looking at 11 who bowed—the dream fulfilled.

Joseph received their gifts without comment, but in them he saw the largess of a man who would be no man's debtor, and he marveled at his father's generous gift in a time of stark deprivation.

Still through an interpreter and standing at a distance from his brothers, he asked, "How is your aged father you told me about? Is he still living?"

Some of the brothers exchanged wary glances as if asking each other why this man would ask of their father's health with such concern. If three or four of them had a slight intimation of the reason, they kept it to themselves lest they be thought crazed by guilt.

Addressed as a group, each hesitated to be the one to answer, but soon they offered information individually.

"Yes, he is still alive."

"Your servant, our father, is well."

Then, not knowing what to say next in the awkward silence that followed their brief answers, Judah bowed again, and all the brothers followed his example.

The mysterious one looked steadily at Benjamin and asked, "Is this your youngest brother—the one you told me about?"

Without waiting for their answer, which he really did not need, he spoke again. His interpreter gave his words accurately but not with the choke that had been in his master's voice. He said, "God be gracious to you, my son." Of which God, the sons of Jacob wondered, did this Egyptian speak?

His words had been gentle enough, but his attitudes remained enigmatic. At one moment he seemed intimately concerned about their welfare and that of their father; in the next he turned and ran from the room as though offended. They wanted nothing more than to be allowed to load their animals and get away from this unsettling personage.

It never could have occurred to them that the ruler of Egypt had run to his own chamber for solitude to weep tears he had waited for years to shed. There had been an abundance of the earlier tears of anguish and bitterness; these were of joy and of release from resentment. Seeing his brothers again—especially Benjamin—and hearing that his father was alive and well, he felt years of separation melt away.

The grand vizier, now radiant, rejoined his guests. His tears had cleansed away the last vestiges of animosity toward his brothers, and he had washed his face to cleanse away the precious tears.

He ordered the meal to be set on the tables in the dining hall. According to custom, Zaphenath-Paneah sat at a table by himself. There were separate tables spread for the guests— one for the Egyptians and one for the Hebrews. The Egyptians ate different fare and considered the Hebrews drab shepherds. They wondered at their presence at the banquet.

The Hebrews wondered even more, for they were seated in exact chronological order. Reuben was in the place of honor as eldest; Benjamin was at the opposite end of the table. But the youngest wasn't slighted; he was given five times as much as anyone else.

By now Jacob's sons expected the unusual. The food and wine put them in a genial mood, and they actually became relaxed in the presence of their host. But at times each one wondered if the others had noticed the resemblance of this handsome man at the head table to a 17-year-old boy they remembered every day of their lives.

Joseph listened carefully to the talk at the Hebrews' table. He was amused at their confusion and at their delight in the excellent food and wine. He was impressed that they didn't resent Benjamin's receiving the greater portion of food, but only teased him about it in good humor. It was a small indication that their attitude toward this son of Rachel was different from the attitude they had toward him. But it was not enough proof. He had another test for them, a difficult one. Watching them enjoying each other's company at the table, he believed they would pass it, but he had to be sure.

The food had been eaten, and the wine glasses were empty. Joseph motioned to his serving men that the glasses were not to be refilled. He abruptly dismissed his guests and sent for his steward to come to him at once. His instructions increased the steward's amazement at his master's handling of this family from Canaan.

The next morning the 11 brothers were on their way home; they left Menofer at daybreak. As they rode, each thought deeply of the strange things that had happened, trying to find a shred of meaning in it all.

They were two hours away from the city when Joseph gave the signal for his men to move; it was time for the final test. It was an easy matter for swift riders to overtake the plodding caravan. The brothers were filled with terror as Egyptian soldiers surrounded them; they were formally charged with theft. The priceless divination cup belonging to Zaphenath-Paneah was missing and was believed to be in one of the sacks in the captured caravan.

Each of the men had his own reaction to the charges.

"God forbid that we would do such a thing!"

"Before, when money was planted in our sacks, we brought it back. Why would we do that if we were going to steal it again?"

"Search the packs on all our animals!"

"Yes! Search! And whoever has the cup—kill him."

"You not only can kill the culprit, but you can take the rest of us as slaves if you find the cup in our caravan!"

The brothers' boasts were testimonies of their confidence in each other. The steward who had accompanied the soldiers smiled at their bravado and calmly said that the guilty one alone would be punished; he would be taken as a slave. The rest would be free to go home.

Each man quickly brought his sacks to the steward for inspection, each certain that his own would not contain the missing cup. They were annoyed at the delay and longed to be far enough down the road to Canaan to be beyond the reach of the unpredictable grand vizier.

Very deliberately, each sack was opened and searched. In each one was found the pieces of silver that previously had been paid at the granary. The steward disregarded this; they could keep their silver. He was looking for the heavily jeweled cup that his master treasured. It was found in Benjamin's sack.

Benjamin stood with his hands pulled behind his back; his wrists were roughly tied by a rope. The steward held the end of the rope as Benjamin was made to walk along beside his camel back into Menofer.

The steward called back to the panic-stricken men standing by the side of the road: "Stay there in the sun if you want to, but it will do no good; you might as well be on your way home. You are free."

Free? Haunted by the memory of another brother who had

walked beside a camel, tied as a slave? Free? Faced with taking news of Benjamin's fate to their father whom they already had crushed with grief too many times—and that one time in a very particularly permanent way? They had been prisoners of their conscience; now they were prisoners of their caring—for Benjamin and for their father. In the ritual of sorrow they tore their clothes.

Reuben, having so easily volunteered the lives of his children if anything happened to Benjamin, felt wild trembling in his heart. He was inconsolable. Simeon and Levi sat immobile in the dust of the road, their faces revealing the remorse that had haunted them for so long.

Judah, the last of the four who had a part in the despicable selling of their brother, reloaded his donkey, mounted it, and turned it toward Menofer. As he began inching toward the city on his indifferent animal, each of his brothers followed.

Reuben had turned over the responsibility for the rest of the caravan to his own steward with instructions to go on home with the desperately needed food. They would follow as soon as possible or would try to send word of what happened.

Judah led the men to the palace where so recently they had feasted. They were given immediate admittance to see the grand vizier. He masked his joy and pride in them with a final challenge.

"What have you done? Did you think I wouldn't know about your theft?"

Judah had spent time on the way back to town asking the God of his father to help him know what to say. He was given an eloquence he never had before and would never have again. To his words was added his genuine humility. He was past the point of offering excuses or reasons for their problem—past the point of denying the guilt of Benjamin or of any of them. He simply pleaded for mercy.

Please, my lord, let your servant speak a word to my lord. Do not be angry with your servant, though you are equal to Pharaoh himself. My lord asked his servants, "Do you have a father or a brother?" And we answered, "We have an aged father, and there is a young son born to him in his old age. His brother is dead, and he is the only one of his mother's sons left, and his father loves him."

Then you said to your servants, "Bring him down to me so I can see him for myself." And we said to my lord, "The boy cannot leave his father; if he leaves him, his father will die." But you told your servants, "Unless your youngest brother comes down with you, you will not see my face again." When we went back to your servant my father, we told him what my lord had said.

Then our father said, "Go back and buy a little more food." But we said, "We cannot go down. Only if our youngest brother is with us will we go. We cannot see the man's face unless our youngest brother is with us."

Your servant my father said to us, "You know that my wife bore me two sons. One of them went away from me, and I said, 'He has surely been torn to pieces.' And I have not seen him since. If you take this one from me too and harm comes to him, you will bring my gray head down to the grave in misery."

So now, if the boy is not with us when I go back to your servant my father and if my father, whose life is closely bound up with the boy's life, sees that the boy isn't there, he will die. Your servants will bring the gray head of our father down to the grave in sorrow. Your servant guaranteed the boy's safety to my father. I said, "If I do not bring him back to you, I will bear the blame before you, my father, all my life!"

Now then, please let your servant remain here as my lord's slave in place of the boy, and let the boy return with his brothers. How can I go back to my father if the boy is not with me? No! Do not let me see the misery that would come upon my father.

35

"I'm convinced! My son Joseph is still alive."   *Genesis 45:28*

Before Judah's plea had ended, it was answered in Joseph's heart. But for the moment the two men faced each other in a room grown suddenly quiet.

Joseph stared at the unexpected gentleness on Judah's face and heard the compassion in his voice. His hands, which had tensely gripped the arms of his great throne chair while Judah spoke, now relaxed. He smiled slightly but still hid his unspeakable joy. Judah had become a marvelously new person. He cared enough about a brother to take on himself the heavy life sentence from which his own innocence would have exempted him. In a precious way Judah now seemed closer to him than his full brother.

Joseph drew his eyes from Judah and looked at his other brothers, who were silently standing behind Judah, demonstrating a support Joseph would not have imagined them capable of having. He needed no further proof of what kind of men his brothers had become. He had no wish to test them further. He was losing control of the pent up emotions in his heart, but this time he would not run to hide his tears. He ordered everyone out of the room except the sons of Jacob-Israel. Then he wept unashamedly, so loudly that the eavesdropping Egyptians had no trouble hearing him.

Then to his astounded audience he said, "I am Joseph!"

The brothers heard the words they had dared to hope for from time to time as they thought they noticed something familiar in this man. They had never experienced such sharp, sudden joy before. But after the first burst of elation, some became terrified. Guilt was still their taskmaster.

Joseph asked again, because he wanted to hear the answer again, "Is my father still alive?"

"He . . . lives." Judah's eloquence had ebbed; he now could scarcely voice the two words.

Joseph stepped down from the platform where he had sat while he listened to Judah. Since his brothers were still stunned into speechlessness by surprise, fear, relief and joy, he would speak to them.

In words they would treasure forever Joseph told them not to be angry with themselves any longer for what they had done to him because God had gloriously used it for good. He was in a place, because of God's leading, from which he could save the house of Jacob from starvation.

He told them of God's revelation that the famine was worldwide and would continue for an unprecedented five more years. He offered them and their families the security of Egypt's fertile countryside called Goshen. And he did want them to bring Jacob—right away.

Joseph wanted to say much more, but his voice was giving way to sobs of gladness as this fellowship with his brothers swept away his homesickness and yearning for his people. They were more his family than ever before. He embraced Benjamin and wept, and Benjamin, usually embarrassed at any public display of affection, wept with him. Then Joseph turned to each of his brothers, and the weeping continued as he kissed each one.

The Egyptians listening at the door had heard enough to merit a quick visit to Pharaoh to tell him Joseph's story. They all, including Pharaoh, rejoiced at this great good fortune in the life of one they had come to love as their own—one who had saved Egypt from starvation and was building up the treasury to unbelievable heights.

Nothing was too good for Joseph—or for his family—if their coming would make him happy. Pharaoh gave the matter serious thought, and by the time Joseph came to tell him of the reunion and of his wish to have his family move to Egypt, Pharaoh was ready with an entire program to be put into effect at once.

The 11 brothers were to load up their donkeys again and go

back to Canaan. They should be given ample provision for their trip, including changes of clothing for each man. Benjamin, because of his closeness to Joseph, was to be given 300 pieces of silver and five changes of clothes.

As they went back home they were to take as many empty wagons as necessary to effect their move to Egypt, but they were not to bring any furniture along. That would be provided from the merchandise of Egypt. They should move only their personal possessions and their most valuable items. When they returned from Canaan, they were to report directly to him, and he would give them the best land for their use. They would lack nothing.

Almost as an afterthought, Pharaoh told Joseph to prepare a special gift for his father. He ordered for him a string of 10 donkeys loaded with the good things of Egypt and another string of 10 loaded with grain and food.

As the grand caravan prepared to leave for Mamre, Joseph came out to send them on their way with a reminder not to quarrel. He didn't want them to revert to fixing blame for something that had happened long ago and was completely forgiven. Jacob's family had been through so many traumatic experiences that they needed Joseph's reminder to put the past behind them and to learn to enjoy their incredibly good fortune.

The trip went smoothly. The traveling time allowed the men a needed opportunity to collect their thoughts—to fully realize the changes that were coming in their lives and to ponder the trading of good for evil that would forever be accredited to Joseph. They also went over in their minds how to tell their father these things. Leah's four oldest sons had reason to be anxious. Having told their father that Joseph was dead, how would they answer his inevitable questions? He might be unable to ask questions; the shock might be too much for his broken heart to stand. They marveled that the younger brothers had not asked any questions since the revelation of Joseph in Egypt had ruined their story of a wild animal eating him. Had their brothers ever believed them? Had their father? As they wondered about it, their faces became hot and flushed—not only because of the desert sun.

They passed through Beersheba with enough wares to open a booth. At one time they might have—prices were never higher. As it was, the thought never occurred to them.

They urged their mounts to go faster as they neared home, and when the last miles were covered, 11 men dismounted amid a wild welcome of cheers and embraces—and more tears.

Judah called for servants to see that the porters Pharaoh sent along were given comfortable quarters, then he and his brothers went to their father's tent. He had been in seclusion since the pack train had returned with the necessary grain—but without any of his sons. He thought he had lost them all!

They tried to tell him about Joseph gently and gradually to keep from exciting him overmuch. But he sensed what they implied and responded with such rapid questions they couldn't delay telling it right out: Joseph not only was alive; he was governor in Egypt!

The old patriarch felt reality ebbing away from him; his mind could not accept all that his sons were saying. It seemed his heart had stopped; he was afraid to breathe lest even that would destroy his fragile grasp of what he just heard. The news, instead of bringing instantaneous joy, enveloped him in bewildered exhaustion. He was shaken. He looked in disbelief at his sons. Surely they would not deceive him again, but . . .

Benjamin, tired of tears and of words, suggested some action. "Father, come and see. We would have no reason to bring empty carts to Mamre—where food is so needed—if we had not been ordered to bring them empty by Pharaoh. He wanted them to be proof of his offer for you to fill them with your choicest possessions and come to Egypt."

Jacob rose to his feet and, leaning on his youngest son, went out to see for himself. Empty wagons. Empty wagons! It was true!

Israel shouted to himself what the others had told him, "Joseph is still alive!"

Then everyone talked. Benjamin, proud of the high position of his brother, said, "He's second in power in all Egypt!"

Comments from the others overlapped and jangled in confusion in Jacob's ears.

"He has saved the world from starvation by his plan of storing grain."

"We're to live in Goshen."

"Goshen is the best land in Egypt."

"We will be near Menofer, where Joseph lives."

The brothers shared a wonderful excitement, but Jacob's eyes were shining with singular delight. He vaguely heard what his sons were saying, but that did not matter very much to him at the moment. For now, all his mind and heart could hold was the fact that his son—his and Rachel's son, Joseph—was alive!

The brothers told and retold their adventures until their father wanted to hear no more. He silenced them with his own cry of victory, "I'm convinced! My son Joseph is alive! I will go and see him before I die."

His decision to go to Egypt—to Joseph—was made instantaneously and seemed right at the time, but when Jacob retired, too excited to sleep, he thought about it again and began to have doubts.

Abraham had been lured to Egypt without God's permission during a famine. Isaac had been warned directly by the Lord God not to make the mistake of his father, and when famine threatened him, he stayed in Canaan in perfect faith that he would survive by the special provision of the Lord God who had provided for him on Mt. Moriah.

Could it be possible that the Lord God would not want him to go to Egypt? He had not spoken to Jacob of Egypt—or of anything else—since that time very long ago during his second pilgrimage to Bethel. Without His specific Word Jacob had sent his sons to Egypt to do the necessary buying. But could he go—even to see Joseph again—without knowing it was the Lord God's will?

He poured out his intense desire to see his son in prayer to El Elohe Israel. The anticipated joy was almost a pain in his heart, but even stronger was the desire to please his God. El Elohe Israel was silent.

Israel walked across the brown, sun-baked grass, looked at the sky that held no promise of rain, and thought of the five more years of drought prophesied by his son. He thought of

Egypt's lush grass in the Nile Delta, well-watered and waiting in spacious fields for his use. Most of all, he thought of Joseph. But El Elohe Israel remained silent.

His sons were eager to be on their way. They already had packed their belongings into the carts allotted to them. They could not understand their father's delay. They were sure Joseph would not understand their not coming at once and would be anxiously looking for them to come with their families. There were 65 persons ready to leave; there was one who was not.

Jacob called his sons together and read from the writings of Abraham about the dreadful vision given to him the night the "horror of great darkness" fell on him. The Lord God had entered into an everlasting covenant with him about the possession of Canaan for his descendants, but there was to be a time when they would sojourn in a land that was not theirs and be in bondage to that people for 400 years. After the time of bondage, the Lord God promised Abraham that he would judge their captors and lead His people out with great substance.

This was part of the writings Israel had not spoken of very much. He usually thought of this prophecy as remote from himself and his children—something for far future generations. He wondered if he was being drawn to Egypt now to immediate safety for himself and his family but to eventual misery for his descendants—400 years of misery.

He continued discussing it with his sons long after he had rolled up the parchment and replaced it in its container. Would their departure to Egypt be for a few years, or would it be the beginning of a long, prophesied exile from the land?

A group of sober men left their father's tent. Egyptian hospitality suddenly looked ominous.

Israel spent the night in prayer. El Elohe Israel was with him—but silent.

Israel finally consented to have his belongings loaded into the carts. The box with the writings was packed securely into a saddle bag on the camel that Israel rode. It had become more precious than ever to him, and if he left the land, those writings would be a tangible tie with Abraham and Isaac—and with the Lord God.

He promised to go only as far as Beersheba. There he would find the altars where his father and grandfather had worshiped when they were in that area. He would go that far and then hope to learn from the Lord God whether to go on to Egypt or stay in drought-ridden Canaan. If he left the land, he would see his son. If he left the land, he knew he would never see it again.

It was not a long journey to Beersheba. They set up camp near a well, surrounded by a grove of tamarisk trees that produced fragile, pale pink, feathery foliage at the end of light green branches. Drought had dimmed their color, but they framed the well with delicate beauty. Israel touched the branches tenderly; Abraham had planted these trees. He remembered his grandfather saying that it was at this well that he first used the name of El Olam, the Everlasting God.

Israel knelt and prayed for the direction he must have.

"El Olam!"

"El Bethel!"

"El Elohe Israel!"

36

God spoke to Israel in a vision at night . . . . "I am God, the God of your father. Do not be afraid to go down to Egypt, for I will make you into a great nation there."
Genesis 46:2-3

father, we've been here at Beersheba five days, yet the road to Egypt still lies ahead of us. We've abandoned our household things, turned our backs on the desolation of Canaan, and Joseph is waiting! What more do you need to know—and what will you know tomorrow that you don't know today? Make the decision. Let's go!"

Reuben had been the spokesman, but Jacob knew he relayed the feelings of the others.

"I will not be rushed into the decision. No one wants to go to Egypt more than I do." Jacob's answer had started in a strong voice, but his chin quivered at the last few words.

"And no one wants to stay here more than you do! In fact, no one else wants to stay here at all!"

"I will not be rushed. I will go only if I know it's God's will. It's too important a decision to make myself; it could involve generations of people."

"You may be taking Abraham's vision too personally."

"I might be, but it will apply to someone, sometime. Why not to me? I will continue to wait, Reuben."

Israel waited several more days—waited and prayed. His sons held their peace with great exercise of restraint.

After one especially hot, tiresome day, Israel retired early. He had slept only a short while when, in the visions of the night, he heard the Voice. It began with that clear, unmistakeable sound—like sparkling energy released by splashing fountains and rushing rivers. The Voice called his name.

He said, "Here I am." Then he waited in exultation. Whether He would say stay or go, he would obey.

"I am God, the God of your father. Do not be afraid to go down to Egypt, for I will make you into a great nation there. I will go down to Egypt with you, and I will surely bring you back again. And Joseph's own hand will close your eyes."

Israel got up from his bed and ran to look at the arching skies. There was no sign of heavenly hosts nor of a ladder stretching up to God, but in his mind the words he had heard echoed and reechoed, burning themselves into his memory, blessing him abundantly.

Beyond the implicit ecstasy of hearing the Voice, he had the Lord God's directive to go to Egypt to be reunited with Joseph! Almost incidentally he rejoiced that his family would have no more worry about famine.

In this seventh and last communication from the Lord God there was a promise that soothed Israel in a most personal way, like a benediction. At his death, Joseph would "close his eyes"—would attend to the last loving rites. Father and son would not be separated again all the days of his life.

The reference to his death did not dishearten him. It was the natural course of events. First he would see Joseph, then, like Abraham and Isaac, he would be gathered to his fathers and to his God.

Before daybreak he began rousing his sons, telling them to waste no more time sleeping. They should be on their way to Goshen. Joseph was waiting!

He sent Judah with a small guard of servants on ahead of the slower moving caravan. He was to tell Joseph that they were coming.

Joseph called for his chariot as soon as he heard Judah's welcome news. He went out to meet his father. Each had wondered what he would say to the other, but in the first moments of their meeting there was no need for words. Father and son embraced and wept together for a good while.

Israel gently pushed Joseph away, holding him at arm's length but not letting go while he looked at him. He was greatly changed in appearance from the lad he had sent off to find his brothers during that much milder drought. It would take a while to get used to his mature look and his Egyptian manner of dress. But these were unimportant things. He was Joseph! There was one thing Jacob had decided before leaving Canaan: He never would call his son Zaphenath-Paneah!

Now he would try to imagine that Joseph had just come back from Dothan, and they would be rejoicing together for as long as .... The Lord God's last words about Joseph closing his eyes flashed into his mind, checking his exuberant elation. Would he die soon since the first part of God's message was fulfilled so quickly? If God willed, so be it.

"Now I am ready to die, since I have seen for myself that you are still alive."

Jacob's first words to his son were of death! Joseph was so surprised at his father's statement that he didn't have an immediate reply. He embraced his father again, this time with no tears but with a hearty, reassuring laugh. Then he said, "Let's look forward to life!" Later Israel would tell his son what the Lord God had said that night in Beersheba, and together they would be glad for the many years yet to be granted to this plain, quiet man.

After father and son adjusted in some measure to the gladness of seeing each other again, Joseph welcomed his brothers and their families. He wanted them to get settled in as soon as possible. They had arrived in Goshen, the best grassland left in the world. Pharaoh had offered this area to them previously, and now Joseph was determined to assure their right to it. He told his brothers that when they were presented to Pharaoh in the immediate days ahead, they were to remind him that their vocation was keeping cattle and flocks.

He then left them to go to Pharaoh himself and tell him of their arrival. He also would impress on Pharaoh that his family were shepherds, people who would not fit into the society of the Nile valley. He wanted a firm edict that they would be given a portion of the semi-isolated section of Goshen. Joseph wanted them to be as free as possible from Egyptian cultural influences. He understood the demands of his father's God;

they were to be separate from those who worshiped foreign deities.

Following the directions Joseph had given Judah, they moved their caravan through the expanse called Goshen to a specific place, the Wadi Tumilat. It looked like paradise to the weary travelers so used to seeing the brown fields of Canaan and, more recently, the stony, sandy desert wasteland.

Goshen was beautiful steppe land extending eastward from the most eastern branch of the Nile, near beautiful lakes including the Bahlia and the Bitter Lakes. It was at its best as the 66 Hebrews passed through it to find refuge. The land was endlessly green with good pasture. There would be no need to move flocks long distances from one pasture to another. A series of canals provided water from the Nile. Twice a year, in spring and in fall, fields were covered by temporary, controlled flooding. During those times animals were moved to slightly higher ground nearby.

The day they entered Goshen, they saw a wealth of green pastures and an abundance of fruit and vegetables in gardens and orchards. They knew there were fish available in the canals, rivers and lakes. The famine-stalked people felt their hearts nearly burst with gladness.

Israel saw and appreciated all the richness, but he was aware of something that pleased him even more. This was a place where they would be far from the sophisticated, pagan life of the Egyptians. They could worship the God of Abraham, of Isaac and of Jacob; they would bow to no other deity.

Part Six

gathered home

From the Word of the Lord to Moses:
  "I am the God of your father, the God of Abraham, the God of Isaac and the God of Jacob" (Exodus 3:6).
From the Word of the Lord given to Malachi:
  "Yet I have loved Jacob" (Malachi 1:2).
From the inspired writing of Paul:
  "Jacob I loved" (Romans 9:13).

Jacob was *tam* . . . living in tents (Genesis 25:27).

Noah was *tam* . . . and he walked with God
  (Genesis 6:9).

Job was *tam* . . . he feared God and shunned evil
  (Job 1:1).

37

Then Joseph brought his father Jacob in and presented him before Pharaoh.
Genesis 47:7

Israel basked in 17 years of peace and plenty, surrounded by his children and their children. He saw them all frequently, except for Joseph and his household.

Government responsibilities kept Joseph in Menofer where he lived with his wife, the lovely Asenath, and their two sons, Manasseh and Ephraim. Whenever he could take time from his pressing work, Joseph made the two-day journey to Tumilat to stay as long as possible, relaxing in the fondly remembered atmosphere of tent living.

During Jacob's early years in Goshen, while famine ravaged most of the world, Joseph's visits were made memorable by the exciting accounts he gave of his various projects. Primarily, he supervised grain transactions in Menofer and other cities. Toward the end of the famine years he devoted more time to relocating people who had lost their land to the government because of their inability to pay for grain they needed. Joseph shook his head at the sad business of handling dispossessed families, but he was elated that Egypt had become, even if for only a few years, chief supplier of the world's staple food.

When the rains came at the end of seven years as God had foretold through Joseph, the famine subsided, and Egypt's influx of grain purchasers dwindled dramatically.

Jacob thought that as the economies of devastated lands recovered, the world would depend less on Egypt. Egypt would depend less on his son, and Joseph could come more often to Tumilat. Instead, his enterprising son plunged into new financial ventures. With the wealth of Egypt largely at his disposal he thrust his country into a thriving commerce in copper and turquoise.

Jacob listened to Joseph's enthusiastic description of his new work and of still another interest in which he intended to be involved—the building of lightweight boats to sail the Nile. He chuckled softly and wondered what had given him the idea that his son, in the prime of his life, would want to sit and talk with him just because the famine was over. He enjoyed Joseph's company and would have liked to have him come oftener and stay longer, but basically he was pleased with his success and encouraged him in his ventures.

When Joseph did come, Jacob reminded him without fail of his Hebrew heritage by reading from the family records. He urged Joseph to pass the teachings along to his sons. One of Jacob's concerns was that his daughter-in-law, the daughter of Potiphera, a priest of the city of On, would teach her sons the religion of her family of sun worshippers. On the rare occasions when Manasseh and Ephraim came to Tumilat, Israel made special efforts to talk to them of the heritage they had through their father—a heritage from the one God, El Shaddai.

He often laughed at himself when he remembered his premature expectation of death, which he thought would happen as soon as he saw Joseph. The Lord God delayed that part of his plan for Israel one golden year after another—17 of them in all.

For the last few mornings now it had been difficult for him to get out of bed. He felt weak, and his vision blurred. He remembered the difficulty his father had with his eyes and then thought more deeply about his father—faithful, unassuming, devoted to his God. He wished he had been closer to his father—to have had words of love and forgiveness from him to cherish through the years.

He thought about Abraham and the delightful days he had spent with him at Mamre—learning, learning, learning. They had a companionship that, although it lasted only through Jacob's earlier years, enriched his entire life. He sighed as he thought of his numerous grandchildren and wondered if he had spent enough time with any of them to have made a difference in their lives. He hoped so.

He had lost the desire to walk across the fields or to sit beside the lakes. It was easier to stay near his tent and think about many things, many people. He thought of Leah, Laban, Esau, Zilpah and Bilhah. He remembered the old potter of Luz—Rekem—and Ishan, the caravaneer. He remembered his mother, Rebekah, that irrepressible woman who loved him dearly and so shaped his early years and much of his life. Most of all, he thought of Rachel—always Rachel.

He remembered the delights of Canaan, that pleasant land. The Sea of Kinnereth, the Jordan River valley, the mountains of Gilead, the wide fields of grain at Meggido, the bazaar at Beersheba, the oaks of Mamre—these and more took shape in his mind.

He relived the rapture of his first meeting with the Lord God at Bethel and the other holy communications at Haran, Mahanaim, Peniel, Succoth, on the second pilgrimage to Bethel, and finally at Beersheba—most precious memories, more treasured each time they were recalled. The wonder of them was only enhanced by the passage of time.

He had been in Goshen so long that he even had favorite memories from there, such as that memorable day he had been presented to Pharaoh. It seemed so recent to him; could it have been 17 years ago?

Joseph had taken him to Menofer as soon as he was rested from his journey and settled in at Tumilat. Jacob had agreed to go partly because he felt it was expected of him, but more because it would give him precious days alone with his newly found son.

They enjoyed the easy trip to the city on the Nile, and Joseph had an opportunity to tell about the years he had spent in Egypt—years of blessings and of burdens—and of God working through it all. Jacob listened in wonder and would, from time to time in the years ahead, ask his son to tell the story over and over. Each time tears would come to his eyes, and he would praise El Elohe Israel!

Pharaoh's palace was all Joseph promised it would be. Jacob-

Israel could not believe it was he himself walking up the wide steps and across the tiled floor of the grand porch that went around the enormous six-story building.

While waiting for an audience with Pharaoh, they sat in a large room furnished with gold and ivory chairs and tables. Grotesque idols were positioned in prominent places. Walls were decorated with hangings of shimmering multicolored silk and highly polished copper panels. Servants brought in basins of water and luxurious towels, and with elegant ceremony they washed and carefully dried the feet of the two men soon to be presented in the throne room.

Word came that Pharaoh was detained, and they would have to wait longer. Joseph was glad for the extra time to show his father through the rooms on the lower floor of the palace. Room opened into room, each more splendid than the one before. The old shepherd's eyes were dazzled by finely carved gold furniture. He marveled at the delicate filigree of ivory screens. He looked from tapestries to thick rugs to mosaic floors in open amazement.

Joseph led him out onto the porch to a place from which they looked down on a terraced garden of flowers, shrubs and small trees. Fountains sent gently sweeping sprays of water into long, rectangular pools. Harpists sang to their own accompaniments. Jacob enjoyed the sights, and Joseph enjoyed Jacob.

During those first days in Egypt Jacob found it hard to get used to seeing unbearded men. Their dress was different from anything he had seen before—the white skirts, the jeweled collars, the ear studs.

He was most impressed with scribes he saw carrying writing tools on strings slung across their shoulders. He looked at their palettes of ink and their cases of pens and thought of his own laborious writing of the family records. It would be nice to have a scribe.

He turned from the incredible sights of the palace to look at his own plain tunic and worn sandals. He was beginning to have qualms about being presented to the master of all this splendor. He looked uneasily at Joseph, who smiled at him as though he were the parent encouraging a bashful child. Jacob would not have his son look condescendingly at him! He straightened his shoulders and walked with the proper dignity of one who bore the name Israel—Prince with God.

By the time he and Joseph returned to resume their wait for the interview, he was overwhelmed, not because of the ostentation of Egypt, but because Egypt was in the hand of his God, serving as God's place to harbor His people until He chose to bring them out as a powerful nation. Mighty Egypt was just a tool for the Lord God.

"Now that you have seen some of the palace, what do you think of it, Father?" Joseph looked a little smug and apparently expected lavish praise for the grandeur assembled under Pharaoh's roof.

Jacob was just as smug. He was about to tell his son of his perspective regarding Egypt and the place it held in the plans of God, but he would have to wait. An escort of palace guards was coming to usher God's plain man into the exalted Pharaoh's presence.

The throne room was immense. At the far side of the room he saw the monarch. He was heavily bejeweled, held a golden sceptre, and was seated on an elaborate throne on a high platform. Courtiers stood at attention at stations all around the room.

Joseph and Israel watched from near the doorway until they were allowed to proceed to the throne. An official was finishing a report to the Pharaoh; he was prostrate before the throne. No one was permitted to look directly into the god-king's face.

Then their moment arrived. Jacob's escort nodded that he might now proceed to the place before the throne for a short interview with the great one. When Israel was presented to Pharaoh, he did not bow. He walked with regal step and stood before the raised platform, looking up into the king's eyes. The officials in the room were outraged but could make no move toward the aged man with Zaphenath-Paneah standing behind him and with Pharaoh descending the steps to stand on a level with him!

Israel had taken the initiative in their meeting and now raised his hand toward heaven. No one in the hall made a sound. Then Israel's voice filled the room as he, in the precious, powerful name of Elohim, blessed the ruler of Egypt for giving sanctuary to His people.

Pharaoh, at a loss for words but observing conventional modes of courtesy in his country, asked a friendly question.

"How old are you?"

Israel thought it a strange question, but answered quickly, "The years of my pilgrimage are 130."

Pharaoh was impressed by the proud carriage, the obvious strength and the keen mind of one so old. In Egypt men rarely reached even 120 years, and if they did, they were usually infirm.

Israel thought his age was nothing to boast of, and he continued, almost apologizing that in comparison to his fathers he had not lived long at all. He volunteered that his years had been marked with wanderings, anxiety and sorrow. At that time Jacob thought his life was nearly over and was ready for Joseph to "close his eyes." He was not complaining or boasting, but merely elaborating on a question, as men even younger than 130 like to do.

Their conversation was short; Pharaoh's reaction to Israel was favorable. Goshen would be the home of his people. They would not be molested. Pharaoh's favor included his protection. The god of Egypt accepted the blessing of the plain man of God, then Israel turned to go.

Pharaoh assumed his favorite position—feet wide apart, arms crossed over his chest, head held high. He watched Israel leave, walking beside his illustrious son. Pharaoh was adept at hiding emotions behind an impenetrable facade, but attendants who managed to look at him out of the corner of an eye had never seen him so mystified. If they could have read his thoughts as well as they read his face, they would have known he was filled with the uncomfortable feeling of having met an equal—or more. Without regal robes, walking with a worn wooden staff instead of a scepter, speaking no witty, sophisticated flattery, Israel still had evidenced royal behavior. He had begun their interview with a gracious blessing, taken the liberty to enlarge on a question that called only for a direct answer, and then actually dismissed Pharaoh with his blessing. Pharaoh considered him presumptuous—magnificently presumptuous!

Israel had thought about that meeting with Pharaoh almost all morning as he sat in the shade of his tent. It was as though he had just then walked through those pleasant scenes instead of having merely reminisced about them. He sat up tall and straight.

He glanced toward the sky and saw the sun directly overhead; it was time for the noon meal but he was not hungry. He went into his tent to lie down.

He had told Pharaoh that his life was largely a wandering, a pilgrimage from one place to another. At that time he had referred to his travels from Canaan to Mesopotamia, back to Canaan, then to Egypt; he also had included in his mind the several major moves within Canaan itself. It had indeed been a pilgrimage, but now that word took on deeper significance.

No matter how long he stayed in any one place, he would be a pilgrim. He was beginning to understand that the vague longings within him would be satisfied, not with a return to Canaan, but with his being gathered to his God and to his fathers. He had kept his staff from Peniel with him as a reminder of his God. Now it was also a pilgrim's staff, a reminder of the transitory nature of everything—everything except El Olam! He was a pilgrim looking for a city where God dwells everlastingly.

38

> May the God before whom my fathers
> > Abraham and Isaac walked,
> the God who has been my Shepherd
> > all my life to this day,
> the Angel who has delivered me from all harm—
> > may he bless these boys.
>
> *Genesis 48:15-16*

Israel had scarcely left his tent for a week. When his family came to inquire about him, his servant said he was busy—thinking, praying, writing, resting—not to be disturbed.

He had finished his portion of the family records, including farewell words to give his sons. They were not words he would have chosen, but they had been impressed on his mind by the Lord God. Israel had complied with divine leading, and now that it was done, he put down his pen and said, "So be it."

Even so, he reflected on how different his own decisions would have been. He would have chosen Joseph as progenitor of the royal line. The Lord God had permitted him to give Joseph only the double portion of inheritance. Judah's line would have the honor of the scepter. The Spirit of God who inspired the penning of each word enabled Israel to accept His judgments, even what was withheld from Joseph.

Israel was not surprised at Reuben's loss of status. The eldest son was denied both the double portion of inheritance and the preeminence of being his generation's link in the chain of God's blessing for all the world. Reuben's act of immorality and his general pattern of weak character through life had been costly to him.

The writing had been emotionally and physically exhausting. God's penman closed his tired, burning, watering eyes. And then El Elohe Israel allowed His prince's mind to visualize the bright beauty of Canaan—from Beersheba to Laish. Favorite scenes thrilled his heart; he felt he was almost home.

The next morning he sent for Joseph. "Tell him to come quickly. Tell him it's important." With restrained, terse sentences he dispatched his messengers.

Joseph left Menofer within a few hours after the messengers arrived; he reached Tumilat two days later. Riding across the wide delta, he thought of the strong shoulders on which he had ridden as a child, of the rapid gait he had difficulty matching as a lad, of the eyes once sharp enough to identify any bird in flight. He remembered the hours of teaching that his father had given him in the sciences and the arts—and in the rich, rich heritage of the knowledge of the Lord God.

"My father, I've come as soon as I could. Is there anything I can do for you? Anything I can get for you?"

"I need nothing, Joseph. Let's not waste time or strength on trivial talk."

Since Joseph's time had been so involved in his government work and his own family lived in Menofer, Israel had learned that the visits with his son were generally all too brief. Joseph felt mildly rebuked as he sat down beside his father. This time he would not be in such a hurry to return to the city.

He heard Israel's soft chuckle, then a nostalgic question. "Joseph, do you remember . . . I thought I would die the same day I first saw you when I came to Egypt . . . because the Lord God told me . . . you would be the one to close my eyes?"

"I remember you spoke of death then, but I scarcely noticed it; I was full of the joy of our reunion!"

"But now, Joseph, I must speak of it again, and you must listen. My life in Egypt has been an easy one—a happy one. Living in this peace and plenty makes me think I am not the same man who slaved for . . . for no money . . . but for priceless, precious . . . ."

Joseph remembered that it always had been difficult for his father to say her name after she died.

"Well now, that's enough reminiscing. I've been doing a lot of that lately, but I want to talk to you of my future."

Israel smiled at the look of surprise on his son's face. How could one so young understand the excitement of the real future?

"You are shocked that I plan for what is ahead, Joseph? Oh, I do, I do! And the word *future* has the richest meaning. My son, it has been unspeakably marvelous to have had even glimpses of the majestic perfection of the Lord God. Imagine . . . being gathered to Him forever!"

That thought pleased Israel so much he stopped speaking for a long while, allowing his mind to try to think of the glory!

Then, rousing himself to address the matter he wanted to settle with Joseph, he cleared his throat and asked his son to give him his oath he would not bury him in Egypt. The thought of his bones being left in this place, when the rest of the family went back to Canaan, could break his heart. Never, never had he chosen to be anywhere but in that land.

Joseph, struggling for a steady voice, did not reply. Israel rephrased his request. "I will lie with my fathers, and you shall carry me out of Egypt and bury me in their burying place."

"I will do as you have asked."

"Swear it to me."

"I swear it to you."

Israel's face glowed; he sighed as though a ponderous load had been lifted. He turned over on his face and lay prostrate on his bed. Joseph knew their conversation was over; his father was now speaking to his God.

Joseph had been back in Menofer less than a week when another messenger arrived from Tumilat. Israel's weakened condition now alarmed the family.

Joseph hurriedly left the city, this time taking his two sons and one of the best physicians in Egypt. Their official chariots rolled eastward along the highway. When they reached the campsite, Joseph jumped down before his came to a full stop. He ran to his father's tent, but a servant kept him from going in.

"He is seeing no one."

"I won't tire him. I must see him . . . I've brought his grandsons, and he will want to know they are here."

"Wait while I look in on him; he may be sleeping now."

Zaphenath-Paneah looked at his gold chain with Pharaoh's crest on it; he turned his signet ring to catch sunlight on the blue sapphire. Trinkets! They might open any door in Egypt to him, but now he stood by a lowly tent, waiting for admittance to the only place he wanted to be.

When the servant told Israel his son and grandsons were there, he summoned the strength to pull himself into a sitting position on the side of the bed with his feet on the floor. He had longed for this meeting and would spend his last energy on it if necessary.

As the three men were brought in, Israel greeted them with words to enrich the memory of his grandsons. He spoke at surprisingly great length and at first with great force and clarity.

"God Almighty, El Shaddai, appeared to me at Luz in the land of Canaan, and there he blessed me and said to me, 'I am going to make you fruitful and will increase your numbers. I will make you a community of peoples, and I will give this land as an everlasting possession to your descendants after you.'

"Now then, your two sons born to you in Egypt before I came to you here will be reckoned as mine; Ephraim and Manasseh will be mine, just as Reuben and Simeon are mine. Any children born to you after them will be yours; in the territory they inherit they will be reckoned under the names of their brothers . . .

"As I was returning from Haran, to my sorrow Rachel died in Canaan . . . while we were still on the way, . . . a little distance from Ephrath. So . . . I buried her there . . . beside the road to Ephrath."

Israel's mind digressed into memory and he was disoriented from his present surroundings for a brief time.

"Who are these?" He pointed to Manasseh and Ephraim.

"The sons God has given me," Joseph gently answered.

"Bring them here so I may bless them."

Israel scarcely could see them, but he put his arms around the young men and kissed them. He turned his head toward Joseph and said in open happiness, "Once I thought I'd never see your face again, but the Lord God has allowed me to see your children, too."

Joseph drew his sons away from their grandfather, enough so they could kneel before him—placing Manasseh, the elder, by the patriarch's right hand to receive the larger blessing. Israel, now fully aware of what he was doing, deliberately reached out to place his right hand on Ephraim's head. Then crossing his arms, he placed his left hand on Manasseh's head. The Lord God had ordained their portions as He had those of Israel's own sons—as He had ordained the portions of Jacob and Esau so many years before.

Concluding the blessing of his grandsons, he turned in loving communication to Joseph. "May the God before whom my fathers Abraham and Isaac walked, the God who has been my Shepherd all my life to this day, the Angel who has delivered me from all harm—may he bless these boys. May they be called by my name and the names of my fathers Abraham and Isaac, and may they increase greatly upon the earth."

Israel had adopted Ephraim and Manasseh into his family. Each would have a full portion of his inheritance, representing the double portion he was permitted to allot to Joseph.

He rested then, refusing to see the physician who still waited to be called to attend him. Israel wanted some time alone.

Lying back on his bed, he thought of his two adopted sons and took pride in them. Then it seemed the darkness of his eyes was spreading through his body, weaning him from all the things of the earth. He sent for his 12 sons.

In giving his last words to them he would be relaying God's will and making it his own. It was one last test of full obedience—of negating his conflicting natural desire.

Through the darkness someone's voice came to him, saying his sons had arrived.

"Gather yourselves together . . . listen to Israel, your father.

"Reuben, my firstborn, you are as unstable as water—a man of good intent, but not excelling in action—a man of immorality."

Israel's face registered grief and shame. He cried out, "You went up to my couch and defiled it! The double share of the firstborn will not be yours but will go to Joseph's sons; the excellence of power, the line of Shiloh, will be Judah's.

"Simeon and Levi, you are alike—instruments of cruelty. I will scatter and disperse you in the land. Cursed be your fierce anger!

"Judah, your brothers will praise you. You will prevail over your enemies. The scepter will not depart from Judah, nor the ruler's staff from between his feet, until Shiloh comes, to whom it belongs.

"Zebulun, live by the seashore; become a haven for ships.

"Issachar, strong as a donkey, enjoying rest and ease, you will be submissive and enslaved."

Israel knew he was disappointing his sons by not smoothing over their sins and inadequacies. The necessity of speaking this way to them in his last moments was trying to him. He especially drew back from the next prophecy, but it had to be said.

"Dan, strong and dangerous to your enemies, you will be a serpent by the roadside, a viper along the path, that bites the horse's heels so its rider falls backward."

For a moment he stopped his words of praise, blame and prophecy. The association of the word *serpent* with Satan was indelibly fixed in his mind. His message to Dan recalled to him the satanic force that had tried to destroy God's people since the beginning of time. Israel called out to the Lord God with a prayer to embrace those assembled at his bedside and their descendants, for Satan would continue to strive hard against the children of Israel. In love, anguish, hope and fear he cried, "I look for your deliverance, O Lord!"

Turning back to his sons, he knew Gad was next in line. "Gad, you are courageous, but you will be harrassed by enemies.

"Asher, you will be prosperous, enjoying delicacies fit for royalty.

"Naphtali, you are freedom loving, eloquent and helpful.

"Joseph . . . Joseph." It seemed no further words would come from Israel. Then in a torrent of eloquence the dying father, unable to give the highest inherited privilege to his favorite son, gave him a legacy of his love.

"Joseph is a fruitful vine near a spring wall, whose branches climb over a wall. With bitterness archers attacked him and shot at him with hostility. But his bow remained steady, his strong arms stayed limber, because of the hand of the Mighty God of Jacob, because of the Shepherd, the Rock of Israel, because of El Shaddai, who blesses you with blessings of the heavens above, blessings of the deep that lies below, blessings of the breast and the womb.

"Your father's blessings are greater than the blessings of the ancient mountains, greater than the bounty of the everlasting hills. Let all these rest on the head of Joseph, on the brow of the prince among his brothers."

Israel's face was lit with expressive delight; his glowing words to Joseph hung in the soft, warm air that surrounded them all. No one spoke for a long while, but soft sobs of remorse mingled with those of sorrow.

Israel remembered Benjamin was waiting—Benjamin, the son of his right hand. Israel longed to give this son a crown of praise also, but was moved to say only that he was "keen and fierce as a ravenous wolf."

He had spoken to each of his sons according to the honor or disgrace they had brought him and according to events of the future. He loved them all; none was disinherited. Rewards or losses were the result of how they had chosen to live in the past and of coming choices that were foreknown by the Lord God. Israel was satisfied that he had spoken rightly; he released his family completely into God's care.

He was ready—eager for his long-awaited journey into the real future. He reached for the old staff by his bed. It was worn smooth; it was sturdy.

There were a few more words to be spoken—Israel's last request. In it he reminded his sons of their homeland and charged them that they should bury him no place but there. As though announcing a marvelous new thing, he spoke of what was to come, at first with jubilant excitement, then with increasing detachment.

"I am about to be gathered to my people. Bury me with my fathers in the cave in the field of Ephron the Hittite, . . . in the cave . . . in the field of . . . Machpelah . . . near Mamre . . . in Canaan, . . . which Abraham bought . . . as a burial place . . . from Ephron the Hittite, . . . along with the field. There Abraham . . . and Sarah . . . are . . . buried. There Isaac . . . and . . . Rebekah . . . were buried. And there . . . I buried . . . Leah. The field . . . and the cave in it . . . were bought from the Hittites."

Israel was silent. He pulled his feet up onto the bed and lay down, still holding his staff. His sons saw him smile, raise his head from the pillow and lie down again—in the joy of one who had finished a long, difficult pilgrimage and was welcomed home.